Dear Par

'A moving and inspiring journey th[...] and all they can be. If you have a young person in your life, or know somebody who does, please read this book.'

MORRIS GLEITZMAN, BESTSELLING WRITER AND AUSTRALIAN CHILDREN'S LAUREATE

'Gabbie Stroud's *Dear Parents* is a crucial bridge between two important pillars in education—parents and teachers—but most importantly, it holds at its passionate heart the best interests of children. If you want to understand the way your children are being educated in these challenging times, and whether the system is fit for purpose, you must read this funny, informative, and eye-opening book.'

LUCY CLARK, JOURNALIST AND AUTHOR OF *BEAUTIFUL FAILURES*

Teacher

'An achingly heartfelt personal reflection on the way bureaucracy dehumanises and compromises our teachers and our children . . . how the joy of teaching can be turned into despair, and how children are becoming less important than outcomes. Heartbreaking.'

NONI HAZLEHURST AM, ACTRESS, WRITER, DIRECTOR, BROADCASTER

'Gabbie documents the inside story on the harm done to kids and teachers in our stressed-out, test-driven schools. Schools, especially primary schools, need to be based on relationships and a love of learning, yet we are doing the very opposite. Intense, personal, and impassioned but also crystal clear about what has gone wrong, and therefore how to fix it.'

STEVE BIDDULPH AM, PSYCHOLOGIST AND BESTSELLING AUTHOR

'Moving. Insightful. Funny. Sad. Gabbie Stroud was a gifted teacher. She loved and nurtured her students, she was proud of their achievements, they made her laugh and cry. But the system ground her down, and teaching left her. She is a loss to the profession, and the children she might have taught. Her journey is a lesson for everyone who cares about education and the future of our children—and the country. How can the system be made to work better? How can we respect, recognise and reward the professionalism of teachers? Gabbie Stroud brings these questions to life . . . with a passionate insider's insight, from the classroom, staffroom and the principal's office.'

JULIANNE SCHULTZ AM FAHA, PROFESSOR OF MEDIA AND CULTURE, GRIFFITH UNIVERSITY AND FOUNDING EDITOR OF *THE GRIFFITH REVIEW*

'What do we want for our children when they start school? What kind of teacher does any family want for their young ones? I want a teacher like Gabbie Stroud. PLEASE! Gabbie's story of a gifted teacher's experience shows what might be possible if we changed the policy settings to allow good teachers to do their job, attending to their students rather than documenting forever to demonstrate "standards" and "be accountable". Every citizen needs to read this book, feel the author's love for teaching and think about what would need to change to keep good teachers influencing our children.'

MARIE BRENNAN, PROFESSOR OF EDUCATION, VICTORIA UNIVERSITY

'*Teacher* is the story of one teacher's love of teaching and her ultimate heartbreak as the education system finally took everything she had to give and left her broken. Unfortunately, Gabbie's story is shared by many other teachers.

'The love and commitment she shows to her students, the guilt that she experiences as her students get the best of her, and her own daughters get the crumbs that are left, the overwhelming exhaustion she feels as her plate is piled higher, the frustration of spending so much time being forced to do what she knows does not benefit her students, all these things are palpable in Gabbie's story.

'This is such a valuable story to tell and to be heard. Gabbie was broken because the system is broken. Teachers all over the country are breaking and, even worse than that, students are breaking too. The joy has all but been sucked out of classrooms as standardised instruction and assessment have taken over from the creative art that once was teaching.

'Gabbie's story needs to be shouted from the rooftops. She very eloquently shows us why and how education needs to change. Teachers like Gabbie (once a teacher always a teacher) have so much to offer. Passion and wisdom are powerful things and she has them in abundance. *Teacher* made me laugh and cry. I loved it!'

KATHY MARGOLIS, EDUCATION ADVOCATE

'In this powerful and poignant memoir, we share Gabbie Stroud's lived experience of what it really means to *be* a *Teacher*. Her wonderfully creative and compassionate teaching journey highlights each day's joys and challenges and increasing demands—until finally it all becomes too much. Beautifully crafted, honest and authentic, this memoir has the potential to help us understand—and potentially rescue—the profession. A must-read for all who care about the future of the teaching profession.'

ROBYN EWING AM, PROFESSOR OF TEACHER EDUCATION AND THE ARTS, THE UNIVERSITY OF SYDNEY

'Gabrielle Stroud details the minutiae of one teacher's life in a brutally honest individual account so well that it becomes a universal story. Her slow burn of passion, compassion, emerging skill, hope and dread, but above all the humanity of the most humanising of professions, provides great insight into the costs and benefits, triumphs and tragedies of teachers' work. You'll laugh and cry. But you will really learn about life as a teacher. A must-read for all considering the profession.'

PHILIP RILEY, ASSOCIATE PROFESSOR OF EDUCATIONAL
LEADERSHIP, AUSTRALIAN CATHOLIC UNIVERSITY

'*Teacher* by Gabrielle Stroud is a heartfelt and moving memoir about one woman who wanted nothing more than to teach our children and inspire them with her own big-hearted warmth, generosity and love of learning. Instead she finds herself broken by a system that cares more for data and demographies than young minds and spirits. She shines a penetrating light on all that is wrong with the Australian education system and how it fails both our children and our teachers. Impossible to read without choking up, this is an eloquent rallying cry for change and should be mandatory reading for all politicians and policy-makers. Luminous and heart-rending.'

KATE FORSYTH, BESTSELLING AUTHOR OF *BITTER GREENS*

'Gabbie Stroud has written a poignant book that explores her personal story of the good, the bad, the inspirational and inex-plicable in the life of a classroom teacher. She was incredibly capable, passionate and committed—and yet she was eventually defeated by the forces of curriculum change, the pressure of incessant accountability and the sense of disempowerment and disrespect that has affected the teaching profession. Her story is becoming sadly all too common, and it is our children who suffer and who are missing out on a better education.'

MAGGIE DENT, BESTSELLING AUTHOR, PARENTING AND RESILIENCE EDUCATOR

'A comforting reminder that somebody gets it . . . A must-read for teachers and those who value Australia's educators.'
GOOD READING

'Stroud is unflinching in her criticism, yet her frustration with a system she sees to be broken does not overshadow the joy, humour and love that spring from the pages . . . A compelling analysis of the way our children are being taught, *Teacher* is a book for all of us with an interest in the future of our education system.'
WEEKEND AUSTRALIAN

'The stories in this book are irresistible and will encourage parents and teachers to value similarly complex and touching experiences of their own . . . this book powerfully records what can happen when teachers are put under too much pressure and when peripheral issues are allowed to take centre stage. It is a plea to educate our young in a context of hope, joy and common sense.'
SYDNEY MORNING HERALD

'Stroud does a sterling job of conveying both the highs and lows of the job, from knowing that you've changed a life forever to fearing you can never do enough. Impassioned, empathetic and eloquent, Stroud's work should be widely read: teachers will recognise much of what she covers, and others—including, hopefully, policy-makers—will come to understand how passionate and talented teachers will leave the jobs they love in a flawed system. ★★★★★'
BOOKS + PUBLISHING

'Stroud is a gifted teacher, and this is a lesson our society should take to heart. ★★★★✓'
THE ADVERTISER

'An insightful memoir about the art and struggle of being a teacher . . . essential reading for any parent.'

MANLY DAILY

'If you're a parent with a child in school or about to attend one, you need to read this memoir . . . powerful and moving, and may even involve some tears.'

MUMS AT THE TABLE

'Harrowing and poignant . . . Your experience as a teacher might not parallel that of Stroud's, but you'll be able to relate to many elements. Teachers resist the urge for fight or flight that's the crux of the book. How you manage it determines your mental health, your capacity to teach. I think Stroud offers us a route, a maxim we're all echoing.'

EDUCATION HQ AUSTRALIA

'This book is essential reading for anyone in, or anywhere near, a school. Many will reject aspects of her critique, but we can't afford to ignore its overall message . . . In our efforts to create something better, *Teacher* is a timely warning that we ignore the teaching profession at our peril. If we don't take them with us, we'll go nowhere. It is also a plea to politicians, pundits and principals to follow three steps to make a difference for teachers and kids: give them support, give them trust—and then get out of the way.'

INSIDE STORY

Dear Parents

GABBIE STROUD

Letters from the Teacher—
your children, their education,
and how you can help

ALLEN&UNWIN
SYDNEY · MELBOURNE · AUCKLAND · LONDON

Grateful acknowledgement is given for permission to reprint p. xi excerpt from *Up the Down Staircase* by Bel Kaufman, copyright © 1964. Used by permission of Scribe Publications, Melbourne, originally published by Prentice Hall Press, New Jersey. All rights reserved.

First published in 2020

Allen & Unwin
83 Alexander Street
Crows Nest NSW 2065
Australia
Phone: (61 2) 8425 0100
Email: info@allenandunwin.com
Web: www.allenandunwin.com

A catalogue record for this book is available from the National Library of Australia

ISBN 978 1 76087 526 8

Internal design by Bookhouse, Sydney
Set in 12.5/16.9 pt Fairfield LH by Bookhouse, Sydney
Printed and bound in Australia by Griffin Press, part of Ovato

10 9 8 7 6 5 4 3 2

The paper in this book is FSC® certified. FSC® promotes environmentally responsible, socially beneficial and economically viable management of the world's forests.

For my first and lifelong teachers:

Mum and Dad,
with gratitude.

And, of course, Jess.

Dear Reader,

Teachers are guardians of a great many stories. They are also professionals who honour the privacy of their students. For this reason, it is difficult for teachers to write about their own experiences in schools and classrooms. A teacher's story naturally becomes entangled with students' stories.

Dear Parents is a carefully crafted and curated patchwork of tales inspired by my years as a classroom teacher. All names, characters, places and incidents described come from my overactive imagination and are used fictitiously.

There is truth to be found in the messages within this book, however, any resemblance to actual events, locales, or persons, living or dead, is entirely coincidental.

When you next meet a teacher, consider *their* story and the great many stories they carry, the stories that have been entrusted to them.

Sincerely,
Gabbie

'What is the teacher's responsibility?
And if it begins at all, where does it end?'

Sylvia Barrett, Teacher

From *Up the Down Staircase* by Bel Kaufman

Things to do

- Finish writing programs
- Begin paperwork for Professional Standards ~~bullshit~~
- BPAY my teacher accreditation fee $100
- Update and pay union membership
- Buy glue sticks
- Make a start on Term 2 excursion and confirm accommodation and venue; book buses; establish cost to school and parents/discuss with Principal, etc; draft notes for parents; sleep a lot now . . .
- Update class roll
- Put new backing paper on classroom pin boards
- Check interactive whiteboard works
- Download apps onto class set of iPads (get passwords and permissions from IT person)
- Find out who the IT person is
- Update interactive whiteboard software
- Buy rug to cover dodgy patch of carpet
- Print first day Bingo Game
- Draft my Term 1 introductory letter to the parents

Welcome to the new school year!

DRAFT

Dear Parents & Caregivers,

Welcome to a new school year! I am so excited to be teaching Senior Primary, Stage Three (Year 5/6). I am looking forward to meeting your child and helping them reach their full potential. It is a big year for these students. The Year 5 children will sit NAPLAN in May and the Year 6 children will experience all the highlights of their last year of primary school. My colleague Mrs Fortune will be teaching the other Year 5/6 class and I'm confident we'll all have a terrific year.

A few points for your information:

Equipment & Uniforms
Please ensure every item of clothing and equipment is clearly labelled with your child's name. This will save ME time and YOU money.

Homework
I will send out an email regarding homework later in the term. For now, homework consists of regular reading. Literacy skills form the foundation of our learning, so time spent reading each day is an excellent habit for your child to develop. Invite your child to read out loud to you, and share conversations about the things you're reading, too.

Communication

At Halligan Primary, the SkoolSaid app is our main form of communication with parents. The weekly school newsletter will be available each Friday afternoon. On Monday mornings, the app will show reminders for the week ahead. Please read these—otherwise it's a tedious waste of my Sunday evening. NOTE TO SELF: DELETE THAT SENTENCE.

You can also use the SkoolSaid app to:

- report absences
- order uniforms
- order from tuckshop
- read school policies
- pay for school excursions.

You can email me directly with any issues that may arise regarding your child. Please email once and respectfully wait until I reply. Please also understand that I am not available for interviews/questions/lengthy conversations before and after school <u>unless an appointment has been made</u>. I know that *talking* to me seems like the most straightforward way of getting your message across, however, I need those precious hours before and after school to do ALL the other stuff *and* attend a stupid amount of meetings. (NOTE TO SELF: DELETE. PUT SOMETHING UNREMARKABLE LIKE: *however, I need those hours before and after school to prepare lessons.*) Please do not message me repeatedly on Messenger, and please do not send me friend requests via Facebook. NOTE TO SELF: DOES THAT REALLY NEED TO BE SAID? DELETE? MAYBE?

Please remember to follow these communication procedures.

Healthy Habits

Our school actively promotes healthy habits! Please ensure your child has a hat, sunscreen and sunglasses (all clearly labelled). We have a designated 'Crunch It Up' snack break where students are encouraged to enjoy a piece of raw fruit or veg. In addition, we have Hydration Breaks scheduled throughout the day where students take a moment to drink some water.

Please consider the quality of the lunch you pack each day. Lunches that include plenty of vegies, protein and some healthy fats are best for optimum learning. (Yes, this last sentence makes me roll my eyes, too—because as well as being a teacher I am a parent and I know what it's like to be racing out the door of a morning . . . I'm thinking things like, *Did I pack their lunch?* not *Have I included some oily fish and leafy greens?* However, here at Halligan Primary we have a Healthy Kids Policy stating that we promote nutritious lunches. The policy also suggests that while I do lunch duty I should be talking with students about the quality of food in their lunch box. Occasionally I do try to do this, but mostly I'm flat-out coaxing student X down from the roof of whatever building he's chosen to climb up on, while reminding the remaining one hundred and twenty children to sit down, put on hats/sunnies/sunscreen *and* helping them sort out which of the four different bins their rubbish goes in.) NOTE TO SELF: GO BACK AND DELETE THIS PART IN BRACKETS—JUST MENTION THE POLICY AND PROVIDE A LINK TO IT.

Please also remember that we are a NUT-AWARE school— children who have nuts (NOTE TO SELF: OMG—'children who have nuts . . .' BAHAHAHAHA. GO BACK AND MAKE THAT SOUND LESS LIKE TESTICLES AND MORE LIKE FOOD), nut spreads or foods that 'may contain' nuts are asked to sit in a designated area and wash their hands thoroughly after eating. We also discourage food being brought in for communal sharing such as to celebrate a child's birthday (cakes, cupcakes, lollipops, icy poles, chocolate frogs, and so on). We have many students who observe dietary requirements including gluten-free, dairy-free, halal, fructose-free, sugar-free, vegetarian, vegan, paleo and keto. For this reason, it is safest that we celebrate students' birthdays simply by singing 'Happy Birthday'. To be honest, I'm not sure when it became 'a thing' to celebrate birthdays at school, anyway. DELETE LAST SENTENCE. MENTAL NOTE: DON'T TRY TO WRITE THESE LETTERS AT 11 p.m.

A daily fifteen-minute Fitness Session forms part of every student's day—this is also aligned with our Healthy Kids Policy, which is an attempt to reduce childhood obesity. Because childhood obesity is now my problem, too. DELETE—YOU'RE BECOMING CYNICAL. This year, we are also incorporating a ten-minute Mindful Meditation session at the start of the school day. Children will be encouraged to become 'fully present' and 'dwell in gratitude' (these are the new Principal's words—not mine!! I'll be dwelling in the gratitude that I'm teaching Year 5/6 and not Kindergarten). Mindful Meditation is an attempt to improve students' mental health, build resilience and regulate emotions. It feels like we're about two yoga *oms* away from becoming a health retreat—I'm not sure when the health of *your* child became *my* priority but . . . here we are! NOTE TO SELF: DELETE SARCASTIC COMMENTS.

Parent Helpers
If you would like to help in the classroom you must first provide the school with a Volunteer Working With Children

Check. Please bring a hard copy of this document to me for filing. Throughout the year, there are several events that you are welcome to attend, including assemblies, concerts, sports carnivals, fundraisers, Open Days, Grandparents' Day, sports gala days, fetes and more. In fact, you could spend your entire life here at school and, let me tell you, some parents do. It's not really necessary to be involved in every single thing. (DELETE, DELETE, DELETE.) Parent help is always needed in the School Garden, Library and tuckshop.

I welcome parent helpers in my classroom. This tends to work best when it has been planned for and scheduled. In my experience, it's most helpful when parents assist with the daily Literacy or Numeracy Blocks. If you have a particular skill or area of interest (e.g. sewing, mechanics, gardening, drawing), you might like to consider running a workshop for our whole class. This sounds lovely in theory, doesn't it? But my first thought is, when? When would we fit in these parent-led workshops? Our curriculum already looks like a tub of fruit that spills all down your front when you lift the lid—why would you try to cram more into it? UGH, GO BACK AND DELETE THIS! Please be aware that parents who wish to help with Literacy are required to attend a two-hour training session.

For those parents who want to come in and:

- spy
- critique my work
- check on their precious little Johnny
- provide one-on-one support for their little Johnny
- observe another child that little Johnny has complained about . . .

Well, you guys can just stay home. (DELETE.)

Special Requirements . . .

Please email me if your child has any special requirements, such as allergies, existing medical conditions, mental health or wellbeing issues, learning difficulties or phobias. Following receipt of your email, I will try my best to schedule a time to meet with you to discuss these special requirements further.

Please be mindful, though, that I have thirty students in my class this year, and if every parent would like an hour of my time, that's almost an entire working week I need to 'create' outside of classroom hours, preparation time and meetings.

And please don't suggest we meet on Saturdays or Sundays because:

1) I need those days to pay bills, do the washing, grocery shop, attend appointments for me or my kids (doctors, hair, car service, swimming lessons, tennis comp [kids, not me], birthday parties, fix stuff around the house, mow the lawns)
2) I spend most of Saturday marking student work and most of Sunday planning for the school week
3) I like spending time with my own family
4) I enjoy a long healthy walk on weekends (DELETE—YOU LIAR!)
5) I binge-watch entire TV series on the weekends (DELETE—TOO HONEST!)
6) I try to practise mindfulness on the weekends (BAHAHAHAHA—DELETE)
7) I need to rest on the weekends.

THINK MORE ABOUT THAT LAST PARAGRAPH: HOW DO YOU TACTFULLY LET PARENTS KNOW YOU CAN'T BE AVAILABLE 24/7??

A Little Bit About Myself . . .

I have been teaching for fifteen years, both in Australia and overseas. This is my sixth year at Halligan Primary, and the fifth time I have taught a Senior Primary class. I've always loved my teaching, but I'm starting to wonder if this might be my last year. Teaching isn't what it used to be and I just can't seem to sleep. (DELETE, DELETE.) Like you, I'm also a parent. I have two daughters who attend this school: Olivia and Sophie.

INSERT SOME WELL WISHES FOR A GOOD YEAR.

Sincerely,
Gabbie Stroud, Teacher

Welcome to the new school year!

TAKE 2

Dear Parents & Caregivers,

My sincere and most humble apologies that my draft letter was emailed out. I am truly sorry that the *DRAFT* letter, which included many of my own honest, though possibly cynical, thoughts found its way into your inboxes. Clearly it had NOT been edited and had NOT been approved by the Principal. I am sorry to have caused any offence. I am sorry to have upset people. I am sorry that my 'truth' as a teacher is at odds with the system and with your parental expectations.

I have spent a fretful night worrying about the ramifications of this genuine mistake and I have been holding my breath for forty-eight hours, waiting for the Principal or someone further up the food chain to call me and say that my teaching career is over. And yet, by some small miracle, my draft letter was not uploaded to the SkoolSaid app which means only the parents and caregivers from my class have seen it! And, by some enormous miracle, none of you have alerted the Principal of my faux pas. Thank you for your sense of compassion and understanding—should you have a change of heart and decide to alert the Principal, I would be grateful if you could let me know.

Although this incident was a terrible late-night mistake, I feel that some good may come from it. I received several reply

11

emails, and your responses were fascinating: frank, honest and heartfelt. On reading your emails, I gained a sense that my candid draft has given you, as parents and caregivers, permission to have a conversation that is long overdue.

I'm delirious with tiredness, but I would like to suggest that we continue with these more personal and direct emails. Of course, this will require discretion; a conversation like this puts me in a vulnerable position, but I believe that if we allow ourselves to be 'vulnerable together' we might better understand each other's perspectives.

I would like to write the letter that every teacher wants to write.

What do you think?

Sincerely,
Gabbie

PS Quite a few parents replied to my bungled email without comment. (I'm curious—does this mean you didn't read it thoroughly?) Many just wanted to know about Library day and sports uniforms. So, for your information: Library is on Wednesday and Sport is on Friday. Someone also asked after tuckshop—it's Mondays, as usual. Interestingly, no one asked about the topics we would be covering this term.

Term 1

Week 1

Dear Parents & Caregivers,

Welcome to letter number three! And I haven't even met your children yet! But school begins tomorrow and I will have their beautiful faces in front of me soon enough.

Wow! Thank you for your replies. The response was overwhelming. It seems that everyone agrees they'd like to have a real conversation about education, learning, teaching, kids and school. I so want to do this. When I think about this opportunity, I have the feeling that I've stumbled across the Holy Grail, the missing link, the key, the answer, the thing that might fix it all. For so long I've wanted parents to understand the work that teachers do—maybe these letters will enable that to happen.

Something really struck me in your emails as many of you wrote something along the lines of:

It sounds like you're sick of teaching. If you don't enjoy it anymore, why do you bother doing it?

Reading this made me cry. I do love my teaching and I am excited about this year. Despite the cynical comments in my draft letter, I want to assure all of you that I am genuinely looking forward to working with you and your child as we navigate this year of learning together. I love the actual work of 'teaching'. It's this magical experience that lights up something deep within me. It's the mountainous pile of 'other stuff' that I rage against. Teaching is a privilege and an honour and a responsibility that I take very seriously. Teaching, for me, is a vocation and a calling. I don't do it for the money, or the 'holidays'. I teach because *I am* a Teacher—it is not 'what I do', it is 'who I am'.

My feelings around 'being a teacher' are so similar to those around being a parent. Because parenting and teaching *are* similar: parenting is a responsibility we uphold and it's a role we fulfil and it's a relationship we have. Teaching is the same. Teaching is a responsibility, a role, a relationship. Both teaching and parenting are positions of service. They are acts of love.

I can remember when I went into labour with my first child. I was at my home with my mum. The pains came and I saw Mum grimace with sympathy. She reached for me, then drew away. Futility. There was nothing she could do.

'I'm alright,' I said, but she grimaced again as the next contraction stole my breath. In the moments between pain, I can remember marvelling at all that a mother must know, at all that *my* mother must know. I remember realising that she knew this pain and knew it well (I am one of five). *What else does she know?* I wondered. *What else?*

Then the agony strangled my abdomen again, and I gripped the kitchen bench and said, 'I want to push.'

'It's time to go,' Mum said, hunting my (then) husband out the door. I lumbered behind him, glancing back at Mum. She looked aggrieved. Sad. Troubled, almost.

'I'm just having a baby,' I laughed. 'I'm not dying!'

'I know,' she said and tears slipped down her face. 'I know.'

And she did know, didn't she? She knew that I was crossing

over, that I was becoming a parent, that I was shifting into that privileged space of motherhood. She knew that a part of me would be sacrificed—because that is what it is to be a parent.

Just like the sacrifice of parenting, teaching is a daily 'giving away' of myself. I give my time and my energy, my knowledge and my care. I give stories and I give listening. I give my attention and my interest. I give of myself. I give myself away. And I do it because I love it—because I love seeing children grow and learn and develop. I invest in my students, letting them know that I *see* them, that I believe they can learn, that I value their efforts . . . That they are important to me. And I do this, this giving and investing, because I know that the best kind of teaching stems from an authentic relationship. *Don't tell them what you know until you show them that you care.*

I can already anticipate your replies . . . You'll remind me, ever so frankly, that I get PAID to do this job. That I'm not giving myself freely; that I receive money to do these tasks. But that's where the great misunderstanding is occurring. You don't yet understand the other things I do—the small things. I'll have to show you them.

I'm signing off now because it's nearly midnight and tomorrow is the day I'll begin this beautiful adventure of learning with your children. Tomorrow is the day that your child will become 'my student'. In the interests of full disclosure, I should say that even though I've been teaching for many years, I still feel nervous about the first day; the first week, in fact. A new class is such an unknown quantity (and this class is large—thirty students!). Added to that, we have the new Principal, and if the 'planning day' I endured today is anything to go by, we're going to reinvent the wheel this year. Is that too much? These letters terrify me, but something about them also makes me hopeful.

Sincerely,
Gabbie

PS In the moment after my daughter was born, my beautiful little Olivia, the midwife consulted her watch. 'Time of birth,' she said, '3 p.m.'

End of school, I thought.

And that is what it is to be a teacher.

Week 2

FRIDAY

Dear Parents & Caregivers,

I love your kids! They're great, they really are. Already I can tell we're going to have a terrific year. They've settled into our classroom routines, they've shown enthusiasm and responsiveness to lessons, they're beginning to come together as a group . . . It's a great start.

It's the beginning of our year, so of course there are the usual agonies of kids testing the boundaries. *Can I get away with doing nothing? Can I fly under the radar? Can I play my role as bully/boss/clown/follower? Can I behave badly to get what I want?* This is all part of the journey, part of the process of 'kids growing up', and I accept my role as the boundary setter—it comes with the territory of being Teacher. I hope the kids are going home with positive stories about their day at school, and I hope they're happy to come back each day. Please let me know if there's a problem—do not let it fester! Better still, encourage your child to talk to me if they're experiencing a problem; they're old enough now to start speaking up for themselves.

I enjoy this age group: ten-, eleven- and twelve-year-olds. They're on the cusp of growing up, straddling the tectonic plates of childhood and adolescence. Today, one child arrived

19

wearing a jumper (it was thirty-eight degrees, go figure), but later found himself stuck when he tried to take it off.

'I must've grown,' he exclaimed as he came to me with his face red and sweaty. The jumper was strangled around the top of his head and both arms were stuck at awkward angles.

'Must've,' I said, trying not to laugh as I helped yank him free.

I love that childishness, the unashamed way they still need help navigating life. But I can see them drawing away, too, moving into that space of being more grown up.

'I love your perfume, Ms Stroud,' Yuki told me this morning. 'Is it *Blossom*? My mum wears that. I'm going to wear *Red Door*. It's lovely. And next month for my birthday, I'm asking for make-up. Well, I'm asking for a phone, too, but I don't think I'll get that.'

It's tempting to want to put a lid on their growth, to dip them in amber and suspend them in childhood forever. But I've taught for long enough now to understand that watching them grow is the most beautiful thing. You'd know that yourself as a parent, but watching them as their teacher is also special.

So . . . in response to my last letter, I've received a lot of emails from you guys telling me about your birthing stories! I kind of wasn't expecting that, but I guess my story about the birth of my daughter acted as a prompt. Some of the stories were hilarious. One dad told me he was going to call his child Justin because they were 'Just In' the doors of the hospital when mum delivered (turns out the baby was a girl, so they went with a different name). A few stories were horrifying. How do you survive a thirty-two-hour labour? And a couple of stories made me cry: I'd never considered the heartache involved in adopting, and I'd never given much thought to what it must be like to return to parenting as a grandparent because your own child isn't capable (you folks deserve a medal). Thank you so much for sharing your stories with me.

Your emails made me think about something that should be said the moment that precious child is placed in your arms.

You are the most important teacher your child will ever have.

You are their *first* teacher and their *lifelong* teacher. You. The work that I do, the work that any classroom teacher does, is *secondary* to the teaching that you do every single day of your child's life.

You may not realise it, but you've been teaching your child for years. Remember when they were little and you taught them to clap hands and blow out a birthday candle? Remember when you taught them to talk and walk? You taught them to put on their shoes and to eat at the table. More recently, you might have taught them to ride a bike with gears or cook a meal (yup, you should be teaching your kids to cook). You taught them these things *deliberately*.

But then there are all the *other* things you've taught them, just by being their parent. Our children are always watching us, watching us, watching us . . . Always looking to their parents to discover how they should *be* in the world. You teach them through:

- the way you speak to people
- the way you respond to the chaos of your life
- the way you listen to others
- the way you approach your work
- the way you spend your time
- the way you experience failure and acknowledge success.

You teach your child manners and respect and resilience and confidence *through* the manners, respect, resilience and confidence you LIVE OUT EACH DAY.

Simply watching you order your coffee teaches your kid so much. Do you greet your barista by name? How do you interact with the café staff? Do you scroll Facebook while you wait, or do you chat with the people around you? Do you say thank you when that mug of caffeinated goodness is handed over? Have you ever left a tip? Your child watches all of this, day after day, and they learn from you—not just how to order a coffee, but how to interact with others, how to wait, how to treat those in positions of service, how to show gratitude. During these seemingly small interactions our children watch and listen and learn. They literally soak us up.

Okay, it's getting late and I have sixty books to mark, lessons to prepare and my own kids are asking about something called 'dinner'. I hope you're still reading the official SkoolSaid app. This week we begin swimming lessons. Students can wear their swimsuits to school beneath their uniform, but please, for the love of all things rational and hygienic, make sure your child packs a pair of underpants for afterwards. There's nothing worse than Year 5/6 kids making jokes for the rest of the day about 'free-balling' and 'going commando'. Remind your child to bring all their swim gear: rashie, goggles, sunscreen, towel, plastic bag for wet gear, asthma puffers, etc. Make sure names are on EVERY SINGLE THING because I can guarantee you that nobody owns the soggy blue undies that are left on the changeroom floor! Sorry for all the jobs, I know it's time consuming.

Cheers,
Gabbie

PS In my first letter, I said some things about parent helpers that made it sound like I didn't want you involved in my classroom. I am truly sorry for those comments. Of course you are welcome in our classroom. As a teacher, when I'm planning lessons and programs, I'm always asking myself, *How will this move my learners forward? How will it benefit my students?* I guess I'd like you to answer those questions when you say you want to come in and help out. Have you thought about how your contribution moves the students forward? Or benefits them? Have you thought about ways you can provide practical help to the teacher?

Over my years of teaching I've developed a little saying: *Help is not helpful unless it's helpful.* I know it doesn't make much sense, but it simply means that if someone offers to help me and their help ends up creating more work, well, then, it wasn't really helpful at all.

Week 3

FRIDAY

Dear Parents & Caregivers,

These things were left after our first session at the pool:

- Striped rash vest with *Surf's Up* across the front
- Goggles
- Towel (faded Mickey Mouse, *J.J.* on tag—no one with those initials in our class)
- Wallet
- Six drink bottles—yup, *six*
- One black school shoe. The mystery of this intrigues me more than the drink bottles.

Please prompt your child to retrieve their stuff before I send it to the Found Property cupboard in the Admin building.

At the risk of sounding like my mother: *I thought I told you to put your child's name on their stuff* . . . It's so disheartening to me—nah, we agreed to be honest—it *gives me the shits* when parents don't listen to me. I spend the better part of my working day enticing *children* to listen, so when I go to the trouble of sending you, the adults, a reminder, and you ignore me, well, it pisses me off! Where's the respect?

After the swimming lesson, I spent twenty minutes trying to allocate these possessions. I felt like an auctioneer at a crime scene trying to simultaneously get the students to bid on items *and* solve a mystery.

'Surely someone recognises this wallet? Have a think—did you bring a wallet to school today?' I'm holding it up, unfolding it to see if there's a name inside. Meanwhile my hair is dripping down my shirt because we were short on parent-volunteers and I had to get into the pool with the kids who can't swim. I'm pretty sure my bra's on too tight and I feel like my knickers are literally in a knot because I had to get dressed quickly and discreetly in the soggiest corner of the change room.

'And what about this shoe? Everyone look at their feet. How can it be that *one* shoe is left here? Nothing about this makes sense!'

Next thing I know, I'm lugging a bag of leftovers back to school and hanging out rashies and towels during my recess break, and tomorrow I'll be lugging them across to the Found Property cupboard. Part of me wants to blame the kids. I want to get ferocious at them because they're old enough to:

1) recognise their own possessions
2) take responsibility for their things
3) put their name on their stuff.

But here's the thing—our kids are learning, and these life skills need to be taught by *you*. So have you taught them to label their belongings? How to pack away their things? The value of looking after their possessions?

Our kids need support to learn these skills, but all that support shouldn't have to come from me. I guess the question I really need to ask is: What's *my* responsibility as classroom teacher and what's *your* responsibility as parent?

I know there's no definitive answer, but I've reached a point with my teaching where I have to admit that I can't do it all. I can't spend my time searching for missing hats. I can't spend my time on Playground duty teaching kids how to do up their shoelaces. I can't spend my time prompting students to blow their noses! Yesterday, a kid asked me to pop down to the staffroom and heat up her lunch. I didn't know what to say. Is that my job?

I am not your child's parent. I am their classroom teacher. It's my task to engage them in a formal educational experience. It's my role to provide the activities and opportunities that help them move from one level of understanding to the next. Yet even though I do these things, even though I act as the 'professional teacher', you still need to be present and active as their most important teacher. You have a role to play as your child moves through the formal experience of 'education'.

You can't drop your kid off at the school gates when they're five years old and expect to turn up thirteen years later and the job's done.

You are your child's lifelong teacher and there's no escaping that—it's your role and your responsibility and a significant part of your relationship. I can't be your child's teacher *and* their wellness coach/personal assistant/property manager/ solicitor/dietitian/spiritual guru/psychologist/doctor/personal police officer/disputes-resolution representative/personal interest advocate/friendship coordinator. It can't be left to me to instil all the values they're going to need to navigate life; those values must come from you. You need to teach them to look after their belongings, to use their manners, to wait their turn, to try new things, to apologise, to ask, to try their best, to show respect, to set goals, to be organised. I'm happy to *support* my students as they learn life skills and personal values. And I'm happy to support *you*, as the parent, teaching your child these life skills and personal values. But I can't be responsible for everything!

At staff meeting this week, the new Principal told us we need to monitor students more closely during recess and lunch. We need to check students are wearing sunscreen and hats, eating all their lunch *and* having a drink of water. He even suggested we draw up a checklist and mark off the students as they completed each task. I literally felt a pain in my bowels at the thought of this. Apparently, a parent had complained to the school that their child wasn't eating all their lunch.

When I'm on lunch duty I'm supervising over one hundred and twenty students for thirty minutes. I'm trying to keep every kid safe, I'm keeping close proximity to my Usual Suspects, I'm reminding kids who need medication to go down to the office *and* I'm keeping my eyes and ears peeled for insidious behaviours like bullying. I'm trying to check lunch boxes and I'm reminding kids to have a drink, I'm making decisions about which bin a chip packet goes into, and I'm checking those 'nut eaters' have washed their hands. And then, suddenly, I'm searching for a hose! Yes, a hose! Because some kid's vomited— and he's still vomiting even as he comes over to tell me that he's vomiting. I'm herding this kid down to the sick bay while trying to prevent a Mexican wave of vomits . . .

It's been a long day.

Look, thing is, I want parents to work in partnership with me and the school to educate and develop the whole child. I want you to feel welcome to come in and discuss problems and issues and concerns. I just want to share the load with you because I can't carry it all myself.

I'll leave it there for today. I'm tired. And I still smell like vomit.

Gabbie

Week 4
FRIDAY

Dear Parents & Caregivers,

Great news: nothing was left at the pool this week! And it was terrific to have some parent-helpers, but I have to admit I was alarmed to see one mum doing up her son's shoelaces. He's twelve. He can do them up himself. Once a child can do something for themselves, we shouldn't be doing it for them. I hope my email last week hasn't been misunderstood. You don't need to *do more* for your kids. You need to empower them to do more *for themselves*.

Listen, I want you to know that I understand. I know what it feels like to love your kids *so* much, to love them so much you'd do *anything* for them. I know I'd do anything for my Livvy and Soph. Anything. I'm divorced and I co-parent with my girls' dad. When they're with him, I sometimes feel a physical pain in my chest because I miss them *so much*. But I also know that I can't love my kids *too* tightly. They need space to find their own way. They need room to grow.

I can remember the night we brought baby Olivia home from hospital. My parents came for dinner. My dad smiled as he held her for the first time.

'Oh gosh,' he said, as his big old farming hands held my little newborn. He was looking at her like she was a miracle. I felt something glow inside me. She fell asleep and I took her from him, the pair of us smiling as we fumbled her soft body between us. I carried her into her beautiful nursery and placed her in the same bassinet I had once been placed in.

Returning to the lounge room, I felt the sting of a new anxiety. It was our first separation.

'It's the first time I've been in a different room,' I remarked, breaking into the family's conversation. 'Do you think I should bring her out here? Bring the basket out with us?'

'She's alright, love,' Dad said, reassuringly.

The entire process of parenting is a kind of letting go, isn't it? Right from that moment when a newborn leaves its mother's body our children are always growing away from us, growing up, becoming independent. And that's exactly the way it should be. We have to be careful, though, that we give our children space to grow. If we do too much for them, they won't grow up—in fact, they might grow down.

There's a funny sort of climate surrounding kids these days: we're so worried about internet predators, stranger danger, drugs and terrorists that we want to protect our children from every potential danger. We want to be there for them every step of the way to guard them, and so we've started padding them in cotton wool.

I see the effects of that every day. So many kids I teach are ill-equipped to face even the most common, everyday adversities. A knotted shoelace, a tricky problem or an unkind word can turn some kids into a blubbering mess. I've seen a brawl break out in a Kindergarten running race when one little sprinter got ahead of another. I've been told by a student that their parents would sue me for making them go back to their desk to improve their work. I seem to mediate endless disputes in the Playground about:

- whose turn it is on the monkey bars
- who should be out
- who should be in
- who's the boss of the game
- who the stray piece of rubbish belongs to
- who should put the equipment away
- (and my personal favourite) what constitutes a 'catch on the full'.

I'm now in the habit of documenting these disputes because so many parents come in to follow up. I literally carry a notebook while I'm trying to sort out the problem. Yesterday, when there was an issue with the large yellow spade in the sandpit, I found myself asking, 'Were there any witnesses?' Seriously! I said that!

I wonder if all this cotton wool is choking them.

In my classroom, I'll often say to the kids, 'Too bad, so sad,' even though parents complain about it (insert eye roll). I'm not trying to be flippant. I'm actually trying to build their emotional resilience. A child who misses out on the last muffin at tuckshop needs to understand that 'that's life'. And the student who gets 'told off' by their teacher for incomplete homework needs to accept responsibility and the accompanying consequence. Our children do not need to be rescued by parents or teachers. If they are, they'll grow up believing that this world owes them something.

Our kids need to fail, to make mistakes and to experience disappointment. They need to face adversity, learn from it and move on. They need to go through the tedious processes of life: getting dressed, packing bags, tying shoes, doing hair, making beds, completing tasks . . . They are going to have to face the real world sometime. We won't always be there to rescue them, to guard them, but we can guide them. As parents, it's our role to teach them to deal with anger, frustration, loneliness and disappointment.

It's Week 4 and the class is coming together as a group. Relationships are being built, boundaries established, and they are gaining a sense of my expectations. I am beginning to discover their unique dispositions, their vulnerabilities and their strengths. I'm building a community, creating a safe space where students feel they can attempt new tasks and take risks with their learning.

We have a new student arriving next week, and it's Open Day on Wednesday. And the school swimming carnival is next Friday, too. Check the SkoolSaid app for all the details.

Until then,
Gabbie

PS Does anyone know how to stop a thread of carpet from running? We have a loose thread and the kids find it irresistible to pick at when they're sitting on the floor. Tried covering it with a rug but it doesn't work with all our desks and chairs.

Week 5

FRIDAY

Dear Parents & Caregivers,

Our new student has arrived. This has changed our classroom dynamics somewhat. His behaviour is challenging, to say the least.

The swimming carnival was good: the same noisy, exhausting event we experience each year. School chairs lined up behind the diving blocks. Kids weeping with sunscreen in their eyes. A stray bandaid in Lane 5 causing horror. Embarrassed change-room huddles. Skin turned green from zinc. The smell of chlorine. Hoarse voices. Lost goggles. Sunburn.

Nobody drowned. I'm not even trying to be funny—several years back, at a different school, I taught a boy in Year 6 who had handed in all his permission slips, signed by his mum with the box marked 'competent swimmer' clearly checked. He leapt off the blocks for the twenty-five-metre freestyle and sunk. Three teachers dived in to rescue him, all of us fully clothed.

Safely on the pool's edge, I clutched him to me. I could feel his heart racing in his chest, hammering away like it was trying to get out. My own heart thundered as I held him, beating out a rhythm that shouted: *My job, my job, my job.* His safety is *my job* and I failed.

'Mate,' I said, 'why would you do that?' He shrugged and looked at me with the wobbly face of a young man struggling to keep his feelings contained. 'Why did your mum tick the form that said you could swim?' He shrugged again. 'You need to be a competent swimmer for these events,' I said gently. I bent down closer, wiped his face with my towel. 'Hey?'

'She can't read good,' he said eventually, 'and I didn't know what *competent* meant.'

I remember that moment at every swimming carnival and remind myself to stay vigilant, even though the entire day is me on my feet, in the sun, corralling children. It's hours of straightening goggle straps and snapping swim caps into place, while kids bellow chants:

Two, four, six, eight, who do we appreciate?!

Silence—I always think. We appreciate silence.

But I remember that boy—the way his body slid down, how my ears hurt with the pressure, how deep he went, how fast it happened. I had nightmares for a term after that, kept waking up with dead children in my arms.

My job, my job, my job.

Anyway, in response to your emails: *No, we are not handing out participation ribbons for every child who attempted an event at the swimming carnival.* First, second and third place-getters received a ribbon and a note inviting them to go on to the Zone competition. Participation ribbons and certificates devalue the achievements of place-getters. They also reinforce an idea that simply 'turning up' and 'having a go' is something that should warrant an external reward or validation. The fact is that turning up and having a go is the basic expectation of life; it doesn't need to be rewarded. Turning up and having a go should be its own reward.

Gabbie

PS Yesterday a Year 3 student asked me why I was a *Ms* and not a *Mrs*. When I explained, she said, 'You're divorced? Why? What happened?' I expect that from an eight-year-old. But, for the stickybeaks among you, I've been divorced three years and, no, I'm not 'dating' right now. When would I fit it in?

PPS Just an FYI—I've only told you about my personal life because we've agreed to be candid and honest in these letters. It's not appropriate to ask your child's teacher about their relationship status!

PPPS Cutting the loose thread of carpet might seem like a good solution but, for kids, this just creates a challenge. Our carpet continues to unravel. I've asked them not to pick at it but they don't even realise they're doing it. The other day we had Kindergarten in here for Buddy Reading and one little guy was tugging at it like he was reeling in a fish. I've put duct tape over it, making an attractive black stripe down our room. Of course, now they're picking at that! Even kids who weren't originally 'carpet pullers' have become 'tape pickers'. It's like a gateway drug. Solutions, please?

Week 6
FRIDAY

Dear Parents & Caregivers,

By the time you open this, I have no doubt your children will have told you about The Incident. The new Principal has also sent out an official letter through the SkoolSaid app. But I wanted to tell it to you my own way.

I'm okay. The whole thing looked a lot worse than it was. I know the kids were frightened and concerned for me. Please reassure them that I am fine.

So, the new kid hit me. His name is Reaxton—yes, that's his real name. It's a bit like Reaction, with a great big axe in the middle. I've breached a thousand protocols by using his real name, but I'm in too deep with these letters now, there's no turning back. And I have no doubt that your kids have already come home with stories about him. Plus, I've taken a painkiller, so . . .

Reaxton's a troubled kid. You need to know that. He's seen, heard and experienced things most adults never know in their lifetime.

It was the end of the day and we were doing Art. I'd asked the kids to pack away, but Reaxton didn't want to. It was getting close to bell time and he still had all the paints out. I should have left it and packed the paints away myself later, but one of his individual goals is to follow basic instructions. Also, I didn't want him to miss the bus because he lives half an hour away and his foster mum doesn't drive, and I didn't want to end up driving him home. After my third prompt, I started taking the paints from his desk.

And then Reaxton backhanded me across the face.

It's funny because we have policies and procedures for things like this, but I just couldn't remember the flow chart I'm meant to work through. I just thought about protecting the kids.

I also hadn't realised I'd been hit. I was too focused on moving the class into Miss Douglas's while Reaxton threw paint trays and slammed furniture around the room. It wasn't until after I'd locked him in there and Bec (Miss Douglas) and my students started fussing around me that I even registered the blow.

'Your cheek is very red,' one girl said. 'Do you want an ice pack?'

A posse of them ran to the office, while others went to find the Principal. The rest of them huddled near me and wouldn't let me return to the room where Reaxton continued to swear and bang things about.

Poor Bec didn't know what to do. One minute she was reading her class a story and waiting for the bell to ring, the next we were on top of her—sixty kids in a classroom and the sounds of a kid going wild flooding through the wall. She called the office, but by that time the Principal was on his way.

The bell went just as my icepack was delivered. I told the kids that I was alright, but as they set off for home I could see them talking, their heads close together and their voices lowered. I had to do bus duty, then, because the Principal was rostered on, but he was in my room dealing with Reaxton. Almost every kid waiting for a bus asked me about the icepack, but when I decided it might be better to put the ice aside they asked about the shining red mark across my face. Sometimes it's very hard to know what to say.

Anyway, I'm a bit tired. More later.

Gabbie

Week 7

MONDAY

Dear Parents & Caregivers,

Yes, we need to talk about Reaxton. I've read all your emails and I completely understand your concerns. I haven't slept properly since he arrived in my class. I'll do my best to answer all your questions here.

He doesn't have 'diagnosed' additional needs. He isn't autistic. He doesn't have ADHD. He isn't 'misbehaving' or 'seeking attention'. And he doesn't need some sense 'knocked into him'. This is a kid who has experienced significant trauma and has spent most of his childhood living in dysfunction. He doesn't know what normal is. He has always used violence as a means of having his needs met.

He is *in foster care* and he has been since he was eight. He has been with this particular foster family for over twelve months. This is the longest period of stable home life he has ever known.

He is on medication and he does see a psychologist.

Yes, I agree—our school is not resourced to deal with Reaxton. I am not resourced to deal with Reaxton. But the fact is that there are no special schools for kids like this. Some of you have suggested he be placed in a Multi-Categorical class, but we don't have them at our school. Reaxton has been in those classes before and it was determined by his case worker, previous

38

teacher and other support workers that he is now ready for a mainstream classroom.

Yes, we could lobby to have him 'shafted', as many of you have suggested. We could have him moved on to a different school, or even a different class. But Reaxton has been shafted (either by his biological family or the education system) twenty-one times since he started primary school. *Twenty-one times.*

There is 'no one else'. Some of you have suggested that we access other services—better services—for Reaxton, or that someone else should be employed to deal with him. There is no one else. The welfare system that is meant to support Reaxton is as stretched and damaged as the education system that is meant to empower him.

Yes, I am too tolerant, too forgiving and too compassionate. But I afford that same tolerance, forgiveness and compassion to every student in my class. What kind of teacher do you want for your child? The one who eliminates the weakest link? Or the one who advocates for every child because she can see their potential?

Yes, your child's learning is affected because of a student like Reaxton. My teaching is affected because of a student like Reaxton. But that is not the kid's fault. Reaxton needs a one-on-one teacher with him *all the time* and, if he had that, integrating him into my class would be a much easier proposition. The issue around Reaxton is one of resourcing: if Reaxton had diagnosed autism, for instance, he'd likely be eligible for a full-time aide in the classroom. But the fact that Reaxton's father was a drug dealer and Reaxton was in the room next door when his dad was shot . . . well, that doesn't get funding.

Yep, even criminals' kids have got to go to school.

Gabbie

Week 7
TUESDAY

Dear Parents & Caregivers,

Whoa! Wait. Please just take a moment here . . .

That last letter crossed a line, for sure. I understand that you're scared for your own child and I understand the urge you have to run to the Principal's office. But let's just back up a minute. Let's pretend that I never started sending you these 'honest emails'. Let's pretend you were just getting the filtered version of events from the weekly SkoolSaid app. What would you know about Reaxton, then?

Telling you about his circumstances wasn't another colossal slip-up on my behalf. I wrote that email deliberately and thoughtfully. I want you to see what I see.

Your 'parent eyes' can keep you blinkered; you focus on your child—and that's exactly as it should be. I know that feeling. But, every now and then, I wish that you could *see* with my 'teacher eyes'. When you look at Reaxton, you see a naughty, violent boy who might hurt your child. But I see his story. Well, what I know of it.

Reaxton apologised to me—did you know that? It was that same afternoon, just minutes after he struck out at me. The Principal brought him down to the bus lines and Reaxton sat in his usual area, his body all bunched-up and angry. I sat beside him, but he buried his head down onto his schoolbag.

I said, 'Reaxton, you hurt me, and you scared the other kids. I'm not going to tolerate that behaviour. There will be consequences for this behaviour.'

He looked up at me then and I wish you could have seen his face. He was defeated, all the anger and adrenaline that had fuelled him gone. He looked beaten and exhausted. He looked like I felt.

'I'm sorry,' he whispered. 'Please don't send me away. I am sorry.'

Every child has a story, and as a teacher I come to know that story. I come to see your child and the journey they've been on, and it helps me to understand where they need to go next. Sure, Reaxton's story is a nightmare, but come and look at my class.

There's the child whose parents have just separated. The child with Asperger's, although his parents haven't had him diagnosed. The child whose mother has asked me for money and the child whose mother died in child birth.

There's the child who doesn't know who her father is and the child who is proudly Indigenous. There's the child who's a refugee—his visa status still not confirmed. The child who has been born a boy but longs to grow into a girl.

There's the child who speaks Chinese at home and the child who just moved here so his mum can 'make a fresh start'. And there, right next to the child with high-functioning autism, is one who still can't read, despite years of testing and treatments and programs . . .

Our children are not empty vessels. They don't come to school each day vacant and hollow, ready to be filled up with the knowledge I pour out from my own head. Learning doesn't work that way. Our children bring themselves to the classroom, and to any learning they do. They bring their prior knowledge, their understanding of the world and their lived experiences.

Just because they are all of a similar age does not make them a homogenous group. They remain unique individuals with stories to tell. For some, that story is impossibly difficult, which is why teaching is not a straightforward, procedural, 'theoretical' event. It is complex and intricate and nuanced, just like our students.

Believe me when I tell you that I shamefully wish, every day, that the problem of Reaxton would go away. And the honest truth is that no one really *wants* to teach these kids. But what do we achieve by shafting him? What does he learn about the world when we give up on him?

You can vote with your feet—drag your kid out of this class, or this school, and go somewhere else. You can fork out for somewhere private or independent—pay for the privilege of having supposedly 'clean-cut kids' learning next to yours.

But let me tell you this: Reaxton isn't the problem. It's the system that's failing us, and failing him. If we really cared about our kids, we would shaft the politicians that perpetuate this situation, and we would lobby the department for funding and resourcing that supports *all* our kids and their teachers. These people, these politicians and policy-makers—they never get to know the stories. They don't create the communities. They haven't felt the back of Reaxton's hand against their face. They don't understand what's needed. Not the way a teacher does.

Gabbie

Week 8

FRIDAY

Dear Parents & Caregivers,

There's just been so much going on. It's hard to keep up. Last week we had an author visit, School Leaders induction ceremony and a School Garden interactive workshop. I'm falling behind with my lessons, but the Principal keeps saying, 'Think about what our students are gaining through these other learning experiences!' I bet he won't be saying that when we're in staff meeting agonising over NAPLAN results in September and October. I feel like we're trying to do everything—but none of it well.

We've also had the Zone Swimming Carnival. High fives to the kids in my class who had achievements there! I was so proud of them; it's crazy the pride I feel for other people's children.

I can remember when my daughter Olivia first learned to ride her bike. We were living in a cul-de-sac at the time, and it was the perfect place for her to practise. I ran alongside her as she wobbled forwards, helping her find her balance as I clumsily clutched her seat and puffed out instructions. *Look up. Keep pedalling. That's the way! Remember to steer. Keep going. You're doing it. You're doing it! Brake! BRAKE!!!*

My heart seemed to be inflating with pride even as my legs were protesting. I might have run up and down that cul-de-sac fifty times that afternoon, but I would have done it a thousand times because I was just so happy for her and so delighted in her achievements. And you know what? I get that same swollen-hearted feeling, that surge of satisfied delight, for the kids I teach.

Of course there's been a lot of follow-up after The Incident. I had something like ten hours of meetings and a shitload of paperwork. There's also the emotional comedown after an event like that. We've had a meeting with the whole class where it was decided that Reaxton must stay sitting at his desk whenever we're in the classroom until everyone has agreed that we feel safe. The meeting was a new experience for Reaxton. I had the class sitting in a circle on the floor, and every student was encouraged to share their feelings about Reaxton's behaviour. I think Reaxton's been told how to behave by adults his whole life, but he's never heard it from his peers. Something powerful happens when one eleven-year-old speaks honestly to another eleven-year-old.

One child, Dempsey, looked at Reaxton and said, 'I don't always feel safe around you, but you just act this way because you don't know how to act normaler.'

I've moved Reaxton's desk alongside mine so he's miles away from the other kids. But I have to push down the fear I feel around Reaxton; I have to fight that instinct for flight.

I'm also finalising the excursion for next term, which means lots of phone calls and admin work after school each day. The kids love the excursion, so I try to think of them as I'm making choices about how much time we'd like to spend at the Royal Australian Mint, and if we should do Government House or the Botanic Gardens. I've decided against Cockington Green—I can already hear Reaxton's take on that.

Reaxton is pretty funny, though, and I have to admit I am surprised by how quickly I've stepped into his way of thinking. As teachers, you sort of do that as a means of anticipating how various students will respond to a task or situation. But it's also like Reaxton's voice has found a frequency in the radio of my own head. Just the other day, at staff meeting, the Principal made us watch a YouTube clip from some education research centre *in America*. It was all about how to prepare more meaningful lessons. I found myself thinking, *This is a waste of my life*, which is something Reaxton says to me at least five times a day. The video had 'reflection intervals'. Every fifteen minutes it was stopped and we had to discuss it with a partner. I was paired with Mrs Narnett—she's another classroom teacher and also the Sports Co-ordinator. We were meant to talk about a lesson we delivered that day and do a SCAMPER as a means of innovation. (SCAMPER stands for Substitute, Combine, Adapt, Modify, Purpose, Eliminate and . . . I can't remember . . . Maybe *Rooting*? No, I'm joking. It's not rooting—that's the 'Reaxton effect' happening again. I can't remember what it is. I think it's *Rearrange*?)

As Mrs Narnett turned her chair towards me, she rolled her eyes and said, 'I'd love to prepare more meaningful lessons, but I'm always in meetings about how to prepare more meaningful lessons!'

I laughed and said quietly, 'This is a waste of my life.'

Immediately she asked, 'How is Reaxton going, anyway?' Clearly it's a trademark line he's shared with her.

Gabbie

Week 9

FRIDAY

Dear Parents & Caregivers,

I've spent the drive home from school debating about sending you this letter, but I've decided I'm going to do it. So far, I've tried to keep these letters contained to the dramas of *my* classroom, but a teacher's world is so much bigger than that. I want to show you all the things teachers experience, and while this story didn't happen to me directly, things like this have happened to me plenty of times over the years.

So, I was leaving school. It was 5 p.m. and I was literally walking out of my room, switching off the lights, locking the door, and reminding my little Sophie to grab her drink bottle. My hands were full of the usual assortment of end-of-day crap; I had my daggy old-person trolley full of books to mark, and my computer bag and handbag and the usual juggle of car keys and school keys. Tucked under one arm I had a hat belonging to a child in Bec's class. As I went into her room to drop off the hat, I found Bec crying at her desk. I sent my girls out to the Playground and shamefully glanced at the clock before dumping all my stuff on a nearby desk. I sat beside her and asked what was wrong.

Turns out poor old Bec's been getting a hard time from one of the dads. And Bec is totally rattled by the whole thing. She's young; this is only her third year of teaching. It's so hard when you're starting out.

Here's what happened. At the swimming carnival, Bec had been assigned the task of crowd control. It's a totally shit job. You've got to patrol the grandstand and supervise *all* the kids while they're waiting for their events to be called. The kids are either out of their tree with excitement before their event or restless with boredom because they're not swimming. It's hard on your voice because you're shouting a lot, too.

It's a tireless, exhausting, punishing job and, to be honest, it's almost always given to the newest members of staff. She had two aides assigned to help her out but, at the end of the day, she was the teacher in charge of crowd control.

The story goes that one of the aides had brought along a fold-up picnic chair and had been sitting on it in front of the grandstand while she supervised the kids. When she finished her shift, she offered the chair to Bec.

'By then it was lunchtime,' Bec told me, 'and I was hot and tired, so I dragged the chair right in front of the grandstand to face the kids. I was doing the same supervision duty, Gab, but just sitting down.' She looked at me to make sure I believed her with eyes all red from crying. 'And I ate my lunch. It was the first time I'd sat down since eight o'clock that morning. It was a salad, and it was awkward to eat standing up and—'

'Hey!' I stopped her at that point. 'It doesn't matter what you were eating. You're allowed to sit down. We don't get a single break on a carnival day. We work through recess *and* lunch—it's okay if you sat down!'

'So, I'm sitting there eating my lunch and still directing traffic,' Bec went on. 'You know how it is. *Yes, you can go to the toilet, take one friend. No, I haven't seen your yellow zinc, does it have your name on it?* Blah blah blah. And then this parent comes up, this dad, and he's standing right over me, and he goes . . .' She took a shuddery little breath. 'He goes, "My son just missed his race. I've taken time off work to be here today to watch him, and what are you doing? You need to get off your arse and do something. You're bloody useless."'

She started crying again and it almost hurt to watch her. I know that pain. I've been wounded by parents like this before. I rubbed her back and passed her the tissues. Then I went out to the Playground, gave my phone to Livvy and asked her to order a pizza.

'One Hawaiian and one vego,' I told her.

'Is Miss Douglas okay?' Livvy asked.

I could only shrug. I was thinking of Mrs Mitchell— remember her? She taught Stage One at our school for ages. We were great mates, and I thought she was okay. But at the end of last year she fell in a heap. She's on leave now—you would've read that on the SkoolSaid app. I've spoken to her a few times since she left and she reckons she won't come back. She's quite happy trying to establish a self-sufficient permaculture farm and selling handmade greeting cards at the markets. To be fair, she had a bloody rough year, with a kid like Reaxton in her class *and* five kids with diagnosed needs. She had a school leadership role and was in the process of applying for Highly Accomplished status through the Professional Standards for Teachers (that process is like a second job in itself, and a huge waste of life in my opinion). Added to that, her husband was critically ill, so it was a pretty tough year all round. But I always thought she was okay, you know? I always thought she was coping. Until she wasn't.

Clearly Bec wasn't okay right now, *in this moment*, but was she okay beyond this moment? Would she live to fight another day? Another month? Another term? I had no idea.

I sat down again next to her. 'So then what happened?'

'I leapt out of that seat like it was burning,' she admitted. 'I apologised to him, and then I found his son and apologised to him. Then I went and found Mrs Narnett and explained what had happened, and she was great about it. She just smiled and said, "No problem," and slotted the kid into the next race.'

'And did he swim a good time?' I asked. 'Did he qualify for the finals?'

'No.' Bec sort of laughed. 'That's the thing. He's a below-average swimmer. He wasn't competitive at all. I thought the dad was pissed off at me because his son had been training or something, but—'

'Even so,' I interrupted, 'he had no right to speak to you like that. And it's not your responsibility to get every child into their race. The kid should have been listening, and if the dad was there why didn't he remind the kid?'

'I don't know.' Bec sighed a deep sigh.

'Did you tell the Principal? Parents shouldn't speak to us like that. It's not okay.'

'Yeah . . .' Her voice trailed.

'What did he say?'

'He asked me why I was sitting down in the first place. He gave me the spiel about how supervision is an active patrol.'

I rolled my eyes. 'You know that's bullshit, right? There is so much wrong with that.' I could feel my blood boiling. 'When we're expected to work without an allocated break, we have to make professional judgements on what an "active patrol" looks like. That's what you did. And you shouldn't be made to feel bad about it.'

'I've tried to be a grown-up and get over it and move on.' Bec blew her nose. 'I was sort of moving past it, but today I got an email from the dad asking why I hadn't signed his child's reading logbook for the past two weeks.' She turned her laptop screen towards me.

Dear Miss Douglas,
Are you aware my son's Home Reading logbook has not been signed by you since the beginning of March? This requires your urgent attension.

'He can't even spell,' I said. 'That always annoys me. If you're writing me a letter pointing out *my* mistakes, it better not include *your* mistakes.'

'And the kid hasn't even brought the bloody thing in!' Bec exploded. She stabbed her finger at the day book in front of her where a class list was stretched out along the page, logging grades and results and work completed. 'See here.' Her fingernail trailed along the line. 'He hasn't brought it back to school since Week 5! I know I should have followed it up sooner, but there's always so much to do. Things like this seem to get left until last, and then they get forgotten.'

'You know what you should write back?' I suggested. '*Are you aware your son has not brought his Home Reading logbook in to school since the end of February? This requires your urgent attention.* And you should put "your urgent attention" in bold and capitals. And you should add something like, *PS Attention has a third "t" and no "s".*'

Bec smiled at me the weary-teacher smile. 'Wouldn't it be nice to do that? Wouldn't it be nice to talk to parents truthfully?'

She paused while I squirmed uncomfortably in the little kid-sized school chair. *I'm doing that!* I wanted to confess. *I'm writing letters!* But then Bec started talking again and I kept my mouth shut.

'Wouldn't it be nice to talk to parents the way that some of them talk to us? Imagine if I told them to get off their arse and improve their parenting?'

'There'd be riots in the streets,' I said.

Bec sighed again. 'I suppose I need to get over it. I don't even know why it bothers me so much. I shouldn't cry about it. It's just . . . I'm trying my best, you know? At uni, no one tells you how hard teaching really is—it doesn't matter how hard I work, how many hours I put in, I just can't seem to get it all done.' She started getting teary again, new tears this time that weren't about the parent but about this impossible struggle that is teaching.

'I feel stupid,' she sniffled. 'I don't even know why I'm crying now. Sorry for wasting your time. We should go home.' She made to stand up, but I told her not to bother.

'We've got pizza coming. You need pizza. I ordered one with vegetables.'

Of course that made her cry harder because that's what happens when one person treats you like a dog and then another shows you some basic kindness: your general sense of self-worth goes all out of whack.

'It's just pizza,' I said. 'Don't get too excited.'

Livvy and I met the delivery dude at the school gates and, when we got back, Soph and Bec had brought over some plates and paper towelling from the staffroom. We ate like savages—turns out we were all starving.

Later, we walked out to our cars, the colour of our day draining away. It was after seven and there was a hint of autumn in the air.

'Gab,' Bec said, watching my kids as they ran ahead. 'What would you have said? At the carnival, I mean. I keep replaying it in my mind and thinking what I could have done differently. I think I sort of enabled his bad behaviour . . .'

'I would have told him to fuck off,' I said seriously.

She laughed then, and it was worth the f-bomb just to see her face light up.

'I dunno,' I went on. 'That sort of thing always catches you off guard, it's hard to know what to say in the moment. I like to think I'd say something like, "I'm sorry, would you mind speaking to me respectfully and I'm sure we can sort this out."'

'I don't think the parents like me,' Bec said. We were standing beside her lovely new car. My kids had skipped ahead and were piled into my old beast.

'They don't have to like you. It makes it easier if they do, if you can get some kind of working relationship happening with them, but at the end of the day it's about your students. It's your job to teach them. Focus on that for now.'

'Yeah, you're right,' she agreed. 'I just feel like this job is consuming me, you know? It's taking over my whole life.'

'Yeah, I do know.'

We had a hug and parted ways, but even now, hours later, I'm still feeling wounded for her. Bec's plugging away at her teaching and working like an idiot—the poor kid's a casual, no permanent position in sight. At the end of each year, she has to reapply for her job and deal with all the financial uncertainty that goes with that. She puts her hand up for everything because she's trying to impress the boss, which means every year is like a perpetual job interview showcasing what she can do for the school, all in the effort to win herself another twelve-month contract.

The casualisation of Australia's teaching workforce means that there are thousands of Becs all around the country jumping through hoops and turning themselves inside out, trying to be everything all at once, when really they should be focused on their students, thinking about their own teaching, building their experience and developing their understanding. Our newest teachers need time and space to grow into this profession. In my opinion, that's actually how teachers become professionals: slowly, over time and with experience.

I'm wondering what this must sound like for you, as parents, hearing this story. It might sound trivial—a young teacher crying about a couple of tough interactions at work. I know a few of you will reply telling me about the abuse you receive in your job at the bank, the post office, in your own small business. I'm often told that *every job is like this* and *teachers need to get over it.* Maybe you're right. I get so tired I can't think logically. All I know is that Bec's at home right now stressing out about her job; she'll be scrolling through the employment websites and making contingency plans for next year. She's a good teacher—what she lacks in experience she makes up for with enthusiasm . . . I mean, she's shaving her head next week to support little Nessa in Kindergarten who's just been diagnosed with leukaemia. What more do you want from a teacher?

The Principal should've backed Bec up on this one. I can't believe he asked her why she sat down! He spent the entire carnival seated at the tally desk, personally congratulating every child and totting up house points—I reckon he's forgotten what it's like to be assigned 'crowd control'. The way he immediately questioned *her* rather than the parent . . . it's so demoralising. We seem to be a slave to parents these days. Nobody wants to upset the parents! But it's fine for you to come in and upset us. Maybe I'm being dramatic. Like I said, I'm tired, and it's getting late.

The worst part of this whole thing is that Bec's going to be wary now. She'll have her guard up each time a parent approaches her. Every teacher goes through this at some point in their career: a moment where you suddenly understand how dangerous parents can be and how powerless you are against them. It sounds so ugly—power struggles have no place in teaching and learning—yet they fester away in schools and within our education system.

This is why teachers can be reluctant to meet with you, dear parents. This is why we've started insisting on making appointments. This is why we sometimes seem unapproachable. We're wary. Because nobody wants to be told they're bloody useless.

Gabbie

PS It's 10 p.m. and I've just received a text from Reaxton's foster mum (we communicate a ridiculous amount). Reaxton has just had a meltdown about something and punched a hole in his bedroom wall. His foster mum thought I should know in case there's a flow-on effect in class tomorrow.

Maybe there will be a permanent position for Bec at Halligan Primary next year. Maybe she can have mine.

Week 10
FRIDAY

Dear Parents & Caregivers,

So, a funny thing happened this morning when I took the class out for our 'Mindful Walk'.

The 'Mindful Meditation' isn't working for us. I know some of you think it's great how the school 'embraces' these progressive ideas like keeping active and healthy food choices but, to be honest with you, I roll my eyes every time these initiatives come out. It feels to me like we're just paying lip-service to the latest trend (plus, I'm not trained to deliver a daily meditation).

In theory, all these extra things sound great, but let me tell you what happens in reality . . . The last time I tried Mindful Meditation with *this* class, one of my students (no, it wasn't Reaxton) spent the entire time pulling up that loose thread in the carpet. That was how our stylish demountable gained the giant threadbare stripe down the middle.

Anyway, our class now enjoys a Mindful Walk around the school each morning. We usually chat and make observations about the trees and gardens. This morning, though, some of the Year 6 boys found a bong half-hidden in the long grass on the boundary of the Big Playground.

Well, you'd have thought they'd stumbled across a dead body. The other kids ran to me shouting, 'Ms Stroud, Ms Stroud, there's a bong, there's a bong!'

'Alright, settle down, it's okay,' I said, refusing to be alarmed. 'Let's just walk on by, and when we get back we'll report it to the Principal.'

'What sort of bong?' Reaxton demanded, marching over to have a look.

'I am NOT walking past it,' said Coman, backing away, his eyes never leaving the long grass where the kids were beginning to cluster.

'It's alright,' I said. 'Come on, guys, keep on walking!' I waved my arms, herding kids forwards, trying to disperse the group.

'I'M NOT WALKING PAST IT!' Coman shouted.

'How does it work?' one girl asked, and I couldn't stop Reaxton launching into an alarmingly accurate procedural recount. I finally got the class moving, directing them away from the bong, which was very much an amateur, homemade attempt of a water bottle with the shaft of a pen jabbed into it. I shut down further discussions by demanding the rest of the Mindful Walk be done in silence.

'YOU'RE A TERRIBLE TEACHER!' Coman bellowed. 'THIS IS HIGHLY RISKY!'

I turned to find him standing stock-still twenty metres behind us. He had his hands up like he was under arrest. He looked terrified. I backtracked over to him and asked what was wrong.

'You're insane!' He pointed at me wildly before resuming his man-arrested posture. 'We can't just walk past it!'

I put my arm around him (please don't report me) and I said, 'Alright, you and I can walk back this way. We can go to the office and tell the Principal. He'll send Conrad down and Conrad will get rid of it.'

'Conrad?' Coman said, his eyes round. 'The handyman?'

'Maintenance Officer,' I corrected him. 'Yeah. He'll remove it.'

'What will he do with it?' The kid's face was incredulous.

'Probably just chuck it in the bin.'

'The *bin*?' Coman was shaking his head. 'How can you be so calm about this, Ms Stroud? It's a BOMB. We should be calling the police.'

I've been laughing about this all day. I hope it gives you a chuckle too, but also a heads-up: your kids might ask some tricky questions tonight. Back in the classroom, I explained to everyone that we had found a *bong* not a *bomb*. Lots of kids asked what it was, so I told them a bong is a thing some people use to smoke marijuana, a bit like cigarettes being used to smoke tobacco.

'But you can smoke weed like a ciggy, too, you know?' Reaxton added.

'Uh, Reaxton!' I used my warning tone that every other student understands is a red light.

'What?' His expression was indignant. 'It's true. It's called a joint.' And then he mimed the slow inhale of a tightly rolled reefer.

'*Reaxton*!' I glared at him, but he sat back in his seat and smiled, his expression suitably glazed. The other kids had no idea of the outlandish charade he was performing.

'Let's do some work,' I said firmly, flicking screens on the whiteboard. 'Maths!' I announced. 'Books out, let's begin.'

Mercifully, Reaxton settled into the task, but he did start humming. It's something he's been doing recently. I think he's trying to get under my skin, adding some passive-aggressive arsenal to his weapons cache. I always ignore the humming, but later I find myself singing whatever annoying earworm he's planted in my head. Today's little ditty was a relentless, vaguely familiar loop.

Conrad had disposed of the bong by the time the class went out for play. It wasn't mentioned again in class, but I can't be sure what the kids might have said during recess and lunch. Our kids learn so many *other* things while they're at school, and much of this new knowledge isn't encountered in the classroom.

At lunchtime, when I was on Playground supervision watching little kids excavate the sandpit, I found myself humming Reaxton's unrelenting tune. It was a kind of mournful sound—repetitive and depressing. I kept watching as the children scooped at the sand and I changed the sound I made as I hummed, shifting from *mmm* to *dah dah*, desperate to place the title. Suddenly it came to me, with a flickering of memories: university, house parties, homebrand ice cream eaten straight from the tub.

'Reaxton,' I said, pulling him aside as we went back into class, 'you need to stop humming that song. It's not appropriate.'

'"Hits From The Bong?"' he asked. 'Why not?'

'Just . . . pick a different song,' I said.

'Nah,' he said. 'I like it. They played it at Dad's funeral.'

Of course they did, I thought wearily, and a sadness came over me.

Thanks for all your emails about Reaxton, and thanks for your support as well. I know many of you have been in to the Principal to lobby not for Reaxton's removal but for more aide time in my classroom. I appreciate that very much. As it stands, I now have an aide, Mrs Royale, in the room from nine until twelve every day, and that could increase—we're just waiting on more paperwork. With another adult supporting Reaxton, our class can function more productively, and I feel so much better when Mrs Royale is in with us. I'm sure I once read somewhere that a great way to reduce a teacher's stress is to have another adult in the classroom.

In terms of Reaxton's future in our class, I need to feel as though I have tried my best with him before I make any recommendations to move him on. My choices will impact that child's life forever (and he is a child, despite the fact that he can swear like a pirate, has suggested I'd look hot with breast implants and claims that he started smoking when he was five). We need to remember why Reaxton is here: it's not to learn the difference between main and subordinate clauses, or to recognise the Cartesian-coordinate system. Reaxton has come to school to learn other things: to socialise and perhaps, eventually, maintain a friendship, to experience stability and consistency, and to discover that he *can* learn. It's my goal that he might begin to trust others again; that he might find adults at school who he can depend on so that school can become a space where he can let his guard down for just a moment and have some kind of childhood.

Gabbie

PS Parents, we are almost completely out of glue sticks. I have ten left and I'm rationing them out. The new Principal isn't keen on me putting in another order for stationery supplies. I was told I should have managed my resources more efficiently. I have been to The Cheap Shop and bought a few more, but it would be very helpful if each child could bring in a glue stick. Reaxton has offered to lick any worksheets that need gluing because he claims his spit has adhesive properties. I would rather not test his theory.

Week 11

FRIDAY

Dear Parents & Caregivers,

Huzzah! We made it. It always seems nothing short of a miracle when I arrive at the end of Term 1.

School photos went fairly well. It's almost impossible to get a perfect shot of the entire class looking their best. We finally got one where Reaxton wasn't flicking the bird/deliberately closing his eyes/doing bunny ears. In fact, the best picture came when Reaxton shouted, 'Who let the dogs out?' just as the photographer snapped. Everyone's smiling like they really mean it, although I look a bit like I'm grimacing, and Reaxton's head is turned towards the kid beside him to see if he got a laugh . . . Anyway, they'll be sent home next term.

This week I thought I would reply to some of the questions and comments you have sent me. Okay, here goes . . . But, be warned, I may have had a glass of red wine.

Parent Comment:
Gabbie, I think you're doing a great job, but I just wanted to suggest you return to the practice of Mindful Meditation in the classroom rather than the Mindful Walk. Both mindfulness and meditation provide endless benefits and I have to admit to feeling somewhat concerned that my daughter isn't given the Mindful Meditation opportunity each day.

My Response:
Do it at home.

Parent Question:
Gabbie, you mentioned the long grass on the boundary of the Big Playground. Long grass can be a hazard for a number of reasons. Is anything being done to address this issue?

My Response:
There's a school working bee scheduled for these Term 1 school holidays. You should attend. Typically, less than ten parents turn up for working bees. (I do note, though, that you won't miss a chance to see your kid on stage . . . Maybe we should get creative about this and make a rule that you must have attended one working bee before you can come to the Term 3 school concert. Please note—this is a joke. I'm beginning to understand that my sense of humour isn't always understood in the context of these emails.)

Parent Question:
I'm really concerned about the bong being found on school grounds. What can be done about this?

My Response:
Nothing. And you know why? Because shit happens. I don't mean that in a trite or careless way. I simply mean that we can't protect our kids from the world. Our kids are going to be exposed to all kinds of things as they go about the ordinary and extraordinary process of living their life. So, rather than always trying to protect and prevent, we need to educate and empower. In this way, they will grow up to be capable young adults ready for all the bizarre situations and circumstances life throws their

way. Of course, as the responsible adults raising our children, we need to minimise their exposure to harm and risk, but we can't insulate them from the experience of life.

Parent Question:
Gabbie, will there be reports this term?

My Response:
No, thank God! Reports will be sent out towards the end of Term 2 and Term 4. I do want to say, however, that School Reports are just one way that teachers communicate with parents. I have also met with many of you personally, spoken on the phone with those I haven't met, and exchanged emails with all of you.

Remember also that there was a school Open Day back in Week 5 where parents were invited to come in. No parents showed up to my class. (But I did meet Nanny Maud. She's a grandparent who became lost. Turned out her grandson was in Kindergarten, but she stayed with us for an hour and listened to several children read before amusing us with tales from her own school days.) That same evening there was an Open Night for those parents who work. The school even offered sparkling apple juice* and cheese! Two parents from my class showed up.

Today I'm sending home three workbooks with each child: Numeracy, Literacy and your child has chosen the third. Over the holidays, please find some time to sit with your child and read their work. Ask them about the things they are learning in class,

---

* *Sparkling apple juice.* Because the last time the school offered wine, parents started fighting. Yup. For reals. Two dads had a punch-up, and one mum got in on the action, too. No one can remember how it started or what it was about. Some teachers say it was because their kids had an altercation in class; others recall that it was a pre-existing argument that got dragged in from outside the school gates.

ask them about the things they have found interesting and the things they have found challenging. Ask them what their school day is like: what they look forward to and what they dread? Ask who they sit next to and who they play with and what book they're reading in class. Ask them: Are you happy at school? How do you think you're going?

Your child can tell you just as much as my report card can.

Parent Comment:
When I was at school . . . (I've deliberately left this sentence unfinished.)

My Response:
I have received lots of emails that begin with 'When I was at school . . .'

'When I was at school, we weren't allowed to . . .'
'When I was at school, our teacher . . .'
'When I was at school, we never . . .'
'When I was at school, we always . . .'

It's not fair to compare your experiences of school with those experiences of your child. The world has changed and education changes with it—exponentially, at times! It's quite likely that we do a few things differently at school since you were last attending as a student. Try not to be blinded by nostalgia! And also please remember that your child is not duplicating your childhood. Their experience of school might be quite different to yours. If you had a positive (or crappy) time at school, it doesn't mean your child is having the same.

Also, just because you once went to school doesn't make you a teacher. Just sayin'. It's pretty freaking annoying being told *how to do my job from someone who's a plumber by trade. I get enough of that from the politicians who govern education with their business degrees and interests in economics. Sorry, I think the red wine is beginning to talk.*

Parent Question:
Where do all the glue sticks go?

My Response:
Good question. My best guess:

- *Reaxton has stolen three.*
- *The Kindergarten class borrowed six and only four came back.*
- *Two are probably in the back of Yuki's desk but it's so tightly jammed with paper and junk that we may never know for sure what's festering away in there.*
- *One fell behind the bookshelf in such a way that we can't retrieve it, not even with the metre ruler (or 'measure stick' as Megan calls it—sigh—this time next year she'll be in Year 6).*
- *Two were lost to heat exhaustion when lids weren't secured and we had that weekend of forty-plus temperatures.*
- *One snapped clean off when a student did the ol' wind it all the way out trick. We did reinsert that one and it is still in circulation but it frequently falls out and is getting fuzzy from all the time it spends on the floor.*

It's time to sign off now—school holidays beckon. I hope your kids all have a refreshing break from the classroom.

Gabbie

PS Here's a list of things I took to the Found Property cupboard today (all without names). Why not come in for the working bee during the school holidays and have a rummage through the pile? I've got:

- Three empty pencil cases
- One pair of goggles
- Four drink bottles
- Three lunch containers
- Two lunch box lids
- Two sports T-shirts
- One sock—yes, *one*. And, before you ask, I don't know
- Four school jumpers.

School holidays

Dear Parents & Caregivers,

No, I don't plan on sending the emails out during the holiday period. Why? Because it's the holiday period. I also can't help you if your kids are bored. I won't be emailing out activities for them to complete, recommending apps you can download or sending links to educational websites. That's not my job. Besides, being bored is good for kids. Once they're bored, they start to get creative.

Letters from the teacher will recommence in Term 2.

Until then,
Gabbie

Term 2

Week 1

FRIDAY

Dear Parents & Caregivers,

And we're back . . .

Thank you to everyone who has already emailed and asked after my school holidays. I had a good break! Technically, teacher 'school holidays' are called 'stand-down periods' because we aren't officially on holiday. And, contrary to popular belief, teachers do continue to work throughout this time. Yes, we try to get away for a 'holiday' when we can (and we pay premium prices for that privilege), but the reality is that most of us engage in sustained periods of work throughout the 'school holidays', preparing all the programs, lessons and assessments that we will deliver during the term. And there's never enough time. I always return to school with a sense of self-loathing over all the work I didn't complete during the break, as well as a generous serving of guilt about all the time I squandered reading, watching TV, catching up with friends and sleeping in.

My holidays looked like this:

- Attended ANZAC Day service at dawn to support our School Captains who had to deliver readings.
- Attended the Halligan Easter Hat Parade on Easter Saturday put on by the local council. All local schools were invited to attend and it would seem rude if your school didn't turn

up. Twenty kids from Halligan Primary joined in the parade down the main street. The Principal was pleased as punch as he believes this is excellent publicity. Me? Not so much. First up, I don't buy into this idea that schools need 'publicity' to be considered successful; we are not a business or a corporation. Second, attending the Easter Hat Parade meant that I missed a family lunch with my sisters and my nephew who had travelled down from Byron Bay with his baby.

- Came into the classroom on Wednesday, Thursday and Friday of the first week and Thursday and Friday of the second week. I cleaned and rearranged the desks, took down all the old classroom displays, put up new displays, cleaned the window sills, installed and updated software on the iPads and computers, cleaned all the iPads and computer keyboards (disgusting!!!), updated all the spreadsheets and forms that collect and collate student data, and also met with Mrs Fortune to plan programs and the excursion.

- Spent Monday of the first week and Tuesday and Wednesday of the second week working from home. I wrote up more programs, set up online learning spaces, wrote notes and itineraries for school excursions, revised OH&S policies for our excursion, and rehashed the school's enrolment policy. As staff, we have to review all our policies this year—turns out the old Principal fell asleep at the wheel when it came to school policies and now ours all need to be updated. I made eye contact at the wrong moment during staff meeting and ended up on the policy committee. (The new Principal is a big fan of forming committees—already we're calling them chain gangs behind his back.) I had to review the current Enrolment Policy, which is a big document. Could have been worse, though. Mr Lloyd (aka Lloydie, the Kindergarten teacher) got the Infectious Diseases Policy, which is way more involved and a complete bummer considering he pretty much spends his life teaching inside an infectious diseases incubation cubicle.

- Spent this weekend just gone updating, creating and referencing all of my Professional Standards Teacher Accreditation paperwork. I don't want to talk about that. I find it soul-destroying.

The rest of the 'holiday' was spent sleeping, reading, lounging, getting my hair coloured, getting the car serviced, going in to the bank to sort out a bunch of stuff, and trying to come to grips with the update that happened on my mobile phone.

So, yeah, my holidays were brilliant, thanks for asking.

I'm sounding cynical already. I'm just frustrated. I look forward to the break at the end of term just as much as the kids do, but every time I return to school I have this feeling I'm not ready, and it's not just because there's paperwork I didn't complete. I always come back to school feeling like I missed out. I wanted to spend more time with my family. I wanted to take my own girls away for a couple of nights. I wanted to read more books and spend more time swimming before the cold weather sets in. I wanted to do that long bush walk that goes out to the lookout—you know the one? And I had this crazy idea that I might do some cooking: chuck a few meals in the freezer for the busy term ahead. But I didn't get any of that done and now I'm resentful.

As I drove to school this morning, I was thinking about the kind of teacher I might be if I had real time to rest and relax.

I'd like to be returning to school with great stories of the long hike I did and some pics of me and my kids having fun at the beach. I think I'd be a happier, more enthusiastic teacher. And I think I'd feel more connected to my students sharing stories of my holidays, rather than me enviously listening to their tales and feeling—well, yeah—*resentful*. I think teachers need to have time to have a life, too.

Anyway, I'm going to put those feelings aside and choose a better attitude (I'm forever telling Livvy and Soph to choose a better attitude, so I should practise what I preach). The new term is upon us and together we're going to smash it out. Remember Nanny Maud from last term? Lost grandmother on Open Day? She's offered to come in and help the students with art on Thursday afternoons (she's an artist and used to exhibit her work back in the day, and she was once a curator at the Art Gallery of New South Wales, too). She did try helping out in her grandson's Kindergarten classroom, but she said teaching art in there 'was like stepping into a Salvador Dalí painting', plus the chairs were too small and too low. She said her 'backside needs a huge amount of support and should be at least fifty centimetres above the ground at all times'!

Please remember to look at the SkoolSaid app to find all the formal information regarding Term 2. It's a big one for our class because we have the excursion to Canberra and NAPLAN for the Year 5s. Lumped on top of that are reports and parent–teacher interviews. Kill me now. This is the term where I'll take one day at a time, and try to get home before 6 p.m. whenever I can. School swimming lessons are finished (can I get a 'Hallelujah' on that one?). Please note that sports day has changed, so sports uniform should be worn on Tuesday.

I am aware that this may impact students who see the school counsellor *and* those who go out for band/instrumental lessons with Mrs Jethro. I'm not sure how to solve that problem yet . . . Timetabling is an ongoing nightmare.

Gabbie

PS Reaxton was away for the first part of this week. Our class felt smaller without him. The kids asked where he was. 'It's quiet without Reaxton', they said. 'He's so funny.' They told stories of Reaxton's side-splitting antics: the time he tied his own shoelaces together; the time he trapped a blowfly in Yuki's drink bottle; the day he spent in the cupboard refusing to come out; the time he gave himself a thick, black moustache with permanent marker; the day he escaped from our classroom and went to the office and told everyone there was a gunman in our classroom and Mrs Parnell, from Admin, commenced lock down . . . The kids had a treasury of tales about Reaxton, and they told them with a lighthearted nostalgia that made me catch my breath. Each of those incidents had caused me varying degrees of work, stress and trauma, but the kids were oblivious to that. All they recalled was Reaxton, funny and fearless. He was their classmate; he wasn't their problem to solve.

Part of me was hoping Reaxton might be away for a while longer but he returned today. He came into the classroom late, just after ten, and announced that he had a nickname.

'I want you to call me Ax,' he said, standing out the front of the room and holding court as though he'd been teaching for years and was introducing himself to a new group of students.

'Rightio,' Coman said. 'We'll call you Ax. Now sit down. We're doin' Maths.'

Just like that, Reaxton was back and my students were paving a way for him.

I tucked the moment away for retelling in the staffroom. Lloydie (the Kindy teacher) has been referring to Reaxton as The Axe since the day he arrived.

Week 2

FRIDAY

Dear Parents & Caregivers,

Okay, let's talk about NAPLAN. Thanks for all your emails asking me questions and reminding me that I need to be preparing the students. Let it be known that I am painfully aware of this testing regime—I haven't forgotten as some of you suggested and I haven't neglected it as others have implied. I am deliberate and strategic in the way I approach NAPLAN.

The tests are on Tuesday, Wednesday and Thursday of next week. You can read all about the testing schedule and procedure on the SkoolSaid app or by looking at the official NAPLAN website. I have prepared the students as best as I can. Preparation actually started last term. We navigated the online testing space and established our logins and so on. We have completed some practice papers both as a group and under test conditions. I'm confident we have covered an acceptable amount of syllabus content up to this point. I have reassured the students that the tests are simply a way of capturing the things they know, and can demonstrate, at a specific point in time. I have also told the kids that they should try their best, because trying your best—no matter the task—is a basic value I strive to instil in all my learners.

There are two things I no longer tell my students when NAPLAN season rolls around:

1. That the Education Department, and other government departments, are using these tests to collect data. When I gave this explanation to a Year 3 class a few years back, one of my students with high-functioning autism got it into his head that the Prime Minister would be marking the papers. On the day of testing he got himself so worked up that he vomited all over the exams. I was tempted to bundle the entire mess into an envelope and post it directly to the PM, but instead I settled the student and called his mum.

2. That NAPLAN 'doesn't matter', because when I've done that in the past I've felt like a liar. These tests do matter—they just don't matter to me.

I am not a fan of NAPLAN. I think it's unnecessary. I think we lose sight of something incredibly valuable with the regime of NAPLAN testing: the value of learning.

The value of learning. Just that statement alone has so much depth. What is the value of learning?

For me, learning is priceless—too valuable to be measured and weighed and quantified.

I wish I could capture 'learning' and show it to you the way I experience it in the classroom. But I don't know if I can do it with words; it's like trying to explain something divine. Watching children learn is a powerful thing—it's the elixir of teaching, the phenomenal drug that keeps teachers coming back to the classroom day after day after day, even when they're overwhelmed, even when they're exhausted, even when they're frustrated, even when they think they want to quit . . . It's learning that draws them back, time and time again.

Stop for a minute and think about what actually happens when we learn something. It's extraordinary, if you take the time to consider what goes on. In fact, it's nothing short of a miracle. Learning is a kind of magic.

Imagine a Learner, sitting at their desk, and in front of them is a new idea. Beside the Learner is a Teacher, and this person explains the principles and skills and concepts required for understanding. The Teacher could do this in any number of ways: maybe they provide a demonstration, or tell a story, or use real materials, or refer to a simpler problem . . . Whatever the method, it doesn't really matter. What matters is that somehow the ideas and concepts and understandings pass from the Teacher's mind, through the space between them, and into the mind of the Learner.

Learning is literally the movement of ideas, and yet it's even more remarkable than that because when I share my idea or understanding, my own bank of knowledge is not diminished. It's like I've taken a cutting from my own garden of wisdom and transplanted it into my Learner's mind where they can tend to it until it flourishes.

Can you imagine that? I mean, really think about it! These ideas and understandings are being conveyed from *one mind into another*. It's amazing!

After the new idea has been shared, the Learner attempts to engage with it, perhaps through a task or a problem or an activity. At this point, the Learner either succeeds and is guided by the Teacher to develop mastery, or the Learner misses the mark and the Teacher sends out further ideas and concepts and understandings. The process continues like an endless, beautiful cycle until, eventually, the Learner succeeds and takes ownership of the concept and embeds it deep within their own mind.

At this point, this moment of 'learning', the Learner will always look to their Teacher and their shining eyes will ask: *Did you see me do that?* And beside them their Teacher will smile or nod and their heart will sing: *Yes! I saw you do that. I taught you.*

This is the magic of learning. This is The Magic Moment! It's organic, it takes time, and it's different for every Teacher and for every Learner. Many things impact upon this phenomenal exchange, but fundamental to it all is the relationship between the Learner and the Teacher. There needs to be trust, support, encouragement and a space to fail. There needs to be room for feedback and practice. There needs to be praise and direction. Most importantly, there needs to be time. Learners need time to take on these 'cuttings of knowledge' and assimilate them into their own garden. They need time to make learning their own.

So, what happens to this magic experience of learning when we start asking questions like:

- Who learned that best?
- Who learned that fastest?
- Who learned that in time for the NAPLAN test?
- Who can express that best on an exam paper?
- Who can give the single, correct answer?
- Who can't be tricked by this question, designed to produce results that will fit a bell curve?

Let me tell you what happens: enemies of learning creep in and the foundations of learning fall away. Teachers become shackled to time-pressured outcomes and Learners disengage. Magic Moments become fewer and fewer until, eventually, the

Magic Moment is lost. What you're left with is a system that survives on competition and data and accountability, and these are things that should play only a small role in education. They should not be the fuel that feeds it.

Thinking about this actually upsets me. I have tears in my eyes as I write this because it truly feels like a tragedy. I know that some of you will say I'm being dramatic, but I want you to understand that I have very real moral and ethical concerns about NAPLAN and the far-reaching impact that it has. I spent the better part of last year contemplating whether I would return to teaching. I do not like the feeling of being complicit in the myth that is NAPLAN.

That all sounds a bit sinister, doesn't it?

Sigh.

But we've got to stop thinking about learning in Australia as winners and losers, and 'Band 3' and 'Band 6', and 'schools operating to standards', and an economically driven business model. This competitive idea of teaching and learning has no place in education.

I spend a lot of time trying to come up with an image of what schools and classrooms are like; a sort of analogy to help people understand. There's this saying: *You don't fatten the calf by weighing it.* And that image kind of works because our students won't become smarter and well-adjusted by being repeatedly tested. But the idea of my students being likened to beef cattle doesn't sit well with me.

Then there's the idea of schools being like communities and classes being like families. We wouldn't feel right about 'testing and tracking' the progress of our families, would we? What would that even look like? But the image of class groups as families isn't quite right either.

I come back to the idea of gardens quite often because children are very much like seeds, unfurling themselves to become seedlings and trying to flourish in the soil they were planted in. They're growing within the conditions Mother Nature allotted them. And maybe teachers are like gardeners, watering and weeding and tending and toiling . . . There is no perfect analogy because schools are not like anything else, teachers are not like anything else, and students are not like anything else. The entire process of learning is unique and organic and mysterious and difficult to capture—it's certainly impossible to measure in any standardised way. And if all of that sounds wishy-washy and airy-fairy and unprofessional, well, then that's good as we need to remember that learning is divine. We need to shift the belief we currently have that testing and standards and measures and accountability somehow equate to learning. They don't—and, ironically, all the data we've accumulated from that business model shows us that it simply isn't working.

We need to return to the Magic Moment and have faith in that.

Gabbie

Week 2

Dear Parents & Caregivers,

Okay, so it's 2 a.m. on Saturday morning and I can't sleep. But I've had this epic realisation. There's this thing that I'm not meant to tell you. It's about NAPLAN and I think every parent has the right to know. It just occurred to me that since we have this unbelievable email dialogue going on I have a way of secretly telling you the thing that politicians and principals and policy-makers don't want you to know:

NAPLAN is optional.

There's this gross misconception that NAPLAN is compulsory. It's not. Even the official website doesn't say it's compulsory. It very carefully says all students in the allocated NAPLAN testing grades are *expected* to participate. Then it goes on to outline how students with disabilities can apply for adjustments, and students with severe disabilities or who can't yet speak English can be granted an exemption. But if you keep on clicking around, there, in the fine print, you will find out about withdrawing your child from the tests.

See how insidious it is? They opt you in, and it's up to you to find out about opting out. That alone makes me shitty. Why not make it optional from the start? Let people have the choice and be up-front about it. Always remember that NAPLAN is something created by our government, not by educators.

Look, I'm not saying you *should* withdraw your child. I mean, I could lose my job if this gets out, but I'm dancing on a knife's edge there anyway. I just think that there's way too much misinformation about the benefits of NAPLAN being circulated to parents. I think it's time you guys had all the information so you can have an informed voice and maybe even consider how you might use that voice to speak up on behalf of our kids. And maybe, just maybe, on behalf of teachers, too.

At Halligan, the procedure for withdrawing or exempting your child from NAPLAN is to let the Principal know. I believe he will ask you to express in writing why you're exempting your child. You can simply say that you object on philosophical grounds, or you might want to add a few reasons of your own. It's as easy as that—and it's your right as a parent to have that option.

Talk to your child and see what they reckon. I'm not on any kind of brainwashing campaign here, and I'll be in a shitload of trouble if you all withdraw because the Principal will put two and two together—he's an over-achieving workaholic, but he's not stupid.

I should probably go back to bed. I need to *sleeeeeeeep*! This NAPLAN thing is really bothering me. I'm particularly nervous about the way this new Principal might go galloping off in various directions when the results come in.

Anyway, it's one of those wild and crazy ideas that will probably seem stupid in the morning. But I don't care. I'm feeling reckless. I'm going to read over this letter and then press send.

Gabbie

Week 2
SUNDAY

Dear Parents & Caregivers,

I know, I know, it's Sunday, but I have received so many emails from you . . . Clearly there's more we need to discuss about NAPLAN.

So, to clarify, NAPLAN is a particular type of test called a standardised test, which means it's issued in a standard way to a 'standard' group of students and is marked to a particular standard.

The truth is that teachers quite like standardised tests. They're very handy. We can use them to accurately capture what a student knows, can do, or understands at a particular point in time. Standardised tests are also scored in a standard way so we can compare results between students and against the standard performance measures. These kinds of tests are especially good for tasks or skills that have single correct answers, such as mathematical algorithms, spelling of isolated words, basic comprehension and recall of known facts. They can also be administered as short-answer questions, or essays.

Very few teachers have a problem with a good standardised test. Teachers often issue them as a diagnostic measure at the start of the term to find out where their students are at. The beauty of this kind of test is that you can immediately look at the paper or screen and see precisely where the student is secure in their knowledge and where they are unsure.

But NAPLAN has one fundamental difference that makes it so problematic. It's a high-stakes test. The reason it's considered high-stakes is because it is issued nationally *and* the collective results for each school are published on the My School website. These factors raise the stakes considerably: when this data is made available on the My School website, a general commentary can be made about our students' performance nationally. Unfortunately, context surrounding the results is often neglected. What I'm referring to here is the 'story' of each child and each school community. Often the people making comment about these results (politicians, political advisors, policy-makers, journos) have no understanding of how important this *context* is to these results and the national trends.

I find the My School website to be particularly offensive. Parents don't seem to be that concerned about it and I think that's because your child's individual results are not made available on the site. *But our school results are*, and for me that's a really difficult idea to reconcile. I don't believe there's much to be gained in pitting schools against one another. Supposedly the idea behind the My School website is that parents can compare schools and gain awareness of the 'student gain' that's made in each school.

That's a nice way of saying you can find the school where your child has the best chance of winning.

This becomes a problem for me because it buys into this idea that learning is a competition and that you can 'shop around' for your child's education. As I said in my last letter, schools aren't like anything else. We're not selling insurance. We're not generating profits. We're not all about the bottom line. These are schools. This is learning. Magic Moments. Remember?

To be fair, the My School website uses other measures to come up with all its convoluted graphs and pie charts (not just NAPLAN results). I'm not sure that I take much comfort from that but I just thought I ought to let you know.

Second place is the first loser. This is the culture we encourage when we send out NAPLAN data to parents and publish it on websites. We create a climate of competition that's focused on grades and results and getting things *right*, rather than a culture of learning and growth and curiosity. It's argued by policy-makers and politicians and people who have excellent jobs associated with the production and roll-out of NAPLAN, that parents need to see the NAPLAN results so they can be aware of gaps (and successes) in their child's learning; so they can see how their child is *performing at school*. That would be terrific if the NAPLAN information sent to parents also included the child's original test and their responses. Instead it's an envelope of graphs and edu-babble, and I end up deciphering these for parents, which is an incredibly frustrating conversation for me.

Maybe NAPLAN results would be more useful to parents if they held a teaching degree. But most don't. When parents are sent this envelope full of measures, I find they start asking themselves, and asking me, how their kid is going *compared to other kids*. You guys start getting all focused on results and achievement and success when, in reality, learning is as much about failure and having a go and asking questions as it is about selecting the correct circle on a multiple-choice test.

Before NAPLAN, New South Wales primary schools had the Basic Skills Test. This was large-cohort testing across the state. The Basic Skills Test was administered in Years 3 and 5, covered Literacy and Numeracy skills, and provided teachers with relevant diagnostic information on student performance. It also gave teachers access to useful support and resources once student needs were defined. This test was based on the state syllabus. Parents received Basic Skills results in a reasonably parent-friendly format that was useful for dialogue with the teacher. To my knowledge, the school's collective results weren't published in any league tables, newspapers or websites. The collective results weren't in the public domain. Basic Skills was okay but it wasn't ideal: some kids experienced nerves, there was lag time between testing and results *and* as the years went on the test results seemed to drive more and more of the teaching, discussion and decision-making in this state's education system. And then came NAPLAN and My School.

Supposedly NAPLAN was instituted to raise the standard of education across Australia. It was also going to enhance the excellence and equity students experienced when they attended our schools. This was a bit of a slap in the face for me—I'd been teaching for about seven years when NAPLAN came in, and I'd always held high expectations of my students *and* believed equity and excellence were mainstays of my classroom practice. But I guess if a politician says it, it must be right, hey? (Yeah, all of this NAPLAN stuff was started by politicians and continues to be perpetuated by them, too. It's worth asking what they gain from it.)

I can't buy into the idea of this test contributing to equity and excellence. (The test wasn't even aligned with our national curriculum until 2016! How is that even *fair*?) I have watched too many kids develop anxiety and too many kids with additional needs opt out of testing for me to believe NAPLAN is a tool for educational equity and excellence. I have seen too many kids become defeated as the test becomes harder, designed as it is to sort students into their allotted bands. Equity and excellence? Nup—it's second place equals first loser. It's a shit feeling, especially when you're a young human being and you're designed *to learn*.

It's also been argued that NAPLAN would supposedly help schools and teachers to catch those students who were 'falling through the cracks', identify weaknesses in teaching programs, and provide a means of 'tracking student progress'. The reality is that students still fall through the cracks, and in my opinion those cracks are wider now because it's actually *relationships* that prevent students from falling through cracks—that special connection between Teacher and Learner. Yet those relationships don't have enough time or space to flourish in today's educational environment. And if you care to look at all the data that tracks and maps and ranks and measures, you'll discover our students' results are ever so slowly declining.

I spent last night thinking about your emails, tossing and turning because I just can't seem to sleep. Your emails say things like 'a bit of testing never hurt me' and 'NAPLAN prepares them for life'. I have trouble with these arguments. They grate against me every time.

So, a bit of testing never hurt *you*? That doesn't make it right! Just because we were taught in a particular way doesn't mean that's the way we should teach forevermore. What a static place our schools become when we continually roll out the same, same, same. What new and unique future are we preparing our children for when we deliver the old learning procedures their parents endured? What kind of philosophy of learning sits behind the rationale of: *Aww, it doesn't hurt 'em?* And you know what else? *Shame on you!* High-stakes testing isolates our poorest members of society, those living with disability, our Aboriginal community, as well as many others. It puts them at a disadvantage, and yet these groups are the very ones for whom education can be an empowering stepping stone. A bit of testing might not hurt you, but it hurts others, and their learning matters just as much as yours and your child's.

And that pretext that NAPLAN prepares them to cope with life and stress and exams? Ugh! It's not a strong case. You know what else prepares them for life? Cooperative, open-ended tasks. Problem-solving activities with multiple pathways to a solution. Projects that have real-world applications and need to be submitted by a due date. And, really, do we need to be prepared for exams and stress at age eight and ten? I mean, when was the last time you sat a high-stakes standardised test? Were the results pinned up for public scrutiny? Are tests like NAPLAN *really* fixtures of life that students need to be 'prepared for' in order to cope in the real world? Surely we have better ways of preparing our young people for these challenges. I've got more faith in the Mindful Meditation for teaching our kids to cope with anxiety than the argument that exposing them to NAPLAN prepares them to handle stress.

For me, the worst part of NAPLAN is the way this insidious standardised, data-collecting culture has infiltrated our schools. The impact of NAPLAN is *not* just on those few days of testing, as politicians and principals will tell you. The impact of NAPLAN is felt the moment you walk in those school gates for your first days of Kindergarten.

Testing now begins when our children arrive at school. Kindergarten has become the year where baselines are found and graphs are constructed and data is gathered. There's very little play and a hell of a lot of 'sit down and listen'. There are children ploughing through graded readers before they've discovered the joy of stories. There are children sitting at desks and labouring through worksheets before they have the fine motor skills to grip a pencil. There are children being called in at lunch to complete tasks too lengthy for the allocated time because their teacher is under pressure to meet the deadline and produce 'evidence' for the data pile. There are children that don't want to come to school because it's too hard. And, for some, it's impossible!

Once, Kindergarten was this beautiful year of being read to, singing songs and painting big, blobby pictures of your family. It used to be a time of playing dress-ups and playing shops and pretending to be a dragon. Kindergarten was the year you discovered real friendship. It was the year you fell in love for the first time (usually with your teacher). It was the year of growing wings and becoming independent and deciding that school was a pretty good place to go to.

But not anymore. Not since NAPLAN.

There's ever more standardised tests and demands to 'track performance', presumably so we can support our students. Sometimes, though, it feels like we're doing all this testing just to produce evidence that will appease parents. And sometimes it can feel like the evidence is being gathered so the Principal (or policy-maker or politician) will know who to blame when the results haven't spiked. In staff meetings, I've noticed we've started saying things like, 'We need to shift those Band 3s up to Band 4'. I don't think that's the way I should be speaking about my students, lumping them together in bands like cattle being classed for sale.

The truth is all this testing and tracking takes me away from my students. I'm so busy constantly assessing where they're at that I don't have time to prepare for the place they need to go. And when I *am* teaching, well, I find something has happened to my lessons, too.

Before NAPLAN, I used to do this series of lessons in Maths. It was problem-solving using percentages and averages. I'd give the Years 5 and 6 students a scenario:

> *You are part of a team of researchers employed by Legal Eagle Law Firm Pty Ltd.*
>
> *Chunketty Choc Chip Biscuits TM have engaged the services of Legal Eagle Law Firm Pty Ltd. Chunketty have been accused of false advertising. Their biscuit packaging claims each biscuit contains 40% chocolate chips—but a biscuit-loving complainant named Esmerelda Munchalot has made the claim that there is only around 20%.*
>
> *Is it false advertising? Or is it just poorly worded advertising?*
>
> *Research the facts behind this 40% vs 20% claim, and write up your findings and recommendations.*

I bought loads of packets of biscuits and even went to the trouble of adding stickers so the packaging really boasted 40% *choc chips, per biscuit, guaranteed.* I dragged out the kitchen scales, put the class into small groups, and armed them with tweezers and toothpicks. They got to work—mining away for chocolate chips and making a mess all over the room. They were speculating and weighing and predicting and surmising. They did algorithms and posed new questions and felt invested in their results. They calculated percentages of weight and size, and working together to gain accuracy they established averages, and they deliberated on the advice they would give, negotiating the language of mathematics with precision and meaning. Many of them even considered the ethics behind their research (and some very shrewd kids asked how much they were getting paid! It wasn't lost on them that they were being employed by a law firm!). It was a powerful series of lessons that saw students use the practice and language of mathematics in practical, engaging ways. I watched with pride as they all made massive gains in their understandings. I found great satisfaction in teaching them, and I can't tell you how much information I collected about how each child 'performed'.

I don't teach those lessons anymore. I don't teach *like that* anymore. There's just no time. Oh, I try to when I can, but lessons like that aren't valued. Instead we use pen and paper to nut out problems about fifty-six sheep in a paddock; six times as many black than white, how many are black? And inside I'm screaming, *Who cares?*

That's what high-stakes testing does. That's what NAPLAN does: infiltrates so many aspects of my teaching life that I don't seem to recognise the work I do anymore.

And for some reason I just can't sleep.

That'll do for now—it is Sunday, after all. I'm off to visit Reaxton this afternoon. I thought perhaps it might help if I made a connection with his foster family and home life. He has been unsettled; returning to school this term hasn't been easy for him. Just when you think things are improving, he seems to take three steps back, but on the whole I think he's making progress in many different ways. Huge round of applause to many of your children who manage to find compassion and tolerance for Reaxton. They're somehow able to put up with his behaviour for great lengths of time, but they do find him frustrating. We played dodgeball the other day and I noticed lots of kids really pegging the balls at Reaxton when he was in the middle. He kept bellowing, 'Stop aiming at me!' I couldn't help but laugh when Dante shouted back, 'But it's just so satisfying!' Ever so slowly, though, Reaxton is getting the hang of things and our classroom is feeling less like *The Hunger Games* and more like Attenborough's *Life in Cold Blood*, which is probably about right for Year 5/6 at this time of year.

Gabbie

Week 3

FRIDAY

Dear Parents & Caregivers,

We survived NAPLAN. I'm so grateful that we didn't experience any online delays or glitches—our testing schedule ran to course and we got the whole thing over and done with in the designated time. Our kids got through it remarkably well and I was proud of every single one of them. Nanny Maud insisted that we have a little party to celebrate yesterday afternoon. She brought in a watermelon she had carved into the shape of a basket and it was filled with a delicious fruit salad. The kids scooped individual serves into little bowls and we sat around the Playground together, enjoying the juicy, colourful goodness. Lots of kids talked about how happy they felt now that the tests were over.

'You don't *think* you're worried about it,' Coman said thoughtfully, 'but then when it *is* over, you're so relieved, which means you must've been worrying.' He was sitting on top of the monkey bars with three of his mates, their feet dangling over my head, legs swinging in synchronicity. Coman's friends agreed with him, and so did other kids who had installed themselves on the slippery dip; they were bunched together in a snake of traffic, legs hugged around each other like plates stacked in the dishwasher. Megan was at the base of the slide, her weight-bearing back to hold everyone in place.

'I was relieved when Mum said I didn't hafta do it,' she said. ''Cause I'd been freakin' out, but then I wasn't.' She stood up and the sliders stacked behind her inched forwards until the new child at the front leaned back to hold them.

There's a certain intimacy that builds within a class group. The bubble of personal space becomes diminished, but there's something more than that: a collective conscience is developed, built on shared experiences and the ongoing transmission of feelings and ideas. As we sat together in the afternoon sun, I realised that NAPLAN had somehow bonded us together, and I tried to hug that idea to me as the single silver lining on the whole unnecessary ordeal.

Some of you parents decided to vote with your feet on NAPLAN—that was pretty cool! I'm sending you a high five, but let's keep it down low so the Principal can't see. Reaxton had already been withdrawn and two students with additional needs had, too, but then four others withdrew and another four were 'absent' on the mornings of the tests. I can't tell you how empowered I felt to see this kind of push back. It suddenly felt like these risky little emails had paid dividends because you guys, you parents, had stepped up and considered the kind of education you want for your kids *and for all Australian kids!*

The Principal did ask me a few questions about the withdrawals. I shrugged and gave a vague answer. Then he made this funny face that he sometimes makes at staff meetings. He frowns but at the same time sends his eyebrows upward. It looks like his forehead is saying *this is difficult to believe and it makes me cross.* At the same time, his mouth puckers, like he's going to give you a kiss on the cheek—except the eyebrows show it's out of the question. It's all very weird. I'm not the only one who finds his facial expressions a bit *intriguing.* He came into our class to congratulate the Year 5s on finishing NAPLAN, and when his back was turned I saw some girls imitating him. They were frowning and puckering and giggling. I told them it wasn't appropriate and glanced at the Principal; luckily, he hadn't seen. But then, as he was walking out the door, Reaxton called out, 'See ya later, Arse Face.' It's a tough gig being a Principal. I wouldn't want the job.

In any case, I totally understand those of you who still had your child sit the test. One of you came in and said to me on the Tuesday morning, 'I just need to see how he's going compared to all the other kids.' That's fine. I get it. This idea of competition and rank and who comes first and who's the smartest has been so deeply ingrained in our education system that it's really difficult to let it go. It was interesting, though, because one boy became upset during the Numeracy paper, and when I asked him what was wrong, he said, 'I'm not good at Maths. Do I really need to do this test to show that I'm the dumbest kid in here?' Turns out *that* kid has the parent who *just needs to know how he's going compared to everyone else*. It'll be a great day in Australian education when we stop thinking about learning as being a competitive, comparative pursuit and start recognising it as a lifelong human endeavour.

It's tempting now to say that since NAPLAN's over, things can go back to normal. I wish that were the case. But, as I said, the landscape of education has changed under this model of high-stakes testing. I have to continue tracking and testing and collecting data at regular pit stops. In other grades, the testing regimes continue as well, to identify students who don't meet the benchmarks and score low on various other standardised tests. I've heard of some schools that have dedicated 'data rooms', where all the data is piled and compiled and filed. In the data room is a data wall where actual pictures of the students are printed out and pinned up in order of their results on all the endless tests. We don't do that here. Yet. But the new Principal has mentioned it. And it scares me.

Kids learn in their own time. It's a frustrating fact of life. (Remember when they learned to walk and talk and clap hands? They did it when they were ready.) We can push them and push them, and test them and test them, and even teach them and teach them, but until they're developmentally ready the Magic Moment just won't happen. Putting their image at the bottom of a data wall and devising more and more programs in an attempt to move a student from one 'location' to another just seems . . . *pointless*. They get there in their own time, and learning it 'earlier' does not mean it's better.

Take Reaxton, for example. He's eleven and he's just starting to write sentences. He's only now beginning to feel secure enough in his home and school environment to have a go at tasks and take risks with his learning (risks that could include failure, which can be scary for any kid, but is especially terrifying for a young man like Ax).

Other kids were ready for classroom risk-taking when they were four or five. But for Ax the neurological pathways in his brain have been fostered and developed in such a way that he understands conventional learning to be a risk that's always associated with failure. Now, with the support of his foster family and case workers and teachers, new pathways are being encouraged through consistency, routines, nourishment, boundaries and—most significantly—safety.

And this idea about being developmentally ready is not isolated to 'kids like Ax'. I can remember when I was five years old and my parents were talking about daylight saving. Mum had mentioned winding the clocks forward and of course I had asked *why*. My dad had said something about changing the clocks because the hours of daylight were becoming 'longer'.

'When is daylight saving?' I asked.

'Next weekend,' Dad said. 'Isn't that right, love?' And he looked to Mum for confirmation.

She checked the calendar and gave a nod. 'Sunday.'

'How do you know?' I asked, glancing at the calendar. 'How do you know it's on Sunday?' My farm-kid experience had taught me that Mother Nature was not something to be relied on. I had shared my sisters' bathwater often enough to know that rain may not come despite the forecast. How could Dad be certain that Sunday would be the exact day that Mother Nature would extend our daylight so much so that we should adjust our clocks?

'Well, it's on the calendar,' Dad said. 'It's always around this time.'

'But how do you *know*?' I pressed. 'How can you be sure?'

'Well, the government decides,' Dad said, shrugging as he stood and made to leave, ready to shift sheep or fix fences.

'The government?' I remember feeling incredulous. *This government is mighty powerful*, I thought. *It controls time and daylight.*

I carried this misconception for a long while, believing that the prime minister I saw on the television had authority over the sunrise and the sunset. I wondered how he got the message to the Sun, telling it to stay out later. I wondered how the Sun replied. I wondered, too, why he didn't just ask for rain—if he could control the Sun, surely he could control the rain as well. And everyone knew it was rain that was needed. Good, drenching rain; the kind of rain that meant my sister could pull the plug and I could fill the tub to brimming.

I wasn't developmentally ready to understand the complexities around time and daylight and earthly revolutions and rotations. I had only been on planet earth for five years . . . I had only experienced five summers myself. Days and dates and solstices and seasons were still fluid, abstract, un-understandable concepts for me *at that age*. I didn't have enough real-world, lived experience to understand the premise of daylight saving.

It wasn't until I was sitting in a science lesson years later at primary school that I realised the government only controlled the *date* we were to wind our clocks forward! Mother Nature took direction from no one. She lengthened out daylight according to her own laws and rhythms. Finally, I understood. I was ready to 'get it'.

Some kids don't 'get it' because they're just not ready to. Physically, cognitively, emotionally, some kids are just not ready . . . *yet*. They need more time. Just because a group of kids are all ten years old doesn't mean they're all capable of the same things. They're not 'Standard Model Ten-Year-Olds' rolling off a production line. That's why this idea of a standardised test being used as a high-stakes measure of a student's success (and a school's success) is absurd. The students are considered 'standard' simply because of their coincidental default position of being enrolled in Year 3 or 5 or 7 or 9, but that doesn't mean they've all experienced the same life, or developed in the same way, or learned the same things. It's a foregone conclusion that *not all kids are ready* for the content the test will cover, so is it fair to use that kind of test as a means to measure and rank our kids? To measure and rank our schools?

Since we don't all experience life in the same way, we don't in turn all experience learning in the same way. There are many 'other influences' that impact student learning. Things like:

- The number of books in a student's home
- Being read to as a child
- If their father reads
- The mother's level of education
- Complications during birth
- Early experience of trauma
- Quality of diet
- Quality of sleep
- Amount of screen time
- Number of words spoken in the home
- Medications
- Development in utero . . .

So many things impact where a child 'sits' in terms of academic performance. And no matter how dedicated I am as a teacher, no matter how many targeted lessons I deliver, no matter how many resources I access, no matter how creatively I deliver the lesson—if I'm teaching a child that had a rough time in utero, that rarely eats vegies, that averages six hours of sleep per night and has already developed an addiction to Minecraft . . . well, then, it's like I'm pushing shit up a hill.

Make no mistake here, parents. I'm not saying that kids from challenging backgrounds can't go on to achieve great academic success. It is my fundamental belief that every child can learn, that every child is capable of a great many extraordinary things. I have seen kids rise up from incredibly impoverished backgrounds, but they didn't get there because their learning was constantly quantified and weighed and tested and measured.

They got there mostly because of their own courage and fortitude and, perhaps, in some small part, because a teacher's love and care inspired and encouraged them.

Here's the thing. When there's an insistence that teachers should work to ensure every child demonstrates outstanding results on academic, standardised tests, you are asking teachers to carry the weight of something they can't control. We can't travel back in time and erase medical traumas. We can't follow kids home and feed them nourishing meals, or tuck them in at a time that ensures they get enough sleep. We can't provide books for your home (although the library is always available). And we can't change the natural interests, talents and disposition of your child. This is the burden our teachers labour under: the weight of all they can't control.

Yes, the basic skills of literacy and numeracy are essential. And, yes, teachers should work to ensure each of their students gains the very best results they are capable of—*given their circumstances*—whenever they are assessed. And yes, of course, we need to ensure every child graduates school with an adequate level of Literacy and Numeracy.

But now the question that needs to be asked is: *How do we achieve this?* Because NAPLAN just ain't doing it.

Gabbie

PS My afternoon at Reaxton's place was an unexpected delight, thanks for asking! It was reassuring to hear him tell his foster mum to fuck herself sideways. (He's said that to me many times, and I don't know whether to laugh at the physics of it or reprimand him for being offensive.) But there are so many things going on in his life, more things than a kid should have to deal with, and sometimes I can understand his behaviour. His foster parents are the most patient, strong and compassionate people I have ever met. You should see the holes in their walls. But Ax is happy there—I can see it. They have a horse and it's a beautiful thing to watch him interact with it. There's a gentle young man hiding inside that angry eleven-year-old body.

Week 4

FRIDAY

Dear Parents & Caregivers,

So it turns out Nanny Maud sketched a lot of nudes. I didn't know this until she brought in a portfolio of her work to share with the class. She went through the entire thing and talked us through every single picture. Now, already I know that some of you will be sitting there in the comfort of your own home thinking, *That's so lovely—what a great cultural experience for my child.* Others will be thinking, *Nudes! Oh, my! My child has never seen a naked body other than their own!* And a small portion of you will be thinking, *Phhhhhwoarrrr! I knew that Nanny Maud was a saucy one!*

Over time as a teacher, you gain an uncanny ability to think like your students *and* like their parents. But before you start telling me everything I should have done, I want you to understand this: it was a lesson I stumbled into, but it revealed things I never expected. Some lessons just happen that way and they're often the best ones. The ones you remember.

Nanny Maud began with a study of several still life pictures, some by other artists, and some she had drawn herself. Dempsey was sitting forwards in his seat, his clever, young artist eyes skittering across each canvas Maud produced.

'How'd you do that?' he'd ask, pointing with arm outstretched and pencil in hand.

'This here?' Maud would touch the picture. 'That's just hatching—same as that other picture with the pineapple and the reading glasses.'

'But it looks different,' Dempsey pressed. He's a gifted drawer. Already I know there is nothing I can teach him when it comes to Art. This is a humbling aspect of teaching: when you meet talent. Immediately there's the heavy realisation you have the delicate responsibility of cultivating a gift you may not possess yourself.

'It's a different grade of pencil,' Nanny Maud explained. 'This here was 2B, but then I shifted to a 9B. It's a subtle change, but doesn't it make a difference?'

Dempsey nodded and scrabbled through his personal tin of pencils, hatching busily on a scrap of paper to test Maud's explanation.

'Now, look here, boys and girls.' Maud unrolled a canvas to reveal a poster-sized sketch of a naked woman.

I wanted to get up and stop her, but I didn't know what to say. The image caught me off guard. Up to that point, it had been all vases of fruit and portraits of faces . . . The kids giggled, but Nanny Maud just pinned it up and smoothed it out.

'I spent over a hundred hours on this,' she said, and gently touched the face of the drawing. Something about that gesture settled the kids. They said '*Whoa*' in that whispery way they do when they're reading *Guinness World Records*, and there was a moment of silence where I would like to think the students were taking in the beauty of the drawing and marvelling at Maud's talent.

Nanny Maud stood back and surveyed the drawing, tilting her head to one side and frowning like she might step forwards any minute and add to the sketch—perhaps a string of pearls around the lady's throat . . . or some clothes.

'Look here,' she said again, and this time she touched the picture right between the legs. I felt my cheeks flame hot, but Maud was oblivious. 'See how I've used shading for the pubic hair to give it a sense of texture?' she asked.

Now I really wanted to say something, but I didn't know what. The kids were silent, like the proverbial deer in headlights, but imagine thirty-one deer and the headlights were nipples.

'*Texture*?' Ax said eventually. 'She's got a bit more than texture.'

Some kids started giggling and I could feel the gravitational pull of a downward spiral—a class about to degenerate to a place beyond recovery. My mind was racing with ways I could resuscitate the lesson. Maybe, if I stood out the front, I could block their view of the naked lady.

The laughter was getting louder and louder, and I realised that Nanny Maud was laughing, too.

'Do you like the look of her, Reaxton?' she asked.

'Yep,' Reaxton said. 'She's got great tits.'

Maud didn't miss a beat. 'Well, she has *large* breasts, and your *opinion* is that they're great. You're putting a story to the picture. We'll get to that in a minute.' She moved to her easel, a large blank page standing nearby at the ready. She plucked a pencil from her tin and spoke again as she sketched.

'I find drawing forms like this to be a lot like those bowls of fruit. All roundness and curves and rock melons, you know?' She paused for a moment and stepped back from her work. In a few smooth lines she had created a silhouette; the wispy outline of a woman had appeared. Maud had my students in the palm of her clever artist's hand.

'You must understand,' Nanny Maud went on, 'nudes are about representing the human form. They're a chance to think about all the different contours of the body and how to capture them.' She fossicked through her portfolio and unfurled *another nude*, but this time it was a man! He had his back turned. His torso was angular, which made the roundness of his arse look all the more *fruity*. I felt myself blushing.

'Look here.' Maud pointed. 'The scapula and the deltoid. They're fun to draw. Now, this man looks strong, doesn't he?' She consulted the class and the children agreed, nodding and saying things about killer biceps and the amount of weight he could probably bench press.

'Agreed,' said Nanny Maud. 'Now, what can you tell me about his personality? Let's find the *story* behind this sketch.'

The kids were quiet. As the moment stretched, I wondered if maybe they were in shock (there were two poster-sized pictures of naked adults pinned up in front of them), but then Yuki raised her hand.

'Go ahead,' said Nanny Maud. 'What can you tell me about his personality?'

'Well, you can only see a bit of his face there.' Yuki indicated. 'But from what you can see, he's smiling. I mean, his lips go up; it's not a big grin or anything. And his eye, what you can see *there*, it looks sort of cheeky, like he knows a secret. So I think he's probably funny.'

'Pretty funny getting round with ya bare bum showing,' Reaxton said.

'His hands, too,' said Dempsey, ignoring Ax. 'The way he's holding out his hands and how the light is on them . . .' He stopped and held his own hands in the same way. 'It looks

like he's trying to hold the light really softly. So maybe he's
. . . mmm, umm . . .'

'Gay?' suggested Ax. (I think he was seriously trying to
contribute.)

'A gentle giant,' suggested Coman, and he glanced at me.
We had read the *The BFG* together as a class last term.

I grinned. 'He looks way more handsome than the BFG!'
I said, and the kids all made the *ooohh* noise, like I was about
to start dating the dude in the drawing.

'Nanny Maud?' Reaxton called out. 'You should draw me.'
There was a beat and then, 'But only with me clothes on.'

'Would you pose for me?' Nanny Maud had turned away
from Mr Deltoids to peer at Reaxton over the rim of her glasses,
sizing him up, like she was imagining how much canvas she
might need to capture all his sinews and his angst.

'I said I wouldn't get my gear off!' Reaxton blurted. 'But you're
a very good artist. You could draw me, and then I'd sell it and
be rich.' He looked at a few kids sitting nearby, checking to see
if they liked his idea, to see if they liked *him*. 'But I won't let
you draw me starkers,' he said again. 'You're a weird old perve.'

And then the most remarkable thing happened. Nanny Maud
installed Reaxton out the front and perched him on a chair.
She issued paper to all the kids and guided them through
the sketching process. When Reaxton became restless (three
minutes into the task), she gave *him* a piece of paper and told
him to sketch something he could imagine.

What followed was the most focused and enthralling session
of drawing these kids have probably ever experienced. Maud
coached them on proportion and position and shaping and
shading. She asked them to think about ways they could depict
Reaxton on the page and 'not just his likeness'. The outcome was

amazing; these kids captured so many aspects of him. In each picture you could see elements of Ax—his anger, his bravado, his strength—but also things about Reaxton that we had only glimpsed: his wit, his playfulness, his fear and his sadness.

I couldn't believe the work they had done. Dempsey's was remarkable. He had focused on Reaxton's face, capturing the tiny curl of hair that sits just above his left ear. It's a lock I often notice, looped in a perfect circle, always gleaming with sweat after lunch.

And Reaxton's drawing was also surprisingly good. He had sketched a horse, well-proportioned and detailed. It even had a sense of movement, like it was trotting across the page. I studied it with Maud after the kids had gone home.

'So he's an artist,' she muttered, holding the page gently in her palm. 'Well, fuck me sideways!' We both laughed.

Tomorrow your child will be bringing home the Code of Conduct Agreement for the school excursion. Please take the time to read and discuss this with them. If your child feels they can meet the behaviour expectations outlined in the Agreement, please have them sign it (printed name will be fine). As parents, it's important you read and understand these expectations as well. Furthermore, we ask that *you* read and sign the Breach of Agreement section to ensure you understand that you must come and collect your child if they don't meet these expectations. Once signed and dated, please return it to school. We will make a copy to send back home to you. At Halligan Primary, we take the excursion Code of Conduct Agreement seriously.

Gabbie

Week 4

SATURDAY

Dear Parents & Caregivers,

I've been feeling bad about the stuff I wrote to you last week about the new Principal—remember how I described his face? Lots of you replied, sharing commentary about him and other teachers. Yeah, okay, so some of it was funny. I admit that I laughed, but I also felt defensive.

I think it's okay that I bitch and moan about the Principal because he's my boss—you know? Bosses are meant to challenge you and frustrate you; it's sort of how you grow as an employee. But when I heard you complaining about him and making fun of his 1980s fashion sense, it made me oddly protective of him.

I wish you could see the work he does for this school. I wish you could hear him at staff meetings: always advocating for the needs of your kids. You know what he says most often? *We have to think about the parents, too.* It drives me crazy how often he brings *you lot* into our staff meetings and decision-making and discussions. I could happily leave parents to one side when we're engaged in a professional discussion, but the Principal gives you a voice. And even though it makes my workload harder, that's the right thing to do. This Principal understands that parents are the lifelong teachers of their children and that they should work in partnership with the school.

And you know what else? He never says a bad word about any of you! Even those repeat offenders who come in at least once a week to tell us all the ways we're falling short and could do better. *We need more vegan options at the tuckshop . . . We want sensory artwork installed . . . The students need more shade . . . You should do more to acknowledge various cultures . . . All teachers should learn sign language . . .* He never complains about you. He never rolls his eyes. He never swears. He just says things like, 'Every suggestion is an opportunity and I'm glad parents feel welcome in our school.' I would like to see him rolling drunk one day just to find out if he had something else to say. But you know what? He is genuinely a nice man with the best interests of the students at heart.

I complain about my workload, I know I do; I re-read these emails and feel ashamed. But if anyone should be complaining, it's him. Did you know we've had the police here three times this term? Why? Fights between families. AVOs. An attempted break and enter. He deals with all of that stuff. He has to come to the school every time our dodgy security alarm goes off, which is on average once a fortnight. Quick 3 a.m. trip to check on the school grounds, anyone? Nup, didn't think so. Reaxton spat on him once and there are lots of Reaxtons in a school. So put that into perspective and you get a rough idea of the abuse he experiences every day.

He arrives early each morning and he's usually in on a Saturday. He sends the staff an email every Sunday night detailing the week ahead, and on Friday mornings he sends out another email with a lame-arse joke that's meant to help us push through to the weekend.

Yeah, he drives me crazy—*because he's my boss*. Maybe I haven't given him fair representation in these letters, but I can honestly say he is trying his best.

Sincerely,
Gabbie

Week 5

Dear Parents & Caregivers,

Relax. Nanny Maud won't be bringing in the nudes again. Thanks to those of you who sent emails letting me know how inappropriate that experience was for your child. Please rest assured that I will not allow stunning, hand-drawn artworks of healthy naked models to be shown in my class ever again. As an aside, I have two words for you: The Internet. Statistically, your kids will have seen more than nudes before they've even made it to Year 8, so good luck with that. Also, yes, Nanny Maud has a valid Volunteer Working With Children Check.

Sometimes I think you're missing the point of these letters. I'm not writing them as a means for you to spy on the classroom. Some of the emails I've received from you this week made me feel sad. I was sharing with you Reaxton's first Magic Moment. Drawing that horse was the first work he's ever completed, first time he's ever involved himself in the class. You're so busy watching your own kid that you forget about the others. It's an 'every man for himself' way of thinking that is the hallmark of so many things in education (and society) these days.

How does this affect me? *How does this affect* my child?

Teachers can't think that way.

And, believe me, I need those Magic Moments. Without them I wouldn't keep coming back.

Alright, moving along . . . Please repeat after me:

If my child is sick, I will keep them at home.

This week we have had the unholy trinity come through our classroom: head lice, school sores *and* gastro. I've also counted five kids doing battle with the flu. My stomach turns every time I hear mucus being dredged from the nose into the back of the throat, and I also feel physically sick when I have to deal with classroom vomit. Yesterday I had to move a desk that was covered with spew. (Ax was brave enough to carry it with me, and as we arrived outside we found some kids next door doing a measurement exercise, and Reaxton asked, 'Did someone here order some vomit?' I wanted to laugh, but I was trying to control my gag reflex.)

You should be aware that I am not above using these emails for naming and shaming when it comes to exposed school sores and head lice! I will do whatever is required to short-circuit the spread of these cruel and highly contagious 'infections'. One year, both my girls were simultaneously struck with impetigo *and* nits. It felt as though the Black Death had cast a shadow over our household, and it took ages to resolve both conditions. My kids were miserable and completely sick of me combing through their hair and inspecting their skin like we were all chimpanzees in a grooming ritual.

I know it's hard when your kids are sick. I know it's costly and time-consuming and annoying. I know you have to work. I completely understand. I have kids and I have to work, too. And I would prefer to do my work in a healthy environment where I'm unlikely to catch a disease. Please, I beg of you, keep your kid home when they *begin* to feel unwell; let's avoid these classroom pandemics before they can take hold. And if your kid has school sores or nits, please (please, please, *please*) keep them home until they're all sorted. We have policies and information leaflets about this sort of stuff (see the SkoolSaid app). Don't palm your kids off on me when they're unwell—be their parent and their primary caregiver. (And please don't email me back with some sad tale about how you and your partner both have to work and don't have family you can rely on . . . Make some calls today and line up three people you can ask for support when your kid needs care, even if you have to pay them.) I know I sound brutal, but sick kids don't belong at school. It's as simple as that. It's not fair on them, it's not fair on their classmates and it's not fair on me.

And while I'm on the delicate issue of health care—just out of curiosity—did you ever teach your child how to:

- Wash hands
- Clean their ears
- Blow their nose
- Trim their nails
- Brush their teeth
- Attend to body odour
- Wash their hair
- Clean their face?

Who do you think teaches them these things? I am astonished at what I see in and behind kids' ears. I am alarmed at their lack of hand-washing. And it is positively frightening observing them as they blow their noses. This stuff absolutely falls under the heading of *Not My Responsibility*. These are jobs for the parents, I'm sorry to tell you folks, and your kids need some basic 'how to' on attending to their body care. And you know what? Teaching your kid stuff, even simple stuff like this, is really important. It can also be a great way to bond with them.

I remember teaching my youngest, Soph, how to brush her teeth. I had probably dropped the ball a bit with this—second child and all that! And then one day I realised she needed a lesson. As a bubba, she had a baby's toothbrush, and when the witching hours drew to a close each night I would offer it to her as Olivia diligently brushed alongside her. Sophie would suck at the toothbrush, occasionally waving her hand up and down to imitate Olivia's brushing movements.

A few years later, though, when Soph finally had some teeth in her mouth, she'd graduated to a child-sized toothbrush, but I had missed the crucial step of basic instruction. I'd shout, *'TEETH, TOILET, BED!'* and a few minutes later, from any room in our house, you would hear Sophie brushing her teeth. She sounded like a coffee machine.

'What is she doing in there?' I asked Olivia one night. 'It sounds like she's making a couple of lattes.'

'I dunno,' Livvy said, barely looking at me as she read her book.

I heaved my sorry arse up off Olivia's bed and made the effort to observe my child. In the bathroom, Sophie was hard at work at the basin. Perched on her steppy stool, she was busy turning taps and throwing her head forwards to spit. Six or seven times she returned the brush to her mouth, topping up with toothpaste as she went. And each time she brushed and spat, the incredible noise started up.

'Whatchya doin' there, Soph?' I approached gently because she was clearly 'in the moment' and I didn't want to startle her. She stopped mid milk-frothing and looked at me.

'Brushing my teeth,' she said.

'Well, you're doing something,' I said with a grin, 'but I'm not sure it's teeth-brushing.'

I glanced in the basin and suddenly so much about the disgusting state of my bathroom vanity made sense. I reached for my own toothbrush and talked her through the process. She watched with keen eyes as I squeezed a small amount of paste from the tube.

'I bin using way more than that,' she said.

'I know!' I said. 'Now, like this.' Together we brushed. I held her arm and calmed her ferocious scrubbing motion. I angled my head, trying to contain the minty foam in my own mouth as I gave her directions. 'This here,' I gurgled, pointing to the plughole, 'this is the target. When you spit, you want to get it right in there!' I demonstrated and Sophie grinned.

She rose up on tippy-toes, leaning over the basin. She made the almighty noise of milk being steamed, threw her head back and then let rip with a good, hard spit that splattered across the basin . . . and me. She looked up and I saw tiny beads of foamy white spittle shining in her hair.

'I think you missed the target,' I said. 'Have another try.'

Again she threw her head back.

'Stop right there,' I cried before she could start grinding the beans for a fresh cup. 'What's this all about?' I threw my own head back to imitate hers.

'I'm getting spit,' she told me.

'Okay.' The puzzle pieces were clicking into place. 'So, you don't have to "get spit". You just spit out the toothpaste and water and stuff that's already in your mouth. You don't have to add your own spit to it.' I gave a quick demonstration. 'And you aim for the plughole,' I said, wiping water from my chin. 'You try.'

Sophie wet her toothbrush and brushed again using calm, small movements. In our mirrored reflection, her eyes held mine, seeking approval. I nodded.

'Okay, now spit, Soph. Just spit out what's in your mouth.' I pointed to the hole. 'Get it right in there!'

She leaned forwards and spat, neatly and quietly, straight down the plug hole.

'Well done,' I said, squeezing her close to me and kissing her head.

'Thanks, Mum,' she said, reaching up to place her toothbrush in its holder. 'No one's ever taught me how to do that before.' She dragged a handtowel over her face and I watched as a streak of toothpaste was smeared across it. I took a breath, but decided one lesson a day was probably enough.

Even now, Sophie is still a noisy little tooth-brusher. And it can be guaranteed that at least once a week she turns up at school with a stripe of toothpaste down the front of her uniform. But I know she's got the general idea, and I treasure that little memory of the night I taught Soph to clean her teeth.

Take the time to teach your kids—the big things and the small things. I hear people talking about 'daddy-daughter time' or 'mother-and-son bonding', like you have to set aside time in your schedule to make that happen. That's fine, I understand this. But look for the little moments, too—the small, mundane, everyday-life moments where you can connect with your child in a way that no one else ever will.

You could start tonight with a lesson on ear cleaning!

Anyway, if your kids are coming home from school smelling a bit like Glen 20, then you can blame me. I don't know how else to halt the frenzy of disease that's circulating through our classroom at the moment.

I don't have anything much else to report this week. School photos are coming home today. The group shot made me laugh out loud! Reaxton looks like he's singing opera and everyone else's smiling as though he sounds really great. And check out me—I'm actually rolling my eyes so I look like a demon! The funniest thing about it all was *that* shot was the best we could get. I know because I looked at all the pics on the photographer's laptop the day the photos were taken.

Our class is rostered on to present an assembly item next week. True Confession: I have nothing prepared. I've been spending the past two weeks just trying to get the class back into our routine and picking up the things we dropped in the lead-up to NAPLAN.

All excursion payments and paperwork need to be finalised by Monday, please. I'm still waiting on seven Code of Conduct Agreements. Students can't attend the excursion without having these signed and filed. If you have any issues with the Agreement, please make an appointment to see the Principal.

Gabbie

PS I don't really spray the kids with Glen 20. That was a joke.

PPS Glue sticks are on special at both major supermarkets this week.

Week 6

FRIDAY

Dear Parents & Caregivers,

Assembly items! They kill me. Every time. Early in my teaching career, I learned that there's no point devoting too much time to preparing for an assembly item. You can spend hours on the bloody things and then, the day before, the kid who's meant to be doing a major piece of narration says, 'I can't wait for tomorrow. I get a day off school. We're going camping!' Or the Principal sends out a staff email saying, *No item required for assembly tomorrow, NRMA will be here with a presentation on seatbelts*. Or the hall will be closed for floor repairs and the whole thing will be relocated to the COLA (Covered Outdoor Learning Area) where there's hardly any room and the sound system's playing up, so there's no chance you can present the elaborate stage adaptation of *Charlotte's Web* that you've worked on for weeks . . .

The monstrosity my class presented this morning was my attempt at something low key. While it wasn't a complete disaster, it certainly wasn't very good. For those of you who didn't attend, here's what went down . . . I decided to take a gamble on IT and use it as part of our presentation.

Last week, I had each student select their favourite drawing they had sketched this term, and on the weekend I scanned each of them and created a PowerPoint presentation. This took ages, but I figured it was better taking two hours of my own time on Saturday rather than spend two hours of class time trying to knock up some kind of performance or song. I asked the kids to write a couple of sentences about what they had learned during our recent Art lessons. The plan was that each child would read out their sentences at the microphone when their picture was displayed on the screen.

That was the *plan*.

On Wednesday, we went down to the hall for a practice. The projector worked just the way it should. The drawings looked incredible on the big screen. The class lined up patiently at the microphone. Things were going well. Then it was Reaxton's turn. He stepped up very close to the mic and said, 'Tits and bums are really fun.'

The whole class cracked up.

'That's not what you wrote down.' I was too tired to even be amused. That morning he had locked all the toilet cubicles, which created all kinds of drama. Sometimes Ax just shits me to tears. 'What's that even got to do with drawing?' I asked.

'Nanny Maud said nudes are fun to draw.' He shrugged.

'Reaxton,' I said firmly, 'you drew a horse.' I pointed to his sketch now magnified on the screen.

'Oh, *yeahhhh*,' he said in a dopey voice.

The kids laughed again, and I knew I was losing them—the vast space of the hall, the distance between myself and the students, and Reaxton's commanding voice in the microphone had caused a displacement of control and power. It was a tiny shift, almost imperceptible, but I had been there before. It was time to rein everything in.

'Reaxton,' I boomed, reaching for a teacher voice that was low but loud. 'We are not here for your amusement. You need to—'

'Wait!' Reaxton cut me off. 'We've got bleeding back here.' He started waving his hands like he was directing traffic. 'You lot stop there,' he said, palm out as a stop sign. 'You two come here.' His arm curved through the air in a beckoning motion.

From the back of the student line came two boys, one with a nose absolutely gushing, his shirt covered with blood. He looked like he'd been shot. The other kid had an arm around him and a guilty look on his face. Turns out they'd been backstage messing around with props from last year's concert, and one kid had whacked the other across the face with a pool noodle.

'That's disgusting!' squealed Liza. 'There's a trail of blood!' The students scattered, leaping off the stage like seasoned crowd-surfers. They ran around the cavernous hollow of the hall, excitement building.

'Sit down,' I said, reaching again for a booming teacher voice and finding it wasn't there.

'SIT DOWN!' Ax shouted into the microphone and the sound system squealed. The other kids gripped their ears, one collapsing into the foetal position (he has sensory issues associated with his autism).

'Reaxton, please!' I glared at him, but my tone of voice had given me away. I sounded like I was I begging.

'I've got this, Stroudy,' Ax said into the microphone, unhinging it from the stand and walking confidently across the stage. 'Boys and girls, it's time for a game of SURVIVAL TIPS!' He raised both arms in the air like a rock star and the rest of the class went wild, shrieking and shouting. They started running, fast and directionless across the linoleum floor, like ants from a nest that's just been disturbed. Even the child who had been curled up on the floor leapt back to life and joined in, while Coman stepped in a large blob of blood as he raced by, fragments of his footprints tracking across the hall.

'Ms Stroud?' It was Nose Bleeder, standing in front of me with imploring eyes, face smeary with blood. He was bent over and a pool of red had begun collecting at his feet.

'Pinch your nose,' I instructed. I tried to help position his hands and immediately my own fingers were stained with his blood. 'Ummm.' I glanced around, looking for tissues, a first-aid kit, another adult. Even with his nose pinched, the blood continued to stream. I had never seen such a bloody blood nose. I bunched up his shirt in an attempt to capture the flow while I walked him to the change rooms. Within moments, my hands were slick.

'I didn't mean to make him bleed.' The Whacker trailed behind us. 'I didn't mean to.'

I propped the bleeding boy over a sink and searched the space for a first-aid kit. There was none. I held my own bloody hands over a neighbouring basin. Nose Bleeder looked pale and I felt my heart racing. *What if it's broken?* The flow was torrential.

'Can you turn on this tap?' I asked The Whacker, gesturing with my elbow.

The sound of my class going ballistic in the hall was bouncing off the change-room tiles. You could hear Reaxton commentating through the microphone. 'Don't slip in the blood, people! Step around the blood!' He sounded like a television voiceover.

I held my hands over the sink and watched as The Whacker turned and turned the faucet.

'It's not working. There's no water coming out.'

'You're right,' I said glumly, remembering a note stuck to the whiteboard in our staffroom:

No Warter in hall
Week 5 & 6 & prossibly 7
Conrad

Now, I felt like I was 'prossibly' going to lose my mind. I could feel the blood forming a crust on my skin. Nose Bleeder moaned and I snatched paper towels from the dispenser, bunching them under his nose and guiding him to sit down.

'I don't feel great,' The Whacker said suddenly, the colour sliding from *his* face.

'You sit down, too,' I said, directing him to the floor with my elbows and wrists.

I offered fresh paper towels to Nose Bleeder. He dropped the old ones into the bin and I tried not to be horrified by the wet thudding sound they made. I knelt beside the boys, my dry, bloody hands held aloft, and tried to assess my options.

'There's no outta bounds, *bounds, bounds.*' Reaxton's voice wafted through the change room. He had obviously found the reverb dial. 'Play on, *on, on!*'

At that moment, I heard the heavy double doors of the hall rattle open and clank shut. I wondered if students were escaping, but then I heard Reaxton, clear as our school bell, welcoming the Principal into the hall.

That'd be right.

This new Principal is a big fan of the 'pop in'. He often turns up to ask the kids what they're learning. It's a pain in the arse because sometimes they're not 'learning' anything—sometimes they're practising stuff like writing or algorithms. He always looks at my pin board where the *Learning Intention* should be displayed. Honest to God, I'd spend all day adjusting that freaking sign to reflect the stuff we're doing. And, to be extra honest, the only person who ever reads it is the Principal.

So of course he does a popper while I'm in the change room with two boys trying to stem a tidal wave of blood and the rest of my class are running around like imbeciles.

'What are we learning about here 5/6 Stroud?' I heard him ask the kids.

'Tits and bums are really fun! *Fun! Fun!*' Reaxton's voice echoed around the hall.

'Where is the teacher?' the Principal asked, his voice stern and deep and commanding.

'She's in the toilet with two boys and a pool noodle. *Noodle. Noodle.*'

'Oh for fu—' I stopped myself in time, remembering the two twelve-year-olds bleeding and freaking to death beside me. (The Whacker was indeed still clutching the pool noodle.)

'C'mon,' I said to them, edging out of the change rooms.

Standing in the hall, I discovered my class frozen in tableau, as though they'd been playing Musical Statues. The Principal's eyes roamed over the group. As I joined the scene, blood-stained hands still aloft, I saw his eyebrows jump. Surprise. Alarm. Horror. When his gaze landed on Nose Bleeder and The Whacker, his brows leapt higher. Chaos. Risk. Incompetence.

The Principal took a moment to consider the situation, his face slowly scrunching up in that awkward, ugly way it does.

'You should have gloves on,' he said to me.

I felt myself twitch, and I resisted the urge building inside me to rip the pool noodle out of The Whacker's hands and use it to clobber the Principal until his own nose was broken. And both his arms, too.

'This will need to be cleaned up.' He pointed at the bloody trail of footprints scattered across the hall. 'It's not Mr Hallam's job to tidy up after you.'

Then he left the hall, the doors slamming closed. The kids were quiet and still. The popper had ruined the party vibes and the excitement was deflating from them like air from a jumping castle.

'Survival tips? *Tips? Tips?*' Ax suggested meekly.

I snatched the microphone from him.

Back at our classroom, I sent Nose Bleeder and The Whacker to Sick Bay. I told all the kids to grab a device and research something relevant to our upcoming school excursion in Canberra. Once they had fallen into the rapturous coma that screens induce, I went to our wet area and scrubbed at my hands like Lady Macbeth, soaping them up with Premier Blue several times.

'You should have gloves on,' I muttered. *Fuck me sideways*, I thought darkly. I could feel myself seething with rage.

While the class continued to scroll, coming down from their unexpected and dramatic high, I called Mrs Parnell at the office to check the kids in sick bay were okay. She said the bleeding had stopped, his colour had returned, and he wasn't in any pain so we could safely presume the nose wasn't broken. She had cleaned him up and called his mum, who was coming to collect him. Then Mrs Parnell asked if someone could come over to take back the second boy *and* the pool noodle. I sent Dempsey along with Yuki and they returned with The Whacker, the noodle and a folder of paperwork with a sticky note pressed on top. Mrs Parnell had written: *May as well start filling it in now. Please remember to also log online.*

I felt the sense of despair that always comes with administration. I'd only just got the blood off my hands and already I was holding the paperwork required to document the event.

That same afternoon, I received an email from the Principal reminding me that I didn't have a Direction Wheel on my classroom door and that I needed to put one in place before the end of the week.

Direction Wheels allow members of our school community to quickly locate classes when they're not in the classroom, his email preached. *They're helpful when someone wants to pop in with a quick message or salutation.*

I'll give you a salutation, I wanted to reply, but I just closed my email folder and spent the next half hour on the school's online portal, logging Nose Bleeder's epic explosion.

And I didn't practise the assembly item again.

That's why it was pretty rusty. I want to apologise because I know so many of you make an effort to get to assembly and see your child up on stage. But then another part of me doesn't want to apologise because pulling together brief fifteen-minute 'audience worthy' presentations with a group of thirty-one children, every ten weeks, is a bloody mission (no pun intended).

Gabbie

Week 6
SATURDAY

Dear Parents & Caregivers,

Wow! Lots of you replied to the email I sent out yesterday. Someone wrote SHAMBOLIC ASSEMBLY in the subject line and I laughed for ages—the perfect description!

There was also a lot of anger in your emails at the way the Principal responded to the situation. Believe me when I say I was ferociously angry, too. I spent the drive home on Wednesday night shouting all the things I wished I'd said to him. It was quite therapeutic.

All of you agreed that the Principal should have done more. Well, yeah, he 'prossibly' should have done more, but let's not forget that principals are only human. They're not wizards. They're not Dumbledore! The Principal is no better equipped to deal with that situation than I am. Principals don't go through any special initiation ceremony that imbues them with powers to make all the children do their bidding. (And you know what? Come in close so I can whisper this to you . . . A few teachers rise up through the ranks of leadership to become principals because they just can't hack it in the classroom. *Not all of them, but a few.*)

Becoming a good school leader takes time: time to grow as a leader and time to understand the context of the school that you lead. Our Principal is not only new to our school, he's pretty

126

much new to the job. Four years ago, he was a garden-variety classroom teacher just like me, and he's only been Principal at one other school before this one.

Of course, I have my opinions on what I think he should have done and how he should have responded. To be frank: I think it was a shit deal that he left me stuck up Blood Nose Creek without a paddle (or running water). To be more professional: I think he showed a lack of leadership (and common sense), and I also think he should have given me support and assistance. I have worked for other principals who would have handled the situation entirely differently—they would have supervised my class so I could attend to the bleeding; they would have followed up with an after school 'pop in' to see if I needed help with the paperwork.

This new Principal has his eyes on things that I don't tend to value. He's invested in things like displaying Learning Intentions and Direction Wheels. He wants the students to be able to articulate concepts they're learning to any person who might visit the classroom. He needs to be seen to be implementing the latest pedagogies and using the newest buzzwords. Like all of us, he wants to appear to be doing a good job. I understand that. It's just that my definition of what good teaching looks like and his definition are at odds.

And you know what? I just have to suck it up. Because he's the boss. What's more, he's a boss that's doing what he's told. He is absolutely right. I *should* have a Direction Wheel on my door. My students *should* know the Learning Intention for every lesson. And I *should* have been wearing gloves. It's just that all of those things, all of those wheels and intentions and gloves, exist in a theoretical bubble where I have excesses of time and my students are highly articulate and the school is littered with first-aid kits and there's running water at all times . . .

I'm getting off the track. The *theoretical* world and the *real* world of teaching are literally poles apart, and it's probably not anything you parents need to concern yourselves with.

I think what I'm trying to do is gently point out that our anger at the Principal might be somewhat displaced. Shouldn't we be angry at Reaxton for initially hijacking the lesson with his tits and bums comment? Shouldn't we be angry at Nose Bleeder and The Whacker who were fooling around (as kids do) when they should have been lined up, waiting patiently. Maybe our anger should be directed at Conrad because there was no running water? Or at the person in charge of first-aid kits—why didn't the hall have a kit? If you really stretched it out, we could be angry at noses that bleed and pool noodles that are harder than you might first think! So much anger, but where to direct it? And is it worth it?

I think the question that sits beneath the angry feelings is: Whose job is this? When an injury happens—and they frequently happen with large groups of children—who should respond and who then attends to the rest? I know we're straying into procedural territory here, but I still think it's worth considering. Is it a teacher's job to attend to injuries? What should be sacrificed so a teacher can deal with a sick or injured kid? Is it the Principal's role to salvage a lesson if he walks in to discover blood and mayhem? Who then does *his* work while he's mopping up a teacher's mess?

As a teacher, my biggest issue within this shambolic 'Rivers of Blood' assembly story is around what was happening for the kids? Assemblies could be great learning experiences but they've become one of a million 'potentially' great learning experiences crammed within a term. They've become such a rushed and regimented thing that there's no time to enjoy them, to prepare them well and to learn from them.

Perhaps the question we need to ask is: what do students gain from assemblies? I know the easy answer is to say they develop confidence on stage, but I don't believe that's the true motivation behind the assembly. I prepare an assembly item *when* I have to, *because* I have to. I do it because my class is listed on the roster. I try to present something that doesn't cut into too much of my class time because 'developing their confidence on stage' has to sit alongside eleventy million other equally important outcomes. I prepare an assembly item because there's an expectation that I will, because parents want to see something, because there's some unwritten school law that says once per term I should put all the kids in my class on stage.

I'm not against assemblies. I see their value. I just dream of a time where they become something more organic, a genuine learning experience, a true showcase of something great my class wants to share because they want to share it . . . not because it's Week 6 and our name is next on the list.

And what's your role in all of that, Mum and Dad? Nan and Pop? Caregiver? Would you be okay if it was decided that assembly items would be ad hoc, presented only when a class and their teacher felt they had something that warranted a presentation? How would this fit with your Facebook page where you're cultivating a carefully curated timeline of your child's school experiences? How would this affect your perception of the work the teacher's doing? Do you have to see the kids on stage to believe that something is happening in class? Will you say I'm a bad teacher if I only present once a year but Mr Lloyd presents four times?

I can hear myself overthinking this, but rest assured I haven't lost perspective. It's just one assembly practice that went rogue! There are many moments like that within a seemingly ordinary week of school. So often a classroom day unfolds unpredictably, causing chaos and mess and discord, despite careful planning and forethought. But I do think it's interesting to unpack those moments, to actually throw them down under the microscope and see what's going on. They might just be moments, but they have knock-on effects. When you examine a single school moment, you discover it's part of an ecosystem—a live, ever-changing web where everything is interrelated. Systems link to procedures. Teacher competence links to student behaviours. School leadership links to staff morale. Link. Link. Link. It would be oversimplifying things to look at that shambolic rehearsal and lay blame. Instead we need to accept in that moment many human elements were intersecting, producing predictably erratic outcomes.

One parent emailed me and said he was sorry I had such a crappy assembly rehearsal, but he also said: *I laughed out loud reading about it. These stories from the classroom are very funny.* That made me smile—a wry smile, a smile that makes me wonder if you're understanding what I'm saying to you when I share things like this. I know that assembly practice sounds funny because you're safe, reading it as a juicy little email that gives you a fly-on-the-wall insight into your child's day at school. But it's not funny when you're living it; when you're the teacher who has to put your name to it and accept responsibility for it. It's not funny when you're in the moment and trying to regain control, and already you can feel the nuclear fallout from parents: *Why were the children unsupervised? Why were the pool noodles not stored securely? Why wasn't there access to first-aid kits? What was my child doing while all of this nonsense was going on?*

It's not funny when you have to imagine telling a mother that her son broke his nose *while you were in charge.*

It's not funny when you're holding another person's blood.

Gabbie

Week 7

MONDAY

Dear Parents & Caregivers,

Oh my Gawd! I have to tell you about the staff meeting, where the aftershocks of my disastrous assembly practice were still being felt. The first three items on this afternoon's agenda were:

1. Direction Wheels
2. First-Aid Kits
3. Quality of Assembly Items

The new Principal kicked things off with this:

'Staff, I have noticed that there are a few classrooms that don't have a Direction Wheel on their door. Could everyone attend to this as a priority?'

I kept my head down and flicked an email to Bec: *Didn't you say you found a template for Direction Wheels on the net? Could you pretty please send it to me?*

Less than a minute later, my computer pinged with an incoming email. I muted the sound and looked up to catch a wink from Bec. She had sent a PDF of a garish Direction Wheel from some website called Teaching That Twinkles. I hit print and the photocopier in the room next door could be heard churning out the hideous circle.

Direction Wheel—done, I thought. I picked up my pencil and tried to sketch a little something on the edge of my daybook.

Nanny Maud was often telling the kids that drawing was a very calming art form.

'Now, first-aid kits,' the Principal announced. 'Teachers, you need to be aware that your classroom first-aid kit should be with you at all times. As Gabbie recently discovered, there's no first-aid kit in the hall, so when you're down there you need to have your classroom kit with you. And your iPad with the class roll and the school mobile phone since there isn't a phone down there, either. Now, when you're out on Playground duty, you should carry your kit and—'

'What about the Library?' I interrupted, my righteous sense of logic could no longer be contained. 'There's a first-aid kit in the Library, isn't there?'

'Ahhh . . .' He looked uncertain.

'Yes,' Mrs Jethro chimed in.

'And the music room?' I pressed.

'Yes,' Mrs Jethro said again (she's both the Music teacher and the Librarian), 'there's a full kit in each of those rooms, plus a carry-bag kit in each room for Playground duty.' She looked at the Principal and then back at me.

'So . . .' I sat back and frowned, pretending to think. 'We've got a first-aid kit here in the staffroom, one in the office, one in the tuck shop *and* the resource room, and a whole heap of first-aid stuff in the sick bay.' I listed the kits off on my fingers and ignored all the voices in my head that were saying *shut up, shut up, shut up!* 'But when I go to the hall, I have to take my own first-aid kit?' My tone of voice was just this side of lighthearted.

'Yes!' the Principal said. 'And your iPad and the mobile phone. And remember to adjust your Direction Wheel to let us know you're in the hall.'

'Right,' I said.

'Actually, Gabbie,' he said warmly, 'I see the point you're making. It doesn't seem logical that the hall is the only building not furnished with a first-aid kit.'

Here it comes, I thought. I let my head drop to one side and closed my eyes to hide the cynical eye-rolling I've been chastised for in the past. But even with my eyes closed I could see what was coming.

'What I'd like you to do is to make up a first-aid kit for the hall.'

And there it is, I thought grimly. *More work for me!* I wrote *Kit* in my daybook, right next to my sorry little sketch of an apple.

'School assemblies!' the Principal announced next. 'They should be an opportunity for our students to shine!' He smiled. 'I know it can be tricky getting items prepared, but parents don't want to come along and watch a PowerPoint presentation.'

I stared at my screen and tried not to feel bothered. There's nothing like being told your work isn't up to standard in front of all your colleagues.

'When parents come to assemblies,' he went on, 'they want to be entertained.'

A little noise came out of me then, like a grunt meeting a groan. I've come to think of it as my Staff Meeting Noise. It's an inbuilt primal response that I couldn't contain even if I wanted to. It happens every time the Principal gives a directive that is different to my educational philosophy and convictions. *Parental entertainment* does not sit well alongside my intentions and objectives when preparing assembly items.

'I think parents would like to see more singing and dancing,' he said. 'Parents love a good skit, a play written by the students, some musical interludes . . . It's great for them to see the kids in costumes too, and with props and masks and things like that. And the children love it.'

Good grief, I thought. *A mini concert every term from every class.* I glanced at my computer and clicked into the Seeking Employment Page I had bookmarked long ago.

Customer Service for a big name telco.
Meter Reader for local shire.
Night fill at major supermarket.
Team Leader of Transport and Logistics for Green Lea
  Egg Farm.

All were preferable to teaching in that given moment.

'Assemblies should be a time where students can be directors and producers and stage managers!' He was still talking. I was halfway through the job description for Green Lea Farm.

'Bloody hell!' Lloydie interjected. 'This is a bit unreasonable. We're not Halligan Primary School of Performing Arts!'

'Not yet!' the Principal chortled.

I clicked *Apply For This Job* and entered in my email. Transporting eggs sounds really good right now.

Gabbie

Week 7

Dear Parents & Caregivers,

Don't panic. I'm not going anywhere. It was a joke. Sort of. I mean, I did click the link. I often click the link. My inbox has a fair smattering of emails with *Employment Application Form* and *Job Information Pack* in the Subject Header. I frequently open those emails, too. But I'm yet to open the attachments. I haven't taken that crucial next step where you fill out the form and upload it online. It's tempting, though. Sometimes I just like to imagine myself in a job where I'm valued, where the boss says, 'Hey, you pulled that together really well. It can't have been easy!'

I know what you're going to say to me—every job's the same. Alright. I get it.

Gabbie

Week 7
THURSDAY

Dear Parents & Caregivers,

This week I caught up with parents who had been requesting a meeting since Term 1. While they were grateful for my time, and it felt like a productive session, they began by asking what I did with my day and why it was so difficult to pin down an appointment. That gave me the impression that parents think I'm embellishing the weight of my workload and the breadth of my work day as a means of avoiding them. I wanted to use this letter to explain what I do with my time.

I think the work of a teacher is misunderstood. Let's look at today as an example.

I began at 5.30 a.m. I got my sorry arse to the gym (I go a few times a week). I leapt around a room with other stupefied individuals attempting ridiculous things like burpees, push-ups, planks and squats. I got home and brought the household to life, racing through a series of essential but mundane activities, and prompting my children to do the same. For those who share my postcode, you would have heard me bellowing:

'Just get dressed. Get dressed. Get dressed. Get. Dressed.'
'Put the cat down.'
'Put the cat down and get dressed.'
'Well, where did you take them off?'

'We're going to be late.'
'Eat.'
'Stop talking and eat.'
'You need to unpack the dishwasher!'
'Don't put the cat in there.'
(And my favourite) 'You'll just have to get one out of the dirty
    clothes basket and wear it.'

Eventually we were all in the car. The trip to the bus stop
was thrilling because we were travelling with a helium balloon
that I had purchased yesterday for today's Science lesson. The
journey is only a few kilometres, but I think I said, 'Please, stop
touching it!' at least a hundred times. I deposited my kids at
the bus stop (yes, I make them catch the bus most days) and
told them to try their best and be kind. I gave each of them a
kiss and told them I'd see them at school.

Then it was *Game On*. I fanged it into school, running
through a perpetual mental to-do list that included things like:

Check pot plant in classroom is still alive
Make appointment with school counsellor regarding a particular
    Student of Concern
Print out and upload excursion checklists, what to pack & itinerary
Finalise first-aid kit for hall—laminate that stupid list
Ask Conrad about the carpet thread
Mark yesterday's Maths work.

I arrived at school at eight and spent fifteen minutes bringing
the classroom to life (lights, curtains, computers, air con, fruit
bin) and unpacking all my 'luggage' (lunch, student workbooks,
laptop, and assorted items from home for the Science lesson,
which included fruit, eggs, sand, perfume, lentils, flyspray and

that bloody helium balloon—it was already beginning to wilt). Then I rigged up my computer to the whiteboard and brought up all the slides, screens and sites I would need for the day. I went over to the Resource Room and got some readers for my Literacy Groups and more supplies for the Science lesson. I spent the next fifteen minutes in the classroom preparing the activities for the morning.

I also received two phone calls. The first one was from a parent asking if I could send home a printed copy of all the notes related to the excursion because they're having trouble with the SkoolSaid app. The second call was from a parent requesting a time to see me before the excursion to talk about their child's anxieties. By this time, it was ten to nine and kids were beginning to breeze into the room, having a chat and asking about the helium balloon. When Ax discovered it, I decided to hustle it over to the staffroom and made it back to class just in time for line-up.

I was busting for the toilet *and* a cup of tea, but I'd left my run too late.

The morning session always seems to go fast. We do the roll and Crunch It Up, and inevitably there's a small chunk of kiwi fruit or banana or tomato blobbed on the floor and everyone denies knowing anything about it and we have a brief inquisition until some brave soldier mops it up with way too many tissues. We head out for the Mindful Walk, which I have trimmed down to ten minutes. Some students run the course while others amble along and chat—it's a great time for me to listen in to the kids. It gives me a tiny insight to their 'laws of the jungle'.

When we get back to the classroom, we're like a well-oiled machine and move straight into Literacy Groups. It's old-fashioned, but I still try to hear every child read, even just for a minute or two each day. The kids work in groups and rotate through the tasks that are pitched to their ability levels. They spend about fifteen minutes on each task before moving on to the next. My School Learning Support Officer (yes, *Officer*, like they have the power to arrest people if they're not learning!), Mrs Royale, follows Ax during this time, encouraging him to attempt tasks, helping him with his spelling and writing, guiding him with his reading, discouraging his humming, and supporting nearby students where she can.

After Literacy Groups, it's writing time. At the moment we're working on persuasive texts. I also haven't covered enough 'speaking and listening', which is another strand of the English syllabus, so I'm making the poor buggers write persuasive speeches. It's tied in nicely to our work on Government. They've chosen some great topics, too:

Teachers should wear uniforms
Little sisters should be classed as pets
Why Nanny Maud would be a good prime minister
Halligan Primary should have tuckshop every day
Having freckles means you're smarter

And this one . . . Wait for it . . .

iPhones are the new cigarettes.

While the class writes, I work with individual students at my desk. It's a process called conferencing and it's probably some of the best teaching I do: each child gets precious minutes of my time and I give them specific direction and feedback on their writing. Each day I aim to conference with at least six kids, but because of the many and varied interruptions I only ever seem to manage two or three. Once I got through four and swaggered around all day like I was a champion.

Throughout the writing lesson, I notice lots of coughing: some dry and repetitive ('Megan, I think you need to use your puffer') and others wet and hearty ('Go and have a drink now, Pete. You too, Quentin, and wash your hands with soap'). I hear the gentle sounds of viscous phlegm being moved from nose to throat to gut via the deep inhale. I remind students to blow their noses and consider how many germs and sicknesses are festering in the days before we go to camp.

Having Mrs Royale in the classroom at this time is like being given a bar of gold! Her presence completely negates the 'issue' of Reaxton. For this writing task, for example, it has been difficult to get him to decide on a topic and settle in to it. At first, he wanted to do: *Tits, arse and bloody hell are not really swear words.*

That's because I'm on a mission now to curb his swearing, but we often disagree on what constitutes bad language. Eventually he arrived at the idea of writing about animal cruelty after another kid was talking about a racehorse that had to be put down. This interested Ax and so he's writing something about how animals deserve to be treated with respect. Yesterday I heard him arguing with Mrs Royale about using the word 'fucked'.

'But it's the most persuasive word there is,' Reaxton said.

'I think you could be right, Ax,' Mrs Royale replied. 'But we're still going to have to choose *another* word—a word that all the animals would be proud to hear you using as you advocate for them.'

Reaxton paused for a moment, frowned, and then said, 'What about *dog act*? Like it's a *dog act* to kill a racehorse just because it's not a champion? And dogs would be stoked to hear me saying *dog act!*'

Mrs Royale looked over his head and smiled at me. They are small steps we take each day, and yet we're almost always moving forwards.

Our writing lesson concludes with sharing. A few students stand up and read out selected paragraphs. They're coming along, using words and phrases like 'undoubtedly' and 'ashamed' and 'the latest research proves'. We tidy up the room, and Liza collects the books, which get dumped into a tub near my desk for marking.

As the students leave for recess, I say, 'Great effort this morning, 5/6. I'm looking forward to reading your work.' But inside I'm feeling dread—at least three or four minutes on each child's book, multiplied by thirty-one students. Nearly two hours. For one foolhardy moment, I wish to teach Kindergarten again where marking can be done in minutes (or half-hours, at most). But then I remember all the preparation, the mothering, the nurturing, the nose wiping and tears. My pile of books looks time-consuming but less onerous.

Reaxton's latest earworm has been 'Eye Of The Tiger', so I'm humming that as I throw on my high-vis vest, grab my first-aid kit, hat, sunnies and whistle, and strut out for recess duty on the Junior Playground. I sing a few lyrics to a Stage One student who's gnawing on a fluorescent strip that looks a lot like futuristic leather. He says, 'My grandpa sings that song.' The kid next to him eyeballs me and asks, 'Are you pregnant Missus Trout?' I firmly deny the allegation and try to suck my stomach in. I lap around the eating area, trying to burn calories. I think of the toast I ate for breakfast. That third piece wasn't necessary.

A Kindergarten girl comes to me, bleating with sadness because a yoghurt pouch has exploded in her lunch box. I kneel down to her level and feel my bladder protesting—I've been needing to go for ages.

I get the child settled and eating. I empty her lunch box and try rinsing it at the tap, but my bladder won't allow it. I employ the services of a Stage One boy who blasts the box full of water, splattering his own clothes with yoghurt. He's not bothered, but I document the whole thing in the notebook attached to my first-aid kit just in case his parents come in to question it. Finally, Bec arrives and relieves me, and I race down to the staff toilets and relieve myself. I think of my doctor telling me that I have to stop holding on like I do—it's caused me problems in the past. 'But when can I go?' I always lament. 'I can't leave the class unsupervised.'

In the staffroom, I make a cup of tea and scoff down the vegies and hummus I have packed. I'm racing against the clock— raw vegetables are time-consuming to eat—so of course I bite my tongue. The bell is being rung and my tongue is hurting like a demon. I tip my tea down the sink, but there's no time to wash my cup. I tuck it into my little pigeonhole because Mrs Parnell will kill you with her bare hands if you leave a dirty mug in the sink.

Back at my classroom, the kids are waiting in something that resembles a line. There's been a drama concerning two of my girls in the Playground. The teacher on duty chats to me discreetly and I mentally add the information to the list of things I need to tell the school counsellor. I feel the concern that has been growing for a particular girl shift up a notch. I take a breath and usher the class inside.

It's Maths and they know the routine. There's a times table warm-up already alight on the whiteboard screen and the kids are working through it. Reaxton has a separate task to complete because he's so far behind with his Maths. For once he gets started without me having to cheerlead him into it, so I take the chance to check in with the girl I'm worried about. At my desk, she reassures me several times that she's fine and that there's no real problem. That's actually what she says—'There's no real problem, Ms Stroud'—and it makes me think about real problems and pretend problems, and what the difference between them could be. I can't unravel this knot right now so I send her back to her desk, make a quick note about it in my day book, and get back out the front to teach.

Our lesson centres around multiplication. We're using arrays to help us solve complex problems in an informal way. Some students are still using little plastic disks called counters to create the array and their level of 'complexity' is to solve something like 15 x 8. Other students are drawing a 'blank array' to conquer problems like 15 x 14. We're building our way to the formal algorithm which some students already know how to do and they use it to check their work.

It's a hard lesson for Reaxton. Mrs Royale works with him but her time runs out partway through. Once she leaves, he spends the rest of the lesson trying to flip the counters up so that they land on the blades of the ceiling fan. Today, the Behaviour Gods are smiling on me and no other students join Ax in his game of Ultimate Tiddlywinks.

I work the room, trying to get around to every child to see how they're managing with the task. A small group of kids have become confused; they've lost their way and their answers are unreasonable.

'This can't be right,' Megan says. 'There's no way the answer could be in the thousands.'

'We've done something wrong,' Jeff agrees.

They call me over and I spend time with them, trying to back-pedal through their thinking and figure out their misconception. It's a complex and authentic moment for me as a teacher, requiring metacognition and relational understanding as I attempt to step into my students' way of thinking. It takes me a few moments to see what has happened. They've become so focused on following the newer, more challenging process that they've neglected their basic knowledge. They're making errors in the first step of the multiplication, which has thrown everything out of whack. I challenge them to solve the same problem again on a fresh page, this time talking aloud as they solve each step.

'Ten times ten is one hundred,' Megan says slowly, while Liza documents the calculation. 'And then ten times four is four hundred.' Megan watches as Liza writes it down. 'No! Wait!' she exclaims. 'That's not right, it's *forty*, not four hundred.'

'Oh, yeah.' Jeff laughs and reaches for an eraser, tosses it to Liza. 'No wonder we kept getting such huge numbers.'

I commend them on checking their work and for seeking help.

'Our answers were totally outrageous!' Megan grins. 'But we get it now.'

I feel a sense of satisfaction; it was a little Magic Moment, but it buoys me along as a teacher. I glance at the clock and have a minor freak-out. We need to change gears and get the Science lesson started.

I end Maths abruptly and hear myself saying, 'It doesn't matter if you're not finished.' I say that far too often and it troubles me. Why do I bother asking them to start something if they never get to finish? What kind of work ethic am I promoting? I shake off the guilt and send Yuki over to the staffroom for the helium balloon.

While she's gone, Reaxton turns on the fan and counters fly across the room. I tell him he'll have to stay in at lunch for five minutes because that's our agreed consequence whenever he touches any switch without permission. He tells me that's a *dog act* and a waste of both our lives, but then asks if he can help me because I'm pulling a bunch of things out of a basket, and his interest is piqued and he doesn't want to miss out.

The Science lesson is messy, but lots of fun. It's a revision of solids, liquids and gases. The students have to sort the various materials according to their properties, but they also have to note down the observable features and justify their choices. All the students are engaged and enthused, although it gets noisy, and my student with particular sensory needs has to wear his noise-cancelling headphones. Other than that, it's a rich but exhausting lesson. Every student achieves success as they fill out their online worksheet. They ask good questions, especially about gas and how it can be contained. The lesson takes us right up to the bell and I send them off to lunch. The room is a bombsite. There's honey spilled on one desk and a million fingerprints in it, and Pete has dropped an egg on another desk. I don't care about the mess. I feel like a superhero as I put lids on containers and canisters. The lesson was a triumph. *Why hadn't the Principal popped in for that one?*

I find the dustpan and the cloths, the cleaning spray and the fruit bin. I remember a time, not that long ago, when I could have asked some students to stay behind and help me clean up. I know there are many kids in my class who'd be more than happy to spend a few minutes tidying up. They would chatter away about different things, make lame jokes and laugh at one another. But I've learned my lesson there. I've had too many parents come in and question me. *Why did you keep* my child *in at lunch?* My child *shouldn't be required to clean!* (Said with utter disdain.) My child *missed time to have lunch—they're entitled to their allocated eating time!* Parents, no matter how pleasant they may have seemed at earlier meetings, have been known to transform into angry union officials representing their worker when you ask their child to do something additional, even if it's something that contributes to the common good of their classroom society.

In my experience, arguing with parents will almost always end in defeat. They will go above you, beyond you, around you and through you until their requests are ratified. Being *teacher* was once a role of 'service' but for some it's now seen as the role of 'servant'.

As I wipe down desks, I remember I'd told Reaxton he had to stay in. Following through with his consequences is paramount at this stage of our relationship, so I drop everything and trek outside to the Big Playground. He's easy to find, following Mr Lloyd the teacher on duty. As I get closer, I can hear Reaxton attempting to wear Lloydie down with his broken-record strategy.

'Please can I play? Please can I play? Please can I play? Please can I play? Please can I play? Please can I play?'

Mr Lloyd checks his watch and says, 'Still four more minutes, Ax. Go and sit down.'

But he doesn't sit down. He just increases the speed of his request and steps in even closer, until he's right in the bubble of Lloydie's space, *PleasecanIplay, pleasecanIplay, pleasecanIplay,* like an automated hashtag set on a repetitive loop.

When I turn up, Lloydie looks at me and says, 'Please shoot me now.'

'Bang! Bang!' I say and he smiles. 'But I'll do better than shoot you,' I add. 'I've come here for this one.' I point to Reaxton, who stops talking and squints at me.

'Come on, Ax,' I tell him. 'Five minutes for turning the fan on. Let's go.'

'Fuck me sideways,' Reaxton says and kicks at a rock.

'Come on, Ax,' I say.

'Fuck me!' He growls it again, and a few kids look up from their lunches to see if maybe he's going to start thrashing things or hit me or howl. I watch him, too, even though I'm walking confidently towards my classroom with the expectation that he will follow.

'Come on, Ax,' I call, keeping my voice unconcerned. Everything has to be a poker face—even your voice.

'Fuck *you!*' he shouts at me.

I stop, turn and look at him. My heart is racing, but I can never let him know that.

'Come on, Ax,' I say again. It's the broken-record technique, teacher-style. Repetitive and deliberate; request the behaviour you expect. And don't negotiate with a terrorist.

'Awwww, fuck!' he says one last time, but he takes a step towards me, so I turn and continue. The expectation has been set.

Back at the classroom, I have him sweep up lentils, sand and sugar. His earlier anger has evaporated and he tells me how fun the Science lesson was. He says next time we should capture farts in jars because farts are gas. The desks are still a mess, but after five minutes I send him out to play and he leaps from the classroom slapping at the doorframe and singing a strand of lyrics from this morning's tune. The earworm starts up again as I grab a bunch of work to do over lunch. I walk to the staffroom muttering about a man and the will to survive.

I'm starving and eat my sandwich at the photocopier, printing out the excursion notes requested by that parent this morning. This is a time-consuming task and I vacillate between feeling resentful towards the parent and frustration at the technology. I also upload the itinerary and what-to-bring checklists to SkoolSaid and print off hard copies as well. In the staffroom, I slump into a seat and start marking some Maths books, still chasing yesterday's work. I only get through five before the bell goes.

I meet my class and walk them up to Library. Again I notice their coughing and snotting, their itching and picking. I remind them to get to bed early tonight and every night until camp. I remind them to wash their hands. Sneeze into their sleeve. Eat some oranges.

It's not our usual Library day—we're normally doing Art with Nanny Maud on a Thursday afternoon—but Mrs Jethro's been sick and everything was rearranged. I wait with the children as they line up at the Library door. When Mrs Jethro appears, she looks grumpy, like she's not going to take shit from anyone, and I tell my class to remember their manners and try their best. I look pointedly at Reaxton, but he's busy stabbing his peers with a thumbtack he's picked up somewhere. I take it from him and he doesn't argue, but as he steps through the Library doors I hear him ask Mrs Jethro if she's ready to rise up to the challenge of our rival. I can't hear what she says, but her tone sounds narky.

I return to my room. There's still fruit and honey and sand on some of the desks. It will have to wait. This is holy time. Divine time. The sacrosanct fifty-five minutes that I live for every week. It's a time devoted to chipping away at the endless administration: submitting information for the school news-letter, updating things to be included on SkoolSaid, securing dates for future activities, tracking student permission slips and payments, entering results into online spreadsheets, updating the roll, chasing Volunteer Working With Children Checks, and returning phone calls to parents. Today I'm on a mission to finalise as much of the paperwork for Canberra as I can before we leave on Monday. I'm required to have emergency evacuation plans and a risk assessment for every venue that we visit. I've been worrying about the paperwork relating to student medication and would like to get across that this afternoon, too.

I'm in the office with Mrs Parnell, confirming the excursion-payment status for each child, when Mrs Jethro phones. Reaxton is on his way to my classroom. He has allegedly undone the beanbag zipper and there are beanies everywhere. I pause my work with Mrs Parnell and we agree to meet straight after school to finish, but then I remember I have bus duty and Mrs P will be long gone by then. We schedule to meet at eight-thirty tomorrow morning.

Back in my classroom, I engage in yet another quasi-counselling session with Reaxton as we continue cleaning the desks. His issues with Mrs Jethro are ongoing; every week he's sent back from Library.

'We've got different personality types,' Reaxton says as he sprays too much cleaner on the honeyed desks. 'Like I've got a personality . . . and she doesn't.' He scrubs at the surface and I see it becoming a foamy, sticky mess.

Last week, he had been sent back for circling 'rude words' in the dictionaries; the week before that, he was searching 'how to blow up a school' on the internet. The week before, two bookshelves collapsed after he removed their screws. He's also glued books shut, trimmed pages with scissors and hidden all the *Where's Wally?* books. (Apparently that was my fault. 'You shouldn't have taught me the definition of irony if you didn't want me to do something ironic,' he said. I thought about making a note of this because it's great evidence that he is learning.)

I return to the Library to collect my class just before the home-time bell, but before I can get there I hear Mrs Jethro shouting.

'Dempsey! There are thousands of books in this Library. Do not tell me that you can't find a book!'

The class look happy to see me. In the back corner of the Library, I see a swarm of beanies cascading out of a deflated beanbag. A few kids have them dotted in their hair and dangling off their hems.

As we walk back to our room, Dempsey sidles up to me.

'Sometimes I think Reaxton's lucky,' he says. 'I wish I could skip Library every week.'

I roll my eyes, and tell Dempsey that Reaxton has been cleaning our classroom and Library is always a much better place to be.

'You reckon?' Dempsey asks. I scruff a few beanies out of his hair and smile at him.

'You're alright,' I say. 'C'mon.'

In the classroom, the kids sit on the floor as we read through the checklist of what to pack for camp.

'Six pairs of underpants,' Dante reads out. 'Ms Stroud, you're hilarious.'

I let them talk and ask inane questions and repeat details they already know. They talk about things they can't wait to see, places they can't wait to go, stuff they can't wait to do. A frenetic excitement builds, becoming almost visible, and for a moment I feel it sweep over me too. I'm eleven years old all over again, counting the sleeps until my class goes to the seaside for four whole nights.

Suddenly it's 3.15 p.m., the bell is clanging and the teaching day is done, but I'm rostered on for bus duty. The duty, however, is a non-event: everyone catches their buses without trouble, and only one parent comes charging down to collect a child who forgot she was being picked up.

Back in my classroom, I smash through some more Maths marking. I get yesterday's work done, but it's already 4 p.m., so I load everything I need into my dowdy old-person trolley. I find a binder and start printing out all the excursion documents I'll need to take to Canberra. At a quarter to five, I head up to the Library again and spend some time scooping up beanies. Mrs Jethro has left the building. She's hardcore about leaving bang on the buzzer when her hours are up. I wish I could be more like her.

Some beanies have been scooped up, but there are still trillions to do. The static is incredible and there's a powerful ionic bond with the carpet. Before long I've got beanies up my arms, all over my shoes, and they're clinging to books on the shelves. They remind me of Kindergarten kids on the first day of school gripping onto their mums, dads, car doors, the school gates—anything to stop them being siphoned into the beanbag that is the Kindergarten classroom.

I think about creative ways of getting the beans back into the bag; vacuuming them and then emptying them in, perhaps Conrad could use the blower vac or maybe I could make it a punishment for Reaxton. I resolve that I'll send a few responsible students up to the Library first thing in the morning. They can miss the Mindful Walk and instead do some Mindful Bean Bagging. Then I think about the potential parent complaints; *child labour, slavery, favouritism, breaching their rights to mindfulness.* I decide that the beanies will become a project for my whole class—together we can get it done quickly in the morning. No doubt a parent will still grumble at the injustice of the entire class being charged to clean up Reaxton's mess, but I can't think of any other time efficient solution. I scrape beanies off my watch and swear. I'm late for an appointment.

I rush from school to Pathology. I have to take a blood test after the shambolic, bloodstained assembly practice of Week 6. I met with my doctor on the weekend and she assured me the risks of bloodborne infection were incredibly low; however, she recommended testing just to be safe. In the Pathology waiting room, I pluck stray beanies from my hair, my cuff, my collar.

After the blood test, I drive home, swinging by the supermarket. I dodge parents in Aisles 2 and 4. I'm served by a student I taught many years ago. She's in Year 11 now and starting to think about options for university. I ask her if she likes working on the checkouts and she shrugs. I always think the checkout looks like an awesome job—it's a fantasy I indulge in. I would scan those items real good and when I went home after my shift . . . Well, I'd just go home. No daggy trolley. No books for marking. No emails. No lessons to prepare. There'd be an expansive space where I could insert my own life.

Finally, I'm home, arriving just in time to meet Matty, my ex-husband, as he's dropping off Soph. Olivia's still at Girl Guides. I slap up some dinner and ask Soph about her day. Some kids in her class told her they heard Reaxton tell me to fuck off. She asks if I'm alright and I soothe her with the words I've often said, 'I'm tougher than that.'

Once Olivia's home, we eat dinner at the bench with the TV on. It's not award-winning parenting by any means, but it's become our Thursday night 'thang' and something about watching re-runs of *Bondi Rescue* brings us all back to calm after our hectic day. In an ad break, Olivia asks after Reaxton, too, and I feel a familiar wrinkle of irritation. It annoys me how Reaxton has come to permeate every aspect of my life.

'He was okay,' I say.

'No funny stories?' she asks.

'No funny stories.'

She's always chasing a laugh that kid, and Sophie's exactly the same. But I also know that Livvy's checking on me, in her own thoughtful way. She understands so much about the wild ride of teaching just by being my daughter.

After dinner, I stalk the girls into the shower and jam as much as I can into the dishwasher. My phone is pinging with email alerts and updates on SkoolSaid, but I ignore them, feeding the cat who's forever under my feet. The girls soon drip out of the shower and into their room. Towels get flicked. Dances are performed. The cat is hugged against their wet, naked bodies. Eventually they are dressed, though still damp, and we cuddle up on the lounge to read.

We're in the middle of a book by Morris Gleitzman—*Once*— a tender, frightening novel set against the backdrop of World War II. I often have to stop reading because my voice catches and the girls want to talk about what's happening. It's a story that's opening up a world I hope they'll never know. My girls relax into me as the words pour out and I feel their bodies melt towards sleep. This is the best bit of my day: the thing

I look forward to the moment I wake up. Reading with my children is my safety and my happiness, my meditation and my dreaming. It's everything. And I know it's everything for them, too. We hug, we kiss, we say goodnight, and I always think for a fleeting heartbeat of the kids in my class. I wish their nights to be just like this, full of affection and stories and warmth and protection.

By this time, it's nearly nine o'clock, and I contemplate going to bed myself, but I'm behind in my marking and reports are soon due. I plough through the rest of the Maths work and begin on the writing books. I manage five before my ability to think clearly leaves me. There's an online professional development podcast I had planned to listen to tonight. It runs for an hour and I need to do it so I can add it to my required PD hours. I click the link, but can't bring myself to log in. It's midnight and I'm just so tired. I add the podcast to my *List Of Things To Do On The Weekend*.

I have a quick shower and then crawl into bed, dragging my laptop along with me. I open school emails. There are two 'envelopes' I'd rather ignore—one from the Principal to my chain gang reminding us that the first draft of policies are now due. There's also another one from the Principal, exclusively for me, reminding me that my *maintenance of accreditation declaration* is due soon and that I need to schedule a time with him to go through this so that he can write up his attestation. (Yup, he really used the word *attestation*.) He suggests we meet next Friday at 4 p.m. He's oblivious to the fact I'll be on a coach with sixty children travelling back from school camp. I don't bother replying because at this stage I haven't finished my accreditation declaration, and with my current workload it's unlikely that I will. I ignore both emails and compose a new one to the school counsellor. I request an appointment to discuss the girl in my class who is presenting as a Student of Concern, outlining a few reasons as to why we need to meet, including some recent incidents and observations. It's a paper trail I'm creating more than anything else—generating evidence to show I've recognised issues and seen red flags. The counsellor only attends our school once a week; I'm not sure my 'noticing' will serve this student in any way, but I have to do what I can.

I fold the laptop shut, slide it onto the floor and try to fall asleep. I'm tired, but I struggle to even doze. This part of the night is usually devoted to worry. I think about all the things I didn't get done, all the things I have to do, and all the energy I'll need to do it. The last time I look at the clock it's 1.36 a.m. and I'm thinking about the plant in my classroom. I wonder if it's still alive.

So that's a pretty typical day. A good day. That's why it can be hard to meet with me.

I'm not sure what you think it is to be a teacher: all holidays and great pay, I guess. I'm not sure how I could ever bust that myth.

Maybe now it's a bit clearer that teaching isn't really a job, it's a lifestyle. It's a massive ton of work that spreads well beyond the allocated hours. It's a juggle that impacts your family, your health and your way of life. It's constant gear-shifting. Emotionally draining. And it's certainly not nine till three.

Don't say it. I know. Every job's the same.

Gabbie

Week 7
FRIDAY

Dear Parents & Caregivers,

It's 9 p.m. on Friday night and I'm still at school. My girls had to go to swimming with their dad so I could stay here and get everything prepared for the excursion. It's late, but I am on a MISSION. I *really* don't want to have to come in to school over the weekend. I *need* to lounge around in my own home, rest in my own bed and soak up the love of my own kids before I have to be away from them. And I promised my girls I wouldn't bring any work home this weekend.

Mindy (Mrs Fortune) was here working through the excursion stuff with me, but she looked and sounded terrible, so I sent her home two hours ago. I have a bad feeling that she's coming down with the flu. Today my class looked and sounded like a zoo: hacking, hawking, picking, itching, blowing, sneezing. Sitting here now, in the ghost town of my classroom, I can feel a niggle in *my* throat and there's this sore on my wrist that doesn't look nice.

Anyway . . . onwards!

You'll all be pleased to know that our classroom now has a Direction Wheel stuck to the front door. I found a piece of fluoro card and scribbled CANBERRA across it and pinned it over the wheel—just to clarify things for 'poppers'. And I can also report that our school hall has a comprehensive first-aid kit with hundreds of surgical gloves included. There's also a typed and laminated inventory Blu-tacked on the wall beside the cupboard where the kit is kept. So that was time well spent.

Excursion begins MONDAY! Please be ready at the school grounds at 6 a.m.

Remember: if a student requires medication, even over-the-counter medications such as Panadol or travel-sickness tablets, it must be labelled with a chemist's sticker stating the child's name and correct dosage. I can't administer medication without the sticker.

No sticker, no drugs.

Teachers Attending: Myself, Mrs Fortune (provided she's still alive), Mrs Royale and Mr Lloyd. There are no parents attending. Why? Because we didn't invite you. Why? Because in the past, parents have proven to be no end of trouble on school camp.

Two years ago, Mrs Fortune had a student in her class named Aidan. Lloydie had nicknamed him The Firecracker* because he was so volatile, prone to outbursts of violence and aggression, apparently without reason. If he was caught out in lunchtime cricket, Aidan would threaten kids with the bat until they let him face another over. He'd punch a kid in the face if he thought they'd looked in his schoolbag. Once he threw a chair clean across the Library like he was tossing a frisbee. The puzzling thing about Aidan was that things that detonated him one day were a complete non-issue the next.

---

* *The Firecracker*. Lloydie only ever said this around trusted staff members, never within earshot of someone who was likely to sue. Is it a bad thing that Lloydie makes up these names?

The other thing I found puzzling was that this kid didn't have any background 'issues'—he hadn't experienced any trauma *that we knew of.* He wasn't diagnosed with any particular needs that would warrant these explosions. He didn't take any medication. Aidan performed reasonably well in all subjects. He could read and write. Maths wasn't an issue. He came from a traditional family: mum and dad (married, both with steady employment) and an older sister, described as a delight by every teacher who had ever taught her.

Because his fits of rage were occasional and random we had managed them a bit like spot fires, extinguishing each one on a case-by-case basis. Of course he faced consequences, and of course we called his folks in. They said, 'He's got a temper, we know it.' Many times Mrs Fortune, the Principal and the school counsellor made plans with Aidan and his family to manage his anger, and for weeks at a time these plans would work and Aidan's behaviour wouldn't be an issue.

So it was that Aidan's potential for aggressive behaviour wasn't even on our radar as we planned for the excursion that particular year. He had gone half a term without erupting, though we still made certain that he and his parents had both signed the Code of Conduct Agreement. We felt that the boundary was firmly in place—*deliberate, aggressive, physical behaviour that harms another student will automatically mean the student is expelled from the excursion and must be collected by parents.* We had organised adequate ratios of adult supervision, including an enthusiastic mum who promised us she could stomach camp food, was ready for the sleepless nights and could manage a small group of students at the various venues.

The excursion commenced and went along in the usual hectic way, but on the evening of day three, when all the kids were tired and frazzled, there was an incident. We were leaving McDonald's and boarding the coach for our evening activity. A student was in the seat that Aidan wanted, and when this student refused to move Aidan choked him. I mean literally put his hands around the kid's neck and squeezed him until he couldn't breathe. Other kids tried to intervene, but it was like Aidan was possessed. It took me and Lloydie working together to prise him away.

The parent 'helper', who had promised us such support, stood nearby. *Filming.* Even as we herded Aidan down the aisle of the coach, swearing and threatening to kill us all, she kept recording.

Outside, Mindy and Lloydie struggled to calm him. Meanwhile, on the bus, the choked child started vomiting, triggering a series of sympathy vomits from other students. I had to evacuate the bus, clean up the spew, settle the kids and try to press reset on an entire evening.

We arrived at the cinema and the students settled in. Aidan was kept outside. Mrs Fortune and I stayed with him, and we called the Principal who agreed that the Conduct Agreement had been breached and that Aidan's parents must be notified. It was decided Aidan should be collected by his parents the following day.

Mrs Fortune rang his folks, ready to tell them calmly but firmly about Aidan's behaviour, and explain that they would be expected to pick him up the following day. The phone barely rang before Aidan's dad answered it. I could hear him shouting down the phone even though I was metres away, on the phone myself and trying to get hold of the strangled student's mum.

'I'll sue you!' he was bellowing. 'And Stroud. And Lloydie. I've seen the footage!' He raged on and I felt my blood become fear, my stomach turn to anxiety. 'You had no right to touch Aidan and I promise you this will end in court.'

Mindy looked at me, terrified.

'I promise,' he went on, 'I promise I'll take care of this. I know where you live.'

It was scary.

Scary because he believed he was right.

Scary because his wife was in the background ad-libbing commentary.

Scary because his voice was so loud Mindy kept blinking with each word he shouted.

Scary because he wouldn't listen.

Scary because he was Aidan's dad and suddenly everything made sense.

But the scariest thing of all was that the parent we had accepted as our trusted parent-helper on camp had framed us. *Sure*, she had all kinds of reasons for filming the scene and sending it on. She thought it would help Aidan's parents if they saw his behaviour. She thought someone should 'collect video evidence'. She thought she was being 'helpful'.

Mindy, Lloydie and I spent the final forty-eight hours of that camp holding our breath. We kept watching the news and checking social media, expecting to see the footage uploaded and shared. It never looks good when two adults are attempting to restrain a twelve-year-old boy. Delirious with fatigue and fear, we kept whispering headlines to each other when the Steven Spielberg–parent wasn't nearby.

'*Hey, Teachers—Leave That Kid Alone,*' Lloydie said as we wandered through the War Memorial.

'*Brave Aidan Survives Excursion,*' Mindy suggested.

We smiled limply at one another, pretending humour was diffusing everything when really we felt like fish in a barrel. Lloydie started smoking again that week.

'Let her put this on Instagram,' he said, sucking in a drag. It was midnight and we were huddled behind his cabin, like high school kids hiding behind the dunnies at lunchtime. It was freezing, but we didn't care. We had bigger things to worry about. The Principal had been calling us, suggesting we might like to apply for leave.

Aidan's father followed up. Police were waiting when we got off the bus, though the Principal had intercepted them and they were in his office. Seriously. And let me tell you, police questioning is just what you feel like after a week-long excursion and a four-hour spew-drenched bus ride with sixty kids.

Things escalated further. There were solicitors and meetings with the union. There were reams of documents—documents with my name all over them—and the Principal seemed to turn grey overnight. And then, suddenly, the whole thing died. A meeting was called and the Principal told us that the whole thing was resolved. Aidan's parents had decided they didn't want to take the matter further.

'And we all know why,' Lloydie spat. 'Because the fuckin' jerk has realised his little habit of domestic violence is going to be revealed.'

'That's a fairly big assumption,' the Principal said. 'You don't know that for sure. And let's bring the language down a notch, Lloydie. You are the Kindergarten teacher.'

There are two little kickers that go along with this anecdote. The first is that Aidan's parents gave all the teachers expensive hampers as Christmas gifts that year. Like we should be grateful for black truffle paste and vintage Champagne.

But the other thing is that same parent, the filmmaker, remains at our school to this day. She has kids in a couple of classes, so she'll be with us for a while yet. I'm anxious every time I see her. I'm guarded every time she approaches. I'm terrified every time I hear her chatting with other parents.

I don't want to feel this way. I want to shake it off. I want to believe the best of parents. But even as I recount that story, my heart races and my stomach churns. The truth is I'm wary of parents and I think most teachers are. We've been hurt by you, and the trust is gone.

Oh, God, I must be tired because now I feel like crying.

See you Monday, 6 a.m.

Gabbie

PS The pot plant in my classroom is missing. I just thought to water it before I left and it's not in the corner. Something about this makes me feel neglectful. I wonder how long it's been gone.

Week 7
SUNDAY

Dear Parents & Caregivers,

Yes, *Sunday*, because you lot are persistent and keep emailing. By the way, writing, *Sorry to bother you, but I just thought of this . . .* doesn't make your email any less intrusive on my weekend. I want to spend time with my family, resting, but there are a few questions that have been raised more than once, so I'll address them here and then everyone will have answers:

Reaxton: He will not be staying with us at the accommodation and he won't be travelling on the long coach journey either. His foster parents are driving him up and they'll be staying with him at separate accommodation nearby. During the day, Ax and The Fosters will travel with us to each venue, and it's hoped that Ax can behave and join us for all activities. This is the first school excursion he has ever been on. On Monday last week, he and Mrs Royale worked out how many hours until camp, and he's been counting them down ever since. Please try not to panic, parents. I think you all read my last letter and imagined Reaxton strangling your child to death while they slept. (My last letter wasn't meant to be about *that* at all. Plus, Reaxton would go for a teacher first.)

Cabin Allocation: I will let the students know their cabin allocation on Monday night when we get to the camp. Two weeks ago, I asked the kids who they wanted to share cabins with, and Mrs Fortune did the same. Then we sat down at the staffroom lunch table and spent two hours allocating bunks. If you've ever planned seating for a wedding, you'll understand how punishing that process was.

Devices: Students <u>do not</u> require any mobile devices. This is a point that bears repeating. Students <u>do not</u> require any mobile devices.

The teachers will all have mobile phones, and we will be bringing class sets of iPads for students to take pictures and record notes. Students do not need to: phone home, receive calls, text message, blog, vlog, create content, update their socials, 'game' or watch movies.

I know that many of you want to justify giving your child a device because you're gripped by a form of anxiety known as *What if . . . ?* What if my child becomes separated from the group? What if my child gets lost? What if my child gets sick? What if my child feels 'feelings' at the War Memorial and needs to talk to me? What if my child is bullied by all the other children and the teachers do nothing and my child spends every single night crying into their pillow? What if the clothes I've packed for them are too warm/not warm enough/too tight/too loose/not on-trend? What if they forget to take their medication/brush their teeth/carry their puffer/put on their coat/take off their coat?

Here's the thing: you being in contact with your kids via a device totally negates the experience of your child going on school camp. I mean, this is *school camp*! This is the part of their childhood where you have to trust that you've given them wings, the bit where they get to have a go at life without you acting as their training wheels, the bit where they learn about the world without you in it.

And let's keep perspective. We're going to *Canberra*. It's not a survival challenge or wilderness adventure.

I can guarantee that some kids will dress too warmly. They'll wear odd socks. They'll swap shoes with one another and give themselves blisters. I'm certain at least one kid will go an entire day wearing their flannelette PJ pants because they got distracted partway through getting dressed. And I know others will sleep in their day clothes, either because they're lazy or trying to be efficient. There's a one hundred per cent chance that one child will return home in the same underpants he or she set off in (with six clean pairs left scrunched at the bottom of their bag).

These things will happen regardless of mobile phones or micro-managing parents because kids are kids and they do kid things and it's how they learn about the world and about life and about *the life they want to live in this world*.

We will contact you in the event of an emergency—not that there will be any emergencies! We have multiple means of keeping you updated: SkoolSaid app, website, Facebook page, email, and I can call you from my phone if required. I promise I will contact you promptly and directly if there is any issue *that requires your attention or intervention*, but please understand that a student coming to me with the problem of a lost hat or an altercation between BFFs will not warrant a phone call to parents.

If something happens back here at home while we are away and you feel you need to make contact with your child during the camp, you are welcome to call me or text. I will respond when I can, given that I will have sixty-four students in my care. My personal mobile number is printed on the excursion itinerary. It's also on your copy of the Code of Conduct Agreement and the excursion summary.

Please take me seriously on this issue, parents, because I'm going to be hardcore on it. Do not send your child to camp with a phone, laptop, tablet, iPad, iPod, smart watch or any other electronic communication device. Do not go and buy 'a cheap little phone that only does text messages', or any other bullshit. I will not tolerate remote-control parenting while we're on camp.

We're teachers. We've got this covered.

Gabbie

Week 8

Monday, 7.22 a.m.

Dear Parents & Caregivers,

Remember what I said about student medication? Even over-the-counter medications such as <u>travel sickness tablets</u> must be labelled with a chemist's sticker stating the child's name and correct dosage. I can't administer medication without the sticker.

No sticker, no drugs.

There are three kids on my bus that are going to vomit their way to Canberra. And there ain't nothin' I can do to help 'em. Shit gets real on excursions.

Gabbie

PS Mrs Fortune sick with flu. Mrs Jethro has been called in to replace her. It's all on the SkoolSaid app.

Week 8

THE SCHOOL EXCURSION

Monday, 12.03 p.m.

Dear Parents & Caregivers,

I've been cleaning up VOMIT. Lots of it. I'm already tired and very familiar with the laundry room at our accommodation. I've got to admit I'm angry at those of you who didn't follow instructions and put your kid's name on their meds!

And to those of you who did give me labelled medication . . . I know *clarithromycin* is an antibiotic, and I can also clearly read the word *penicillin*. I've done the maths. These children have recently had some kind of an infection and no days off school, so you've just been letting their diseases incubate in my classroom. I've got three kids from my class needing these medications this week, as well as all those that need regular meds for various ongoing conditions. At least one was honest enough to admit the truth.

'I've had real bad tonsillitis, Ms Stroud,' she said. 'It just keeps coming back again and again.' Later, when she took a different medication from me, she said, 'I think this one's for school sores.'

I have twenty different daily reminders set on my phone. Twenty. All of them for medications. Oh, and two alarms set throughout the night so I can get up in minus five degrees and toilet a child who still wets the bed but feels anxious about other kids finding out she still wears pull-ups at night.

Thank you, parents. Thank you.

Gabbie

Week 8

THE SCHOOL EXCURSION

Tuesday, 3.16 a.m.

Dear Parents & Caregivers,

So we have some digital addicts—were you planning on telling me about this? I'm just back from Cabin 4. I had to settle the boys inside.

They were playing *Fortnite* on devices they had snuck along from home. I'm relieved to say none of the devices *belonged* to boys from my class, but boys from my class—*your children*—were playing the game. I had a minor battle in trying to take the devices from them. One kid physically struggled to let go, continuing to play even as I was telling him to stop. When I put my hand over the screen, he yanked it away and clutched it harder still, batting my hands and muttering: *justonemoreminute, onemore, onemoreminute*. It was like he was in a trance because he wasn't really with us in the cabin. He was possessed by a virtual life, with virtual strength and virtual goals and virtual friends. It was alarming—frightening, even—to see a child so disembodied from reality.

I confiscated the devices and gave them a whispery yet robust telling off. The kid who had struggled so much started to cry. I reassured him he would get the iPad back at the end of the week.

'That's not it,' he said, still bawling.

'Well, what's the problem, mate?' I tried to soften my voice. 'You a bit homesick?' I wanted to short-circuit things and get to bed. I stepped closer to his bunk and tried to keep the torch light out of his eyes.

'I dunno how I'm gunna sleep.' He rubbed his palms over his face.

'It's easy,' I said quietly, already hearing the sleep-deep breathing of one *Fortnite* player. 'Just close your eyes and relax.'

'I can't,' he said and I was shocked by the desperation in his voice. 'I always just game myself to sleep.'

'Me too,' another boy said.

'Me three,' said another.

Parents, this is a problem. You need to address this.

Gabbie

Later Tuesday, 2 p.m.

Good news! Mrs Fortune's feeling much better and she's going to travel up and join us for the rest of camp. That means Mrs Jethro can be back for Library and Music. The never-ending schedule shuffle! (I'll be so glad to see Mindy. I don't think Mrs Jethro's a fan of school excursions.)

Week 8

THE SCHOOL EXCURSION

Wednesday, 4 p.m.

Dear Parents & Caregivers,

The kids have some free time here at our accommodation before we go to Telstra Tower this evening. They're playing a monstrous game of Kick the Can. It's a bit like hide-and-seek, but with a base that needs protecting and opportunities to creep home and 'make free' everyone who's hiding. Because they're out of school uniform, the game has greater scope and the kids have employed strategies of disguise and espionage to enrich the play.

Right here and now, with exhaustion dragging at my eyelids and a child beside me with an icepack on their knee, I am happy. This is teaching, even now as I'm supervising. This is what I always thought it would be about: getting inside the child's world and helping them navigate its landscapes. I'm belly-laughing as Dante borrows Yuki's skirt to fool Pete who's been counting. I'm thrilled to see Dempsey ignoring dirt and kangaroo poo to commando crawl through the grass. I'm surprised by Coman's leadership as he establishes a reconnaissance mission for a posse of kids. I'm amazed by Liza's speed and impressed by Megan's diplomacy. I'm glad to see Jeff's been included and I'm proud of Reaxton's teamwork.

It is a joy to watch them be themselves, to see them explore their own identities, to play and run and laugh and hide. I see tiny seeds that I have planted flourish in the things they do, the words they say. My heart is full, although my eyelids are heavy . . .

This is teaching. This. Right here. Watching my kids as they play. And now I'm going to join them.

Gabbie

Week 8

THE SCHOOL EXCURSION

Thursday, 10 a.m.

Dear Parents & Caregivers,

Live from Questacon. I just weighed my backpack. Nine kilos. I have been carrying nine kilos of paperwork around with me every day. No wonder I'm exhausted. Coffee anyone? Yesterday I had six.

Everything is going well. Nothing to report. Well, my throat is painful and sore, I've been living on Panadol and caffeine, and I can't wait to get a look in a full-length mirror because there's something irritating on the back of my arms and my left leg. But I'd take six hours sleep before I'd take a mirror.

Do I sound delirious?

Apparently this morning, after breakfast, I told all the kids to go back to their cabins and brush their face, wash their hair, clean their bunks and make their teeth. The kids must be tired too because only a few of them picked me up on the mistake—the rest looked at me like it made perfect sense. Lloydie was sniggering from the teachers' table, and since then he's been reminding me to brush my face, but Mrs Royale thinks I might have aphasia, which is what her mum had when she had a stroke. So there's my level of tiredness—I'm presenting as a stroke victim.

We're off to the National Gallery this afternoon. The kids from my class are especially excited about that because Nanny Maud is going to meet us there.

Gabbie

PS The student yesterday who had an icepack on her knee was from Mrs Fortune's class. So you can all stop panicking. Your children's precious knees are fine. Sometimes I wonder if you guys understand the subtext of these letters.

PPS You can also stop freaking out about Reaxton. He hasn't been sleeping at the camp accommodation. He was just here yesterday to enjoy free play, with his peers, as he is entitled to.

PPPS If you really wanted to freak out about something, freak out about the parent from Mrs Fortune's class who wouldn't take no for an answer when it came to parent-helpers. She tailed the coaches up here in her car, she booked accommodation nearby, she attends everything on our itinerary and has created her own isolated group involving her daughter and a few of her friends, and finally leaves us when we're back at camp.

Naturally, I'm terrified this is all going to end like it did with Aidan's dad. And of course she's given her daughter a phone and told us it's to stay with her the entire time. The daughter didn't like last night's sausages and mash so she called Mum, who brought in Thai—enough for the daughter *and* her four friends. The dish was satay so we had to ask the mother to take the food, the daughter and the friends out of the eating area because we have several kids who are severely allergic to peanuts. The mother looked at us as though we had suggested she eat from a toilet bowl. She left in a huff, taking the girls off to the rec room. Lloydie followed along because we must provide teacher supervision. The mother turned around and called him a perve. Lloydie came straight back and we sent Mrs Royale along instead. These are the kinds of things you should be freaking out about: domineering parents who think rules don't apply to them and can bring down an outstanding teaching career with a single word.

Week 8
THE SCHOOL EXCURSION

Friday, 2 p.m.

Dear Parents & Caregivers,

Coach will arrive at school at 6 p.m. Be ready to collect your child.
    I don't feel well.

Gabbie

Week 8
SATURDAY

Dear Parents & Caregivers,

Yes, that's all I'm going to email about the school excursion. If you want to know more, talk to your child. Ask them about Helen Geier, the friend Nanny Maud brought along to the National Gallery—they actually met an artist who has exhibits hanging in the gallery! Ask them about the hilarious question Reaxton asked during our tour through Parliament House. Ask them about the soldier they researched at the War Memorial. Ask them their opinion on the Aboriginal Tent Embassy. Ask them what they saw at Old Parliament House.

Just talk to them.

This is *my time* now. I need time to be a mother, a daughter, a friend, a sister . . . I need a break from being a teacher.

Gabbie

Week 8
SUNDAY

Dear Parents & Caregivers,

I think I have school sores and my throat is on fire.

Gabbie

Week 9
MONDAY

Dear Parents & Caregivers,

I'm in hospital.

I have ~~tonsilitus~~ ~~tonsilitis~~ tonsillitis (OMG, how do you spell it?).

I also have a peritonsillar abscess that is commonly called a quinsy. Sounds cute, but feels deadly.

Plus, I have impetigo, aka school sores.

I think Mrs Jethro will have the class this week.

Gabbie

Week 9

WEDNESDAY

Dear Parents & Caregivers,

Yes, I'm still in hospital. Thanks for your kind emails. It's nice to hear the students are missing me. And I am aware that things in the classroom would be unravelling faster than that stray thread of carpet. The kids will be exhausted after the excursion. Classes always behave differently for a relief teacher. And, yes, I am well aware that Reaxton will be losing the plot.

But I'm in hospital. I need a minute here. My body is letting me know I need a rest. And it's also letting you know that YOU HAVE TO KEEP YOUR KIDS AT HOME WHEN THEY'RE SICK!

I am not sure when I will be back at school—and really it kind of upsets me that you ask this. I'm sick, people! Getting better is my priority, not school. I can't pour from an empty cup. As it is, I am still preparing all the lessons from my hospital bed and emailing them through to Mrs Jethro each night. I've also started writing up reports. It's hard to detach from school, even when you are unwell. My blood pressure was too high this morning, and when the doctor quizzed me about it I told her I was worrying about work.

The doctors are saying I will be out of hospital tomorrow, so presumably I will be back at work next week. Parent–teacher interviews should go ahead if I am well enough.

Please be aware: I am human.

Gabbie

PS I miss my girls, my bed, my home . . . even my stupid cat.

Week 10

TUESDAY

Dear Parents & Caregivers,

Against my doctor's better judgement, I'm back at school. She gave me a certificate for another week off, but preparing the work for that just felt impossible.

I've arrived back to find my classroom is an absolute disaster. The Principal, in his infinite wisdom, designated my room as the music room while we were away on camp (the music room was having a new interactive whiteboard installed). My benches are covered with instruments and some kid has pulled up a few more metres of carpet thread. There's a marimba (google it) blocking our bookshelf and I've been told it has to stay here until the new cupboards have been installed in the music room, or the CAS (Creative Arts Studio) as the new Principal wants us to call it.

While I was in hospital, Mrs Jethro put the desks in big, long rows, which makes the room feel like a maze. All the tubs of sports equipment and board games from camp are piled up around my desk, along with bags of Found Property (also from camp). On the days that Mrs Jethro taught Library and Music, my class had a relief teacher called Mrs Yankee. The kids told me she was Mrs Cranky and made Mrs Jethro seem like an angel. Apparently Mrs Yankee wasn't keen on marking, and Mrs Jethro wasn't too bothered by it, either, which means my desk has become a mountain of uncorrected books and worksheets. Reaxton's desk has been moved to a corner and I can see he's engraved swearwords down the left-hand side.

My storeroom has been pillaged by other teachers in my absence. I've been left with black paint, a quarter bottle of wood glue that's gone hard, a few sheets of pale-pink photocopy paper and the fat, rusty paintbrushes that give you splinters. All the glue sticks are gone. No sign of the pot plant. And I've just realised the stupid, bloody, God-forsaken Direction Wheel is missing, too.

The class is unsettled and Reaxton's unbearable. His latest trick is to spend recess and lunchtime hiding *inside* the big green wheelie bins. He leaps up when people walk by and frightens the shit out of everyone. When kids try to drop their rubbish inside, he throws it back out. He stinks like a demon, is humming like a maniac, and has regressed to regularly swearing and spitting and shouting. Added to that, the Principal is chasing me down for a meeting to discuss my *maintenance of accreditation declaration* so he can write up his *attestation*.

Fuck me sideways!

Gabbie

PS I'll apologise in advance for the room being a mess when you come in for interviews this week. I don't have the time or the energy right now to clean it up (reports, reports, reports).

Week 10
WEDNESDAY, 6.45 P.M.

Dear Parents & Caregivers,

This is a quick email coming to you LIVE from parent–teacher interviews. I should say Learning Conferences because that's what they are these days. The parent(s) or caregiver(s) and teacher have a conference *with* the child, and in my opinion it feels kind of awkward. It takes a lot of effort on my behalf to make the meeting accessible for the student *and* the parents. Some teachers love the Learning Conference, but they nearly kill me every time—and this lot feel even harder given I'm still somewhat scabby and living on antibiotics.

I've got fifteen minutes before my next interview (conference, whatever). This is my designated 'break time', where I'm expected to scoff down something to eat, use the bathroom and then roll back into the next round of interviews. But since I'm going to wait and eat at home, I thought I'd write you something quick before I forget.

The thing I always notice in the harrowing week of Learning Conferences is the unbelievable range of expectations parents have. You all want something different from me, from the school, from *education!* The following are real statements from parents tonight:

You aren't giving enough homework.
You should cut back on the homework.

You seem to be devoting a lot of time to art.
Do you think you're spending enough time on art?

My child loved every minute of the excursion, thank you for all your work.
I've printed out a list of suggestions as to how you can improve the excursion next year.

I think it's great that the school promotes positive healthy choices.
I'm a bit over all this healthy eating and meditation—waste of time.

I'd like that group of girls to be separated next year.
My daughter's really settled now she's found a place with that group of girls.

I just want my child to be happy at school.
What sort of NAPLAN result do you think my child will get?

Hearing these expectations, each of them contradicting the other, I'm reminded of something my dad always says: *You can't please all the people all the time.* But you know what? As a teacher, I turn myself inside out most days trying to meet the needs of each student *and* the expectations of the parents. In a way, our whole school, and more broadly our education system, is turning *itself* inside out trying to meet everyone's needs and expectations. I can't help thinking that this is part of the problem we're now facing with education. The tail is wagging the dog, and professional teachers are being dictated to by parents and students who . . .

Have to go. 7 p.m. conference time.

Gabbie

Week 10

THURSDAY

Dear Parents & Caregivers,

I'd like to say the interviews were great and that it was lovely to chat with you all but, I have to be honest, I always find Learning Conferences bewildering. So I'm glad to have the opportunity to write to you after they're over.

I want to relay for you a direct script of what happened at one interview.

Teacher: We've talked about all the areas where [Student] is performing really well. Now I want to talk about the areas that need work. [Student] is still well behind where she needs to be with her reading. She needs to practise reading every day. I don't always have time for that in class because by Year 6 we're working on more sophisticated reading skills. Are you reading at home, [Student]?

Student looks at her mother, suddenly unable to talk to me even though in class she has plenty to say. This is another dynamic I find difficult in the trio-style interview.

Mum: [Student] never wants to read at home. She just wants to go to the skate park after school.

Teacher: Okay, I understand, the skate park sounds like a lot of fun. Reading is important, though, so can I make a suggestion? What if you come home from school, have a snack, do your fifteen minutes of reading and *then* go to the skate park?

Mum to Student: Do you think you would like to do that?

Student shrugs. Teacher quietly contains the feeling that she might explode.

Mum to Teacher: I don't like upsetting her.

—End script—

I don't like upsetting her? It's your job to upset her! Wait, that sounds wrong . . . What I mean is, it's your job to help your child face tasks that are unpleasant or challenging or difficult. And sometimes the way to do that is to say, *No, you're not going to the skate park until this is done.* I mean, what's more important? Indulging your child each afternoon or supporting them as they learn to read?

Why are you afraid of upsetting your child? Why are you afraid of your child?

I don't like upsetting her. I keep thinking about that. And you know what? Your child might not like you all the time and that's okay. It comes with the territory of being a parent!

It's okay to say no to your child.

It's okay if your child doesn't have *everything*.

It's okay if your child misses out.

It's okay if your child feels disappointed.

Our children need to experience these feelings. They need to learn how to cope with life, how to rise up after difficulty, how to overcome adversity. More than this—they need to realise that the world doesn't revolve around them, and they need to accept that life isn't always going to go their way and that they exist as a small part of something so much bigger than themselves. From you, they need to learn that parental love isn't about being babied or indulged or pampered, but that it's about being empowered and guided and supported.

I often wonder what goes on in your homes. I feel like there must be some families out there living in hostage situations; like your own kids are holding you to ransom because you don't want to upset them. That's not *loving* your kids, that's coddling them and spoiling them and disempowering them.

Tough love is still love.

Love your child enough to say no.

Love your child enough to say, *I'm the boss.*

Love them as a parent.

When issues arise, don't be afraid to upset them. Argue with them. Question them. Talk to them. Lay down rules and establish boundaries. As a parent or caregiver, your minimum expectation of your children should be that they show *you* respect and understand *their* responsibilities.*

There are lots of descriptors out there these days for how people are 'parenting' (as though you can adopt a particular style like you choose your preference for coffee: latte or cappuccino or cold brew). I see articles pop up sometimes in my social media about *free-range parenting* or *helicopter parents* or *tiger mums.*

---

* *Responsibilities.* Just an aside on this: parents, your children need to do chores! Do you know what I mean by chores? Jobs around the house, like unpacking the dishwasher, taking out the bins, making their beds.

When we were on camp, the kids were expected to wash up after their supper snack. Many of them didn't know what to do! It was a simple plate-and cup-washing exercise and the quality-control was atrocious.

Out of interest, I sat my class down and asked how many of them had chores at home. Ten out of thirty-one kids—only ten. Dante admitted he didn't know what the word meant. Parents, if your child lives at home with you, they should be expected to do chores, and not just to get pocket money either. They should have jobs around the home simply because they're part of a family and in a family everyone contributes.

I try not to buy into all of that, and I certainly don't label the parents that come my way as I'm teaching. But I am starting to notice that more and more parents seem to be treading what I would call The Path of Least Resistance.

'It's easier this way,' parents keep telling me, just like that apologetic mother in the interview script. But you're caving in to your child's demands! And, believe me, I get it. I have two girls of my own, and I've been a teacher for a long time now—kids tend to deal in a currency that adults can find difficult to negotiate, *but we have to stand firm and parent them.*

I've seen it happen and I'm sure you have too . . . You're in the supermarket and a small child has a complete meltdown. *I want this. I want that.* In a desperate attempt to keep the peace and save face, the parent(s) give in to the child. That's The Path of Least Resistance right there. That's parenting based on an idea of *it's easier this way.* Even as they grow older, many children seem to be laying down demands, confident in the knowledge that their parents will acquiesce. *I want a mobile phone. I want to skip my homework. I want to go to the skate park! I want to play* Fortnite. *I want to go to this party . . .*

And you know what, parents? When our kids bring us these demands, this *is our moment* to step up as parents. Because when our children make these demands, they're actually asking if we have boundaries set and expectations in place, and the answer to this has to be, *YES!*

Parenting is a marathon, not a sprint. It's a slow-burn, long-term investment. It's a role and a responsibility and a relationship that you have to contribute to and tend to and live up to—every single day. Dealing with crying, sulking, whingeing kids who are trying to manipulate you into getting their own way is all part of the job description. Parenting is hard, messy, emotional work, but our kids are worth it, and they deserve to have parents willing to do that hard, messy, emotional work. Our children need to be directed, in no uncertain terms, about the behaviour and expectations we have of them.

As a parent, your shoulders need to be broad enough to take on the angst that your kid throws at you when you enforce those boundaries. You need to be able to hear them say:

I hate you!
You're the worst parent ever!
You're so mean to me!
But all the other parents . . .
This is so unfair!

You need to take it on the chin, understanding that they're a child just testing you. And even as they're saying it, you need to keep on loving them.

The Path of Least Resistance. I think we let our kids down when we parent like this. We don't give our children space to grow *up*—we don't raise the bar for them. There's no chance for them to show us the best they can be.

It's easier this way. Is it really *easier this way?* Or is it just easier until next time?

Okay, enough from me. It's time for another antibiotic, and I have to work on School Reports. They're meant to go out on Monday, but because I've been sick I'm behind. They'll be done by Friday, just in time for school holidays.

Gabbie

PS Many of you have commented on how much weight I've lost, and some of you have even asked how I've done it. I never really know what to say when parents put questions like that to me because it is somewhat inappropriate. But I suppose we could call this the Extreme Teacher Weight Loss Program. I lost seven kilos on camp because I was basically doing a weight-bearing exercise the entire day with that backpack, and I lost another three in hospital. It's not a program I'd recommend.

Week 10

FRIDAY

Dear Parents & Caregivers,

Are we there yet?

I can't wait to sleep my way through this weekend and into the school holidays. (The doctor prescribed something to 'help me sleep'.) I've made a promise to myself and my girls that I'm not doing any school work during the first week of holidays. I was even thinking about going away somewhere for a break, but I just don't feel up to it.

All the little things are getting to me this week. The printer jammed when I was running off reports. The kids are bickering with one another. The Principal's still busting my balls about that accreditation paperwork. The Assistant Principal's asking for our evaluations and registers, and mine aren't done. The stupid marimba is still clogging up my classroom . . . It's all so frustrating.

I was determined to solve the loose carpet thread this week. It's an absurd distraction for the kids and I want it done. No matter how much I lecture them on self-control, they still tug at it. It's impossible for them to resist, like when they've got peeling skin or a scab to pick. In the middle of lessons I'm randomly saying: *Stop tugging it! Let it go! Don't pull on that!*

I asked Conrad if he had anything in his shed that we could use to stop it from running. I was thinking of some kind of adhesive, but he brought in a massive orange traffic cone. So we've had that featured in the middle of the classroom all week. Reaxton has done some unspeakable things to it, and a few kids have tried to wear it on their head, but it's surprisingly heavy so they've got a job just lifting it. I'm sick of all this little stuff, all this meaningless, time-consuming *stuff* that has nothing to do with my real work.

School Reports should be somewhere in the depths of your child's schoolbag. I hope you find them enlightening. I met early with the Principal this morning so he could read through them and sign off. Reports are important, of course, but they are such a lot of work. I probably spend about an hour on each one: so with thirty-one kids, that's an extra thirty-one hours I had to find during the last few weeks of term. I always try to start them early, but the computer system isn't always updated and ready for us to use. Plus, I have to wait pretty much until end of term anyway when all of the lessons are finished so I can assign the correct grades and comments.

The worst part of reports for me is the fact that comments these days are so limited. I'm not allowed to comment on your child's personality. I shouldn't say things like, *It's been a delight to have him in my class*, or *Her terrific sense of humour keeps us all laughing.* Everything has to be related to learning and outcomes. Everything has to be backed up by evidence. That's why you get these dry, boring comments like, *[Student] has demonstrated she can independently select and apply appropriate strategies for addition and subtraction with counting numbers of any size.*

I can show evidence of a child achieving that by producing their Maths workbook. But since I can't show evidence of their humour or the joy a student has brought to my days, I'm not permitted to comment on them.

The other tricky element of reports is the space allowed for comments. The system we use here at Halligan actually limits the number of characters you can type into the box! So if a child has a long name, for example, I have to trim back my comments to allow for all those extra letters. I find myself dumbing down reports and using short, simple words to just convey a basic sense of what has been achieved. All of that editing takes so much time. As such, I have the unpleasant feeling that School Reports are a hell of a lot of work for me but of very little use to you.

This afternoon, I had to squeeze in one last Learning Conference. I needed that like I needed a hole in the head, but this shit's just got to get done. After I talked through what I wanted to say, the parent asked how her son was going compared to all the other kids.

This is such a hard question to answer for so many reasons —I had thought I made this clear when I went through all that stuff about the Magic of Learning and how it's not really something that's meant to be measured. It's also awkward to answer that question when the student is sitting right there in front of me. Can you imagine what would happen to his self-esteem if I said, 'He's coming second last. Yeah, he's coming in second last in pretty much every subject. Oh, actually, he's not too bad in Science and Technology. He's coming *fourteenth* in that—so, you know, middle of the heap. But yeah, over all, he's thirtieth out of thirty-one.'

That whole question of placement in learning is really only great for the students coming first, second or third. Everyone else just feels demoralised and generally uninspired to apply effort. And what about the kid that's coming first? Does first place mean they can relax and rest on their laurels, maybe take a week off school while all the rest catch up?

Years ago, when I was teaching Kindergarten, I tried using sticker charts to reward those kids who did their home readers every night. I bought a big piece of cardboard and neatly wrote each child's name down one side. I ruled up rows and columns where they could place a sticker beside their name after each night. It looked beautiful, and I thought the students would love it. I thought they would find it inspiring and motivating. I was certain I would have a class full of enthusiastic little readers before the term was over.

But it didn't take long for one kid to be off the charts with success with the other kids lagging behind. Watching that one kid race forwards did nothing to motivate the others. I had kids stealing stickers and putting them next to their name, I had kids crying when others overtook them, and I had kids hating the one who was blitzing ahead. I had kids arguing that they had read three books on Sunday, meaning they should get three stickers.

The thing I realised was that people aren't donkeys. We don't learn because a carrot is dangled in front of our face. We learn because we're curious and inspired, because we're creative and interested. Nothing about the sticker chart was inspiring or interesting, and it certainly didn't feed into their innate sense of curiosity and creativity. The sticker chart wasn't improving reading or fostering the joy of it! I had simply created a culture of competition and sticker envy, not the passionate love of reading which had been my goal.

We have to shift this competitive mindset that's shadowing education. It's all become one big, ugly sticker chart and that's not helpful to any of us. There are better questions you can ask when you're talking to your child's teacher.

- Has my child made progress? In what areas? Are there areas where progress has been slow?
- Can my child work independently? Can they work cooperatively?
- Does my child put in a good effort?
- Does my child contribute in class? Can they ask for help and direction?
- Do you think my child is happy in class and out in the Playground?
- What sorts of things could we do at home to support the learning that's happening in the classroom?
- What do you notice about my child?

Alright. I'm signing off now. My kids have finished their swimming lessons. It's time to get them home, shovel some food into them, and drop them over at the disco. I won't be staying, despite the disco-fever guilt-trip that was smeared all over us by the Principal this week: *You need to be a visible member of the school community. Teachers need to support the parents who have made this effort. We need teachers to supervise and generate school spirit.*

When he asked me directly if I was going, I told him I would rather sell my kidney and donate the money to the school. He made his weird face and laughed, but I think for a moment he might've wondered what the going rate was for a healthy kidney. I don't usually speak to him like that, it's unprofessional. But in that moment I just didn't care.

All the best for the school holidays,

Gabbie

Later, 9 p.m.

I'm clearing all the school work from my dining table and I just came across notes I made during Learning Conferences. One question asked by a dad made me laugh so hard that I snorted. He goes, *Do you get paid overtime for school excursions?* Even now, it makes me laugh. *Overtime?* Bahahahahahaha!

Term 3

Week 1

FRIDAY

Dear Parents & Caregivers,

I am not ready for this term. I spent the first week of holidays just getting myself better.

I had a quick two-night trip with the girls to my parents' farm. Mum cooked for me and played cards with the kids and did loads of our washing. She's eighty-two and still mothering me, still teaching me. I learned how to grow a cutting, how to perfect my pastry, how to wash a delicate viscose blouse. I'm watching Mum and Dad grow old and wishing that teaching hadn't swallowed me whole. I should be caring for *them*, cooking for *them*, washing *their* clothes. When it was time to leave, they loaded up our car with food: lasagne and soup and apple pies. But there were also old magazines and newspapers for the classroom, meat trays washed clean and ready for painting with Maud, and a few dozen glue sticks they'd noticed on special.

The second week of 'holidays' was spent trying to catch up on everything neglected at home: fixing the trampoline, painting a door, restringing the clothesline, cleaning the car, having the windows washed, taking the cat to the vet for his shots. Then it was back into school to clean my room, which took an entire eight-hour day, and writing up programs and meeting with Mrs Fortune, and finishing all that accreditation paperwork so I can be 'approved' to continue teaching.

I haven't finished writing my Science and Technology program *and* I haven't done PDHPE (Personal Development, Health and Physical Education. It's a KLA, Key Learning Area, which is the sexy name for 'subject').

I think I'll have to print something out from years ago and roll with that. I had grand intentions of writing up a new program that would address a few of the issues that have come up in our class to do with tricky friendship groups among the girls, but I'm just not going to have the time.

Term 3 is going to be crazy-busy. This first week was NAIDOC week, hastily crammed into our school calendar with token activities (we can do better than a flag-inspired mufti day and an afternoon of Art). Next week is Book Week (rescheduled to this term because of NAPLAN testing), Week 3 is Cyber Safety, Week 4 is Science Week and in Week 5 the Principal wants to have a grand reopening and official naming of the Creative Arts Studio, aka the CAS, aka the music room with new interactive whiteboard and new cupboards.

And then, like that's not enough, it's the school concert in Week 9. All of these events somehow manage to become bigger than God's undies and cut into teaching and learning time. Oh, and just so you know, Nanny Maud's away for most of this term. She's had overseas travel planned—lucky duck.

Parents, there's something you need to know. I'm thinking about going part-time. Last term really knocked me around, and at the end there I was very sick. But it's not just because of that. I always feel like I'm neglecting my own kids. In the last half of Term 2, I was palming them off all the time, sending them to their dad's, to my parents', to sleepovers with friends, just so I could do extra school work. Even when I'm home with them I'm forever getting things ready for lessons, or doing marking or creating 'school stuff' on my computer. They're only little for a little while and I want to enjoy them. I want to cook real dinners for them, not just feed them frozen foods and takeaway. I want to have time to do things together on weekends, like bike-riding and bushwalking. I want to have energy when their birthdays roll around to get excited about a party or a sleepover rather than thinking *that sounds exactly like teacher work and I don't want to do it.*

I'm also feeling . . . I don't know, a bit lost, perhaps. I know I make fun of all the mindful crap, but I don't know when I've had a moment where I did something just for me. I want to lose myself in a book or watch a movie without a laptop full of school work on my knee. I want to write—not these letters, not anything to do with school. I want to write stories and dream up characters and take myself on adventures. I want to make a garden. I want to keep my house clean! I want to keep our pile of washing at a manageable level. I want to create space for a life of my own.

It's only Week 1 and I'm already stressed. Or maybe depressed? Yesterday I had parents come in and they were all worked up because I'd torn a page from their son's notebook.

'I pay my taxes,' the father told me, 'and I expect you to teach my child. You should be teaching, not ripping pages from books!'

He threatened to tell the Principal about these emails and the worry of that is doing my head in. Admittedly, these emails are wrong—I know that. I probably deserve to lose my job.

Sigh.

But I don't understand the constant outrage, parents. I try to understand it, but I just can't.

So I tore a page from a child's book? I did it gently and carefully, using a ruler. I did it quietly and discreetly. I explained to the child why I was doing it. I told him that I knew he could do better; he is capable, after all, of more accurate, thoughtful work. I even leafed through his book to show him the quality I expect from him. Of course, the child was upset! His head hung in shame—but not because I shamed him, but because he knew I was speaking the truth. In fact, he even said, 'You're right, Ms Stroud. I was rushing. I can do better.' He did the exercise over again while the rest of the class started new projects. In the end, he produced an outstanding page of work, and I told him I was proud of that and he should strive to produce such quality all the time.

I really can't see the problem. As parents you want me to have high expectations of your child, you want me to teach them and bring out their best, but I keep finding myself stuck between a rock and a hard place. You want me to do my job, but not in a way that upsets, challenges or provokes your child.

Perhaps the issue is context. When your child comes home and says, 'The teacher tore a page from my book,' do you imagine me ferociously ripping pages out and belittling them? Do you even consider the *context* that leads to that point? I wonder if you ever think to ask your child *why?*

Surely my devotion to these kids, this class, has been shown to you time and time again. I don't know how else I can demonstrate my professional work ethic and sense of integrity and commitment to these learners! And yet it feels like you're always just waiting to catch me out, to trip me up, to find a fault . . . It's exhausting, it really is.

Just cover yourselves, that's what the Assistant Principal says at every staff meeting. She's forever reminding us to document and record everything. She never says what we're covering ourselves from, but it's just implied. And it's you, dear parents.

Cover yourselves so parents don't sue. Cover yourselves in case this ends up in court. Cover yourselves because a parent could complain.

I'm tired of it. It messes with my head. Those parents threatening me yesterday upset me.

'We'll tell the Principal about those bloody emails,' the father threatened. 'And you won't teach again.'

I worried about it all last night. But you know what I'm thinking now after I've had a glass of wine on an empty stomach? I'm thinking, *Bring it on*.

Tell the Principal. Dob on me. Sue me. Whatever. It'll save me having to quit.

Gabbie

Week 1

FRIDAY NIGHT. LATE.

Dear Parents & Caregivers,

Alright. So I might have had a few too many wines, but I've got a few things I want to say.

I'm done with being threatened and intimated by you. I'm a damn good teacher. I can honestly say, hand on my heart, that I'm serving the needs of every student in that classroom as best as I can. I'm done with you lot shitting on me at every turn. I'm doing my absolute best, and I can't do any more than that, and I can't do it *differently* either because what I'm delivering is top-shelf, high-quality pedagogy.

I pay my taxes! Well, you know what? So do I! Just because tax dollars go towards education doesn't make you my boss and it doesn't give you any power over me. And you know what else? Even if Halligan Primary was some swanky, private school that commanded bucketloads in fees from you, you still wouldn't be my boss! Because I'm a teacher, and as such I'm a professional with a responsibility to the students I serve. And make no mistake—it's the student I serve. Not you. Not the Principal. Not even the system. It's the student. The learner. That's the relationship I need to develop. That's the role I fulfil.

This idea that *you* are the consumer and I am the *service provider* has got to stop! We're not selling T-shirts here, or data plans. The work I do educates our young Australians and I take that very seriously. I have a moral and ethical responsibility to the greater good. I have to think about all the children in my class. I have to consider the future world your child will graduate into. My day-to-day decisions are underpinned by deep philosophical beliefs, years of study and even more years of research. I'm not randomly ripping pages from notebooks to upset your child or cause you grief. There is method in what you may see as madness.

You know what? As their parent you are their first and lifelong teacher. I know I've told you this before, but does anyone ever even listen? You're a parent.

Role.

Responsibility.

Relationship.

You should know your child better than any classroom teacher ever does. You should hold their history and you should dream of their future.

Even so, you should still respect me.

Because for the year I teach your child, I'm your colleague. You're co-teaching alongside of me. I'm covering the designated curriculum here at school and you're covering the rest at home. And when we work together, when we find the balance and get it right, the child—your child, my student—thrives. But when we are at odds, it's the student who misses out, getting mixed messages and a sense of discord between the two places where he or she should feel safe: your home and my classroom.

And here's another thing. If your kid comes home from school and says, 'I had a bad day and the teacher took a page from my book,' well, that's not your cue to come barging in to school. That's your *opportunity* to teach your child about resilience and self-reflection, persistence and receiving criticism.

Maybe you tell them a story about something that happened to you at work when things didn't go your way, or about how you had to redo that part of the retaining wall because you did the cheats' way first up and it fell apart? Step into that moment of parenting and use it to teach your child, to bond with your child, to grow with your child.

Please don't use it as a green light to accelerate over the top of me and overlook all the amazing and terrific things I've done.

And something else . . . no, it's gone. I had another wine and it's . . . I don't know.

Whatever.

Week 1

SUNDAY MORNING

Dear Parents & Caregivers,

Hmmm. I'm sorry. I shouldn't have emailed after I'd had a few wines.

I was *trying* to say something important in that last email, but perhaps I didn't convey it thoughtfully. Let me try again.

There's an opportunity available to us here—if only we could get it right—where the lifelong teacher (you as parent) and the classroom teacher (me as professional) could work in harmony to bring out the best in the child. But we have to be really careful (and realistic) about how we do this. It can't be a case of you telling me how to do my job and me telling you how to do yours. We need respectful listening, we need healthy conversation, and we need a space between us where we can each allow the other to do their work and the child can flourish and grow.

Gabbie

PS Book Week next week. Costumes to be worn on Wednesday.

Week 2

MONDAY MORNING

Dear Parents & Caregivers,

I've received thirty-one emails over the weekend. Each one of you has written to ask me not to downsize my teaching load. One clever mum wrote me a poem that linked to Maurice Sendak's picture book about the Wild Things.

Oh, Ms Stroud,
Please don't go,
we love you so.

Thank you for that love, parents. It's always nice to be told you're appreciated and valued. I love your children and I love teaching them. But, for me, it's reaching the point where 'love of the job' is not enough. Loving the job doesn't account for the time taken from my own children. It doesn't account for the worry and fear caused by parents. It doesn't negate the impossible workload. It doesn't keep my body strong or my mind at peace. Love of the job has kept me afloat for a long while, but I'm afraid now it's not enough. Full-time teaching is not sustainable for my health or my family.

I also received an email from the Principal over the weekend. After my drunken rant to you, I emailed *him.* (Yes, I'm cringing, I drunk-emailed the boss.) Here are direct quotes from the 'red wine' email I sent to the Principal:

Direction Wheels are unnecessary and a waste of my life.
When you saw my hands were naked, you should have
*   helped me.*
There is no simple answer, but if you would just listen to
*   me you would hear I have plenty of simple solutions.*

And the subject header? *Fuck Me Sideways.*

I have emailer's remorse! After my colossal stuff-up emailing you at the start of the year, you'd think I'd have learned my lesson! It's like I'm actively *trying* to lose my job in the most attention-grabbing way possible. When I drink I'm like Reaxton—all bravado and no filter.

In the same email I told him that I wanted to cut back to three days a week. His reply said he could tell my email was simply a means of me *airing some grievances*; however, he wants to meet with me to discuss the matter of going part-time.

Over the weekend I also received an email from the parents who got angry at me about the page being ripped out. It was an apology—heartfelt and real.

Our apologies, Ms Stroud, the email reads:

We got defensive. The way my son explained things, we thought you were isolating him and victimising him. He told us that you shouted at him and said, 'This work is unacceptable.' He said you tore all the work from his book. We didn't ask him why you might have done that and we realise now that our son was exaggerating.

Everything you've said you want for our son we want for him, too. We want him to do his best and strive towards high expectations. We want you to push him when he's being lazy. Since he started in your class, our son has started talking about his attitude. When his little brother starts whingeing or arguing, our son says, 'You need to choose a better attitude!' That's something you've taught him, Ms Stroud—he told us it's something you say in class. We realised after your email and four red wines that we probably need to choose a better attitude, too. We might need to change the way we think about some stuff related to our kids' school.

I've printed it out to glue in my scrapbook. I've got a collection of books filled with letters, cards, drawings and pictures given to me over the years by students and parents. They're little tokens that have buoyed me along. But, like I said, these nice emails and clever poems and memorable moments with your kids . . . they're just not enough anymore.

Anyway, the lovely email from the tax-paying parents ends with a fair observation:

If there's something I'm bothered about that happens at my kids' school, I want to feel like I can talk about it with you. Your emails make it feel like you don't want to hear from us.

It's not my intention to make parents feel isolated. I think what's happened is that the potential for a healthy working relationship between parents and teachers has become clouded by wariness. There's a general sense of mutual distrust, and I think that's damaging to student learning.

I do want to hear from parents! I think all teachers, in general, want to hear from parents. But we want to hear from you when you've made an appointment. (It feels like you're being ambushed when you're bailed up by a parent as you're walking to your car.) It would be nice if you didn't come in with all guns blazing.

Teachers are happy to engage in conversation, but we're always going to get defensive when you jump straight into threats.

If there is an issue that comes up, make the appointment, and then start the conversation by asking for *context* around the issue. Ask the teacher to explain what was happening in the classroom at the time, what their decision-making process was and how the situation unfolded. You have to be ready to listen to what the teacher is explaining. Then you should speak up, but always engaging in these dialogues with a view to be understood and heard rather than 'winning'.

I'm sorry, folks, I need to sign off there. I'm exhausted by all of this. And Bec's just sent me a text message reminding me that my class is due to present the assembly item this week.

Gabbie

PS One more thing: whenever you meet with a teacher, don't overstay your welcome. Respect their time. It's a small thing, but it's our most precious commodity.

Week 2

FRIDAY

Dear Parents & Caregivers,

What a huge week. It's felt like two weeks crammed into one. I'll give you the highlights.

Swing-Set
At Tuesday's staff meeting, the Principal announced that we're going to be implementing Swing-Set at our school. Don't confuse it with SkoolSaid. It's a completely different thing. Swing-Set is basically an internet portal where teachers can upload pictures and information about individual students and the class, and parents can log in and view it all. In a theoretical world, it sounds bloody marvellous—like parents can tune in and get a sense of what's been happening. But I just felt sick the entire time he was walking us through the online demonstration. *When will I get time to do that?*

Bec has used it before, and she reckons it's a great way to communicate with parents—her actual words were *it stops them coming in to talk to you!* That made me feel bad, too. Is that what we want? Virtual communication? It seems like we've set things up now so that teachers are constantly accessible, yet I don't believe we're getting to the heart of any issues despite all these 'communication points'.

I have so many issues with this, particularly around the workload it creates for me, the way parents will utilise it and I have big questions around whether it's necessary for parents to know all this stuff about their child's day at school. I mean, what do you gain from a picture of your child solving a maths problem? Or a video snippet of the entire class painting? I'll think about this more, and I'm interested in your opinions, too. All I can see now is an impossible workload, and yet another unnecessary *thing* that takes me away from teaching.

You know, if I drop back to three days per week, the biggest danger is that I'll spend the remaining two days doing this kind of 'school work'.

Meeting with Principal

Because of various scheduling issues, my meeting with the Principal was held straight *after* the staff meeting, so you can just imagine how I was feeling. Here are the Principal's reasons why I shouldn't go part-time:

1. There are only three *full-time teachers* at Halligan Primary: me, Lloydie and Bec. If I drop off, we'll be down to two and 'that wouldn't look very good'.
2. It's better for the students to have a consistent, full-time teacher.
3. It will be nearly impossible to find a teacher willing to take my class. (What he's tactfully not including at the end of this sentence is *because of Reaxton*.)

I understand that it's his job to put the students, the parents and the school at the top of his priority list, but it's devastating to realise that your health and welfare as a teacher doesn't even rate. He gave me a few alternatives: sick leave, stress leave, long-service leave. He also discussed all the options around a part-time arrangement. Then he *tried* to talk to me about my feelings.

'I read your email carefully, Gabbie, and I've been thinking a lot about you. It seems you're not coping?' he asked.

I felt my eyebrows leap up in shock. I took a deep breath before I answered him, trying to remain professional. 'I don't think this is about me *not coping*,' I said. 'I think this is about the extraordinary workload of teaching and the toll it's taking on my physical and mental health.'

He nodded, but didn't say anything. I think he was doing a tactical pause or some other teaching strategy, trying to elicit a further response. After a while—a long while, it was almost awkward—he spoke again.

'I hear what you're saying,' he began carefully, as though reading from a script. I felt my heart and mind exploding with his words, broken shards of myself cascading through the cavity of my exhausted earthly body. 'I'm hearing anger,' he went on. 'I'm hearing stress.'

'But you're not hearing *me*!' The words harsh and sharp from my mouth. 'You're just giving me active-listening crap that you heard from some expert who never taught a day in their life!'

'Now, okay.' He moved his hands towards me, gently, like he was trying to catch a bird. 'I understand you're not coping,' he said and I felt new things explode inside me, parts that I thought were fixed and tethered.

'It's fine,' I told him, finding self-control before I completely sabotaged my working life. 'I'm fine. I'm sorry. I shouldn't speak to you like that.' I dabbed at my eyes where tears were threatening. 'Thanks for this information. I'll think about it and let you know.' I took the pages he had printed from his desk and left his office.

'Take care now, Gabbie . . .' his voice trailed.

'Fuck me sideways,' I muttered. 'Waste of my life.'

Book Week

I can't lie to you. Book Week is hard work. Please don't get me wrong—I love books, I'm passionate about children's literacy and I'm completely invested in reading being the heartland of school life. But . . . it's the costumes. They make it hard.

There was a time, years ago, when I loved dressing up for Book Week. These days, not so much. I don't know if it's me becoming old and grumpy or if it's paired with this feeling of teaching demanding so much of me. Years ago, I dressed up because I wanted to, because I had this brimming joy and energy, and there was enough time and space in my life to organise costumes. Now, though, teacher costumes are mandatory. We were even asked about our costumes at the staff meeting.

'My expectation is that you'll all lead by example and come dressed as a character,' the Principal said. 'Because the parents and students love to see their teachers getting into the spirit of things.'

Lloydie passed me a note: *U dressing as a witch? Y or N.*

I circled Y and then wrote: *U dressing as a possum?* I slid the note back.

Way back in his uni days, Lloydie had gone to some fancy-dress event in a full possum suit he'd hired from a costume place. He conveniently 'forgot' to return the costume. He's been Grandma Poss for every Book Week here at Halligan. I followed his lead, purchasing a witch costume that I drag out annually.

Under the table, I flicked a text message to my sister.

Book Week costumes? How are they going?

Nearly done, she replied. *Will drop to urs tonight.*

I've had to delegate my own kids' costumes to my sister. I don't have the time to craft costumes for them. There's something about the whole process of costume creation that makes me feel resentful, like school is sucking yet a few more hours from me. I know that's not rational and I should do it for my girls just because I love them, but my rational thought seems to be strangled by all my emotional *stuff* these days.

Wednesday was the dedicated 'Book Week Day' and all the school came dressed up. I'm always amazed at how many parents turn up for the Book Week Parade. You come to see your kids all looking awesome in their cute outfits. You watch it all through screens on your phones. You rush back to work updating socials as you go.

My little Harry Potter and Hermione! #adorbs

SpongeBob and Hootabelle #mummastayedupallnite

The Avengers! #BookWeek

The costumes *are* amazing—elaborate and homemade or exorbitantly expensive. The characters are mostly from TV and movies. The kids say, *TV shows have a script! That's like a book!* and *Before it was a movie, it was prolly a book.* The whole day is fun and a little bit wild; there's always a sense of excitement when we're out of uniform and costumes heighten that energy. The kids play differently in the Playground, inhabiting characters and role-playing plotlines. The local bookseller colonises the Library and parents open their wallets.

But I always wonder: How many of you go home and read a book together?

The Assembly Item

So I went in a different direction this time. On Monday, I sat the class down for a team meeting and asked them what they thought we should present for Friday's assembly.

'Arse-embly,' Reaxton said.

'Reaxton, that's not helpful.'

'Not helpful, but pretty funny,' he said.

I glanced at Mrs Royale and tried not to laugh.

'Year 5/6, our last assembly was a bit—'

'—of a balls-up?' Reaxton suggested. 'A bit crap? A bit ordinary?'

'Yes,' I said, trying to cut him off, but he was going full-throttle. He had run the Mindful Walk that morning and the endorphins were clearly kicking in.

'It was a bit of a weasel,' he said. 'What you might call a gherkin stuck in a tight spot.'

'Alright, Reaxton,' I insisted. 'That's enough.'

My campaign to change his swearing habits has caused this. He's adopted a classroom dictionary and is reading through it, putting tiny sticky notes alongside words he considers amusing. 'Weasel' and 'gherkin' get a fairly good treatment. *Like a gherkin up a weasel* has become a favourite expression. Ironically, as the year goes on and Reaxton swears less, I'm finding *fuck me sideways* has become a near-daily thought. Not my proudest achievement.

Eventually the class decided they'd like to present something about their trip to Canberra. It was a good idea since we hadn't really done any follow up on the Canberra excursion since I'd been sick. I flicked the whiteboard on and set up a slide show of camp pictures. A generic backing track played music as the images slid by. The kids watched themselves, mesmerised.

'We should just show this,' Yuki said. 'It's really good.'

'It's like the music makes the pictures look better or something,' Megan added.

They stared at the screen, like budgerigars before a mirror. There were occasional bursts of laughter: the wretched image of me and Lloydie sock wrestling on 'talent night', Coman's face of terror as he waited for his turn at Questacon's freefall, the *Fortnite* boys attempting handstands out the front of Cabin 4. A picture of Reaxton flipping the bird outside Parliament House.

'Maybe delete that,' Reaxton said as the laughter died down. 'It makes me look a bit—' he consulted his dictionary '—*barbaric*.'

'I thought that was your best picture, Ax,' Mrs Royale said and he rolled his eyes at her.

'You're being facetious,' he said. 'I love that word. It's a lot like faeces.'

'This music's kind of lame, though,' Dempsey said, reining us back in to the task at hand. 'We should have a better song playing underneath it.'

'Yeah,' Liza agreed. 'We could put a really popular song on and then have these pictures, and it'll be like the stuff they show at the start of State of Origin.'

'Oh, yeah,' Coman said. 'I love that part. Let's do that.'

Reaxton started singing the first few notes of 'Eye Of The Tiger'. 'Dunt, dunt-dunt-dunt,' he sang. Other kids joined in.

'Nah,' Dempsey said. 'That song doesn't go with Canberra. That goes with football.'

'Or tigers,' Jeff said.

'Or people who do stuff with tigers' eyes,' Dante laughed.

'Vets?' Megan suggested.

'Optometrists,' Reaxton corrected. 'But there could be specialist optometrists for tigers. I'll look it up later. What we need is a song about Australia because that's what Canberra's all about.'

'"Advance Australia Fair"?' Quentin suggested.

The class started singing, dredging the tune up like it was a hymn at a funeral.

'No, no, no,' I said, stopping the noise before it could become yet another earworm. 'That just seems to be murdering the mood you're trying to create.'

'Murdering the mood,' Pete laughed. 'You're always so funny, Ms Stroud.'

'Thanks,' I said, glancing at the clock. It was time to start doing some work.

'What if we just said it?' Yuki said. 'Like, what if we just said the words to the national anthem?'

'Mmmm, maybe . . .' I let my voice sound like a question. I was ready to move on, my loathing for assembly items increasing by the moment.

'*Australians all let us rejoice,*' Reaxton said dramatically, standing up on his chair and placing his hand over his heart. '*For we are young and free.*'

'*We've golden soil,*' Coman joined, standing.

'*And wealth for toil,*' Dante stood.

Their voices joined to form a kind of spoken chorus as images slipped across the screen. Megan, Yuki, Coman and Jeff grinning outside Parliament House. Nanny Maud posing with kids in the Sculpture Garden. A queue of bleary-eyed children waiting for breakfast. They kept reciting the words and standing on chairs. They even did the second verse.

They finished in unison, sharing the last line: *Advance Australia Fair.* A selfie of all of us squashed onto my bunk bed was grinning from the screen. My class stood on their seats, looking down at me.

'Your own *Dead Poet's Society*,' Mrs Royale said quietly.

'Ms Stroud's crying,' Reaxton announced.

'Yeah, but I think it's a good thing,' Megan said. 'Anyway, that was awesome. Let's do it for assembly.'

A small group of kids worked for way too long on selecting the pictures to be used for the assembly display, and by Friday I was so tired of our anthem I was ready to take citizenship in any other country. The kids practised it relentlessly, each of them selecting the line they wanted to lead in with, overthinking the intonation and tone of voice, arguing that timing of photos wasn't right and *girt by sea* should coincide with a picture of Lake Burley Griffin and whether the closing image should be the group shot at the War Memorial or the group shot at our cabins. It was wholly *their* assembly item, and even though it may have looked simple when we presented it on stage, it was a collective project that the entire class felt proud of.

Of course, the Principal had a dig when the slideshow started up. He picked his way through the student population to stand beside me.

'I thought we agreed no slide shows at assembly,' he said.

'You're missing a Magic Moment,' I told him.

'What?' His face puckered.

'Shhhh,' I said, nodding at the stage. 'Magic.'

He left me then, almost racing back to the microphone so he could be ready to say wonderful things about Class 5/6 Stroud and their excursion to Canberra.

The Grand Reopening and Naming of the CAS

Teaching staff received an email from the Principal, briefing us on plans for this event in Week 5. We were to prepare something musical to present for the parents. Good grief. It's the same bloody room with two new cupboards and an updated interactive whiteboard! I don't understand why *this* room scored the new whiteboard. It only gets used once a week. Bec's interactive whiteboard is completely stuffed and her class sits in darkness just to see the screen.

Parents, I want you to know I am thinking carefully about the part-time thing. I understand, better than anyone, the way this will impact my students. Mrs Jethro would likely cover the two days and my vivid imagination can clearly picture the showdowns that will play out. I feel your support and I know the kids love me, too. But you need to understand that, most of the time, this job feels impossible.

Gabbie

PS After re-reading this email, I realise I sound like I'm whingeing about Book Week. I'm not. What I really want to say is that the point of Book Week is reading. I'm not always sure parents understand how important reading is. I think parents might think that since reading with their children is easy it can't possibly have so many benefits. It's like you might believe it's too simple, too fun, too cheap an activity to have any impact. But the research shows, again and again, that it really is that simple.

Reading with your child for just fifteen minutes every day will mean they progress significantly more with their learning than longer periods of time spent on any other activities. That nugget of information blows my mind every time. You can spend fifteen minutes reading with your child and it will likely improve their literacy skills more than my fifty-minute lesson on creative writing. I don't think it matters if your child is six months or sixteen—reading books, talking about books, sharing books, giving books as gifts . . . it's all beneficial for our kids.

Reading with your kids, having books in your home (lots and lots of books) and having your children see *you* as a reader (a reader of books, not just a scroller of socials) have a massive impact on your child's literacy skills and development. Before you employ a tutor or sign up for online reading programs, please consider increasing the time spent reading in your home.

Oh, and one more thing on that note: make the reading time fun. Get cosy on the lounge and make it something you look forward to. It's my job as a teacher to teach them *how* to read. It's your job to help them *love* reading. Don't correct all their errors, don't cover the pictures or try to test them. Just enjoy stories. Devour them together, like you're eating chocolate.

PPS Cyber Week next week. I don't really know why we call it Cyber *Week*; it's just a day, really. Someone is going to be here on Wednesday to talk to the whole school, and they'll also do a presentation for parents that evening. You can read all about it on SkoolSaid.

Week 3
FRIDAY

Dear Parents & Caregivers,

I found the pot plant. I meant to tell you last week, but I got on my soapbox about reading and forgot. It was Book Week Dress-up Day and I was in the Kindergarten room before school. Lloydie and I have an annual tradition of selfies in costume.

'Say . . . *Book Week*!' Lloydie took a pic and then scrolled through the images we'd already captured. He zoomed in on a fetching snap of me with long black hair stretched across a rubber nose and warty face.

'Put this on your Tinder profile,' he joked.

'Don't have one.' I snatched the phone from him and pinched at the image. 'That's good, text me that one.'

'I've given up on Tinder,' Lloydie sighed. He had taken off his jumbo possum head-piece and had it tucked under his arm, picking at the whiskers while he spoke.

'*Mwha hahaha*,' I cackled. 'Do you need me to cast a spell on you?' I crowded into his personal space and tried to appear frightening.

He laughed, shoved me back and sighed again.

'No time for dating apps when you've got SkoolSaid and Swing-Set.' He lifted the possum head and put it on.

'Yeah, I know.' I flicked to the next image and zoomed in. '*Hey!*' I shouted, studying the picture before turning around, dark cloaks flapping. 'You've got my plant!' I pointed a black plastic fingernail at the drooping Peace Lily.

'Oh, yeah,' he said, voice muffled. 'I borrowed it ages ago. It was for that Science lesson on living things.' He took the phone, threw his arm around me, and snapped another selfie. 'Oooh, you look really scary in this one . . .'

'I *am* really scary,' I said, picking up the plant. 'Were you just going to keep it here forever? Have you watered it? God, Lloydie, you could nearly use this plant for a lesson on dead things.'

'Oooh, dead things!' he exclaimed. 'That would be the best lesson!'

'You're an idiot. And a thief.'

'Naww, you can't be mad at Grandma Poss,' Lloydie danced a jig, his jaunty tail bobbing along with his moves. 'I've got magic for this and magic for that.' He waved his hands in the air around me.

'Your magic's no good,' I said in a croaky voice. I squinted and pointed a finger at him. 'I've put a hex on you!'

'Oooh, a hex!' he laughed. 'Bring it!'

I turned with a flourish and stalked out of his room, enjoying the swooshing sounds of my cape. I was grinning and relieved. The lily would live and I was lucky to have a mate like Lloydie on staff.

The pot plant is now rehydrated and looking quite happy again in the corner of my classroom. (That stupid bloody marimba is still propped in one corner, but I have a plan to deal with that.)

I can tell there's still concern about me shifting to part-time. Aside from the emails, there have been quite a few of you coming in to class to help out. I love the team that arrive on

Thursday arvo to clean up after Art, and the mums who turn up on Tuesday and Wednesday to assist with Literacy (and I *adore* that coffee you bring me as well!). There's a grandpa who's been coming in for an hour on Friday mornings to run through times tables with each kid. That's having a terrific impact on their learning. There are dads on board as well: one who's going to work with me on some Science stuff later this term and another who put his hand up to manage costuming for the concert. These things help, they really do; they help me and the students in the ways that matter. And I'm grateful. I have to let the Principal know next week what I'm doing with the part-time thing; so, like I said, I'll make my decision and let you all know.

I had a scheduled phone call with a parent the other day. It was a good conversation; this parent was ringing because she was concerned for me and didn't want to lose me as a teacher. She said that after reading all these emails and observing the class herself at various times over the year, she could see two key problems. The first was Reaxton and the second was school leadership. While she was sensitive to Reaxton's situation, she felt that if he were not in my class almost all my problems would be eliminated. She also felt that the Principal needs a crash course in leadership.

At first glance, it's easy to agree with these ideas. Reaxton's behaviour is improving but he is still hard work. I spend many hours each week modifying tasks for him, documenting his behaviour and communicating with The Fosters and his case worker. It's also true that the Principal frustrates me. I wish he had more experience and better interpersonal skills. But Reaxton and the Principal aren't the only things that make a full-time teaching load such an impossible challenge.

The phone call with this parent made me realise that there is still so much you don't see, even though I share a lot in these letters. Teaching a class of kids is a lot like one of those Whac-A-Mole games, where you get a mallet and bash the critters as they pop up from their holes . . . That's what it can be like managing student behaviour. You just belt one kid over the head and it's time to aim for another one. *Clearly that is a joke.* THERE IS NO BELTING. I'm just using it as an analogy.

Right now, Reaxton's behaviour is 'manageable', although he remains a mole that pops up fifty times more than any other and requires a fair bit of clobbering to return back to the hole! But you need to understand there are other kids who consume my time with worry and additional work. These are *your* children. Please don't make the mistake of thinking it's only the troubled child that captures a teacher's attention. We see them *all*, notice them *all*. I think of them. Worry over them.

The week before camp, a girl in my class came to me at recess with two friends and a Mount Franklin water bottle.

'Ms Stroud,' she said. 'I just took a sip of this and I think it's my mum's vodka.'

'What?' I held back a laugh; the idea seemed preposterous.

'You try it,' the girl insisted. 'I know it is.'

I took the bottle from her and gingerly dipped my finger into the liquid. The girl watched as I tasted it.

'It's vodka, isn't it?' She was indignant.

I nodded, gently, slightly. *How do I navigate this?*

'Again!' the child said. 'She's done it again.'

And indeed the kid was right. Conversations with the school counsellor revealed the child is a Student of Concern. It's a sensitive issue. The parent is a fine, upstanding citizen, and active within our school. We tiptoe. This is delicate.

I have two students in my class who can't read. Somehow they've developed adaptive behaviours that have allowed them to sneak under radars (even beneath the supposed saviour that is NAPLAN). Now, at the end of primary school, their literacy skills are not where they need to be. I am causing eruptions as I tell their parents—they're shocked, alarmed, panicking.

Then there's the one who's not ready for high school. Socially and emotionally, he's fumbling along. Crying when things don't go his way. Spending recess and lunch with children in Year 4. Immature in the ways that matter, yet managing academically.

There's the one who can't complete a piece of work independently.

The one who can't shut up and listen.

There's that group of girls who can't be disbanded despite the fact that they're torturing one another.

The one who doesn't have a friend.

The one whose anxiety gnaws at him daily.

The one who lives with a degenerative disease.

A classroom is a cross-section of society, each child with their own story. Remove Reaxton and thirty more remain. Admittedly, Reaxton causes me a great deal of work, he's an emotional drain and managing his behaviour each day is exhausting. But he's just my noisy, needy patient when I'm first on the scene of this crazy accident that is classroom learning! Each child needs something from me and they demand it in their own way.

As for the issue of the Principal and his leadership? Yeah, look, he's a beginner. I have to cut him some slack and remember his context. School principals aren't always given a hell of a lot of guidance until they step into the role and even then, from what I understand, support for school leaders can be thin on the ground. Leadership in our schools is a bit of a lucky dip;

it makes me think of something Kindergarten kids used to say when I was handing out coloured paper: *You get what you get, and you don't get upset.* With a Principal, we get who we get and there's no point getting upset!

I think it's a great tragedy that we don't prepare our school leaders in meaningful ways before they step into the job. So many of them are learning on the run, extinguishing spot fires just like the guy we've got now. All we can hope for is that they're learning as they muddle along and that over time they'll grow into the leader they need to be.

I think it's interesting to consider how teachers become principals. It's a role they choose to take up, presumably because they see something in themselves they believe would make them a good leader. The thing I've noticed, though, is that because our schools are now running under a business model, it's often those who are good at paperwork and administration that tend to rise to the top. To become a principal, you need to work through levels of accreditation and standardisation (which translates to layers and layers of paperwork) in order to demonstrate your ability and competence. The trouble is that being good at paperwork doesn't necessarily make you a good principal.

In my experience, the best school leaders are the ones who are great classroom teachers, who are passionate about learning and who know how to manage student behaviour. The best leaders I've worked for, the best principals, could hold their own in a classroom and were interested in learning and how it happens. The best leaders I've worked for never lost sight of the fact that they were also teachers.

Sometimes, though, it's teachers trying to escape the classroom, escape learning and escape behaviour management who opt in to leadership roles. I'm cringing now because I'm thinking of all the principals I know. They would hate me saying that! But I still think it's true. And I'm not saying *every* principal is an expert paper-pusher who couldn't teach for peanuts, but this is something I've noticed in recent years.

The thing with this guy we have now is that he's just busting himself to impress you, the parents. I've seen enough now to understand that he's driven by a need to have you all feel happy and satisfied. He's fallen for the consumer model of education and he's working himself into a frenzy to ensure you leave feeling like you got your money's worth. He's trying to create for you an Instagram-worthy shopfront. That's what 'reopening' the CAS and the Direction Wheels and the 'no slide shows at assembly' stuff is all about. He wants you to have consumer confidence. He wants you to see the school as shiny and efficient. He wants you to stay and keep enrolments steady. He's just dying to impress you. You are essential to his leadership because *the way he leads* centres around impressing you.

And if he's like every other principal I've ever worked for, he'll want to leave his legacy—some kind of major work that he can look back on in years to come—and say, 'I did that tuckshop renovation for Halligan Primary', or 'I oversaw the construction of that hall', or 'I started that tradition of a street parade for NAIDOC Week.'

I can't begrudge him that. It's part of leadership, I think, the desire to leave a little mark that contributes to the whole. It's just that good leaders need to be secure in their own philosophical beliefs about what good learning looks like, what makes a school great, and what teachers and students need. They also need to spend time understanding the school's unique context and discovering its personality. I'm not sure this guy has given any of that much thought. He needs more time and more experience. But, as a member of his staff, I just have to bear with him.

Anyway, I'm getting to my point now—taking Reaxton out of my class and finding a more experienced leader would certainly make elements of my life *easier*, but they're not the long-term fix that's needed. I'd still be considering going part-time, even if these changes occurred. In fact, I really think that the problems in education today are broader than school leadership, broader than our most challenging students, broader, even than NAPLAN.

In Australian education today, we're doing too many things and none of them well.

We've got an overcrowded curriculum that is impossible to work through to completion. We've got layers and layers of 'other stuff' lumped onto schools as a means of addressing broader societal problems. We've got an obsession with accountability, which means we're continually gathering evidence to show what we've achieved. And we're trying to bundle the entire thing up with a bow to impress some parents who still seem to think teachers are lazy and overpaid.

Schools have become dumping grounds for every issue and challenge we now face in the modern world, and the collective attitude has become a shared belief that the 'teacher will fix it'. We are demanding so much of our schools and our teachers that we've created a perpetual 'to-do list', itemised with box after box demanding to be ticked.

Consider a typical week—this week, for example, we've had:

- Crunch It Up snack break so that the obesity crisis can be averted.
- The Mindful Walk/Meditation for students' mental health.

- Hydration Breaks now combined with the new initiative, Brain Breaks, and we've attended to hydration and cognitive function.
- Swing-Set and SkoolSaid apps? Evidence we're communicating with parents.
- A Cyber Safety talk presented by an expert (at a cost to the school of *seven grand*). Now we can tick the box for keeping kids safe online (six posters included so we dot those around the school as proof for parents).
- A minimum of five fast-paced lessons per day where the teacher closes by saying, 'We don't have time to finish this now.' Each rapid lesson has Learning Intentions on display, so we can say we've made outcomes accessible and explicit for the students.
- A rainbow of garbage bins and multiple compost receptacles placed around the school—that's the environmental angle covered.
- Vegie gardens and chickens, so kids learn the important skill of growing their own food. Sustainable living? Check!

Our school calendar is literally bursting with events, presentations and fundraisers. Every week there's 'something extra': mad hair day, sock day, nude food, the recycle challenge, mufti clothes, bike safety, road safety, tree day, Earth day, clean-up day, book-reading challenge, public speaking, footy clinic, water safety . . . Each lesson I give feels like I'm saying to my students, 'Here's the tip of an iceberg, but we don't have time for you to know anything of its true weight or size.'

I want our schools to be thriving places, I want our kids involved in a rich tapestry of community life.

But this? This that we have right now?

This is too much.

It's like a drive-through takeaway experience, where you eat in your car and feel unfulfilled with sauce on your collar at the end. What we need is a slow food movement . . . but for schools. We need to reduce all these tasks, consider what's important and focus on doing that well.

Please don't get me wrong. I think vegie gardens are an amazing school initiative. I want our kids to learn about their health and how to care for themselves. I want our kids to be educated on how to keep safe. But what I'm trying to ask is:

- How do we ensure we do these things *well?*
- How do we ensure it's learning that matters?
- How do we create enough time in the curriculum for ideas to be explored and taught in ways that will have an impact on the learners?
- Are there things we can eliminate from the curriculum now in order to prepare these kids for their future?

Our overcrowded curriculum* is not only completely over-burdened with content, it's also way too rigid to accommodate all these additional things that schools are expected to embrace. Policy-makers who create this curriculum and hand down these directives about 'accountability' and 'data collection' will tell you that our curriculum is flexible, providing scope for unique

---

* *Our overcrowded curriculum.* You can find this online. You can easily google our state's syllabus documents or the Australian Curriculum. You can read about all the things your child is meant to be covering at school. Strap in, though—it's a rabbit warren, especially once you start spanning across all the subjects. It is written for teachers, but just having a scroll through it would help you understand the monstrous amount of tasks our kids are meant to cover in twelve months.

contexts and allowing for professional judgement. But it doesn't. That's just a story they're telling themselves while they watch teachers drowning, not waving, in a sea of endless content.

And you know what else? While we're in a system that values high-stakes testing, all these other things will always feel like add-ons, and they'll be treated that way, too. The vegie garden and the mindfulness and the Brain Breaks and the Learning Intentions will remain as something extra we try to tack on to our schools like a value-add side of fries or coleslaw.

Gabbie

PS Pot plant found, Direction Wheel still missing . . .

Week 3
SATURDAY

Dear Parents & Caregivers,

Saturday afternoon, and I should be doing any number of things: marking, preparing lessons, grocery shopping, gym, cleaning my car, hanging out with my girls . . . but I wanted to write. I was thinking about the ideas in my last letter and it made me think of something my dad says: *If a job's worth doing, it's worth doing well.*

He's a funny fella, my dad. You could almost call him lazy if he wasn't such a hard worker. Back in the day, when I was a kid, Dad had owned a ski hire—he'd been an enterprising young man and had started one of the first hire services in New South Wales. Along with this business, Dad also had a farm: a stretch of paddocks he'd inherited from his father that were always thirsty for rain but could accommodate a few thousand sheep. For years and years, Dad operated these dual businesses—the farm and the ski hire—and throughout my childhood I watched him switch hats from salesman to sheep wrangler. I've seen my father extend hospitality to busloads of tourists on a Friday night, kitting them out with skis, stocks, suits and boots, and welcoming them back on a Sunday afternoon, listening and laughing as they wearily shared their stories of stacks and snow ploughs. And I've watched my father throw a fleece of wool in the air, launching it up like a bedsheet, so it can splay with even coverage across the greasy wool table of the shearing shed. I've seen his expert hands pluck at the wool, sorting and classing with deftness and speed.

If a job's worth doing, it's worth doing well.

Dad's said this to me a few times over the years: as he checked my Maths homework and declared my figures illegible, when I phoned home from uni crying because an assignment had nearly defeated me, in my first year of teaching when he came in to school to help me deliver elaborate Science lessons. Dad's words have joined the chorus of wisdom from older, wiser folk that resounds in my head as I battle through a working day.

Already, my own daughters know if they do a half-arsed job around the house, I'll ask them to do it again.

'If a job's worth doing—' I'll say, pointing at a roughly made bed or a towel barely clinging to the rail.

'—it's worth doing well,' they'll moan.

They hate it now, I know. But eventually they'll learn to do it right the first time because it matters.

These past few years in teaching, however, I've realised there's a flip side to the 'worth doing well' mantra. *If a job's worth doing . . .* See, you need to consider that first part carefully to uncover its hidden layers. *If a job's worth doing . . . Worth doing.* While Dad worked with pride and diligence on tasks that mattered, he understood the flip side of his working mantra. If a job is not worth doing, well, then, just get it done however you can. I've seen him repair fences using old ski poles from his hire business. 'I'm just repairing it, love. This'll do until I fix it properly.' I've seen him wash up after an entire meal in five centimetres of lukewarm water with barely a drop of detergent. 'I'm a bachelor this week, love. They're my plates and

I'd rather be watching tele.' And for many years his business accounts were filed in a shoebox, a disorderly array of dockets and documents presented to the accountant early in July. 'I leave it for him to sort out, love.'

So, there's the flip side If a job's *not* worth doing, well, why go at it like you want to destroy yourself?

That's the subtext beneath Dad's words and I understand it now more clearly than ever before. As a teacher, every time more work was heaped upon me, I attended to it like it was work that mattered, work I should do well, work that must be important. But I can't believe that anymore. I can't believe that every assessment and fundraiser and theme day and initiative and program that is imposed on me (and my class) is work that matters, is important, is necessary.

And if I telescope out from that, I can see it's an understanding that's billowing up like a mushroom cloud from all these bombs that have been dropped on education:

We're doing too many things and none of them well *because we've lost sight of what truly matters.*

If a job's worth doing—but what is the teacher's job? *It's worth doing well.* We're doing too many things and none of them well.

Wouldn't it be better to do the jobs that are worth doing and do them well?

Gabbie

PS Next week is Science Week. There's information about it on SkoolSaid, and I've had a crack at putting some pictures from our recent Science lesson up on Swing-Set. The site froze partway through, so not every child has something in their Picture Portfolio. I'll try to upload more pictures tomorrow. It takes ages. For me, this is a classic example of too many things and none of them done well.

Week 3

Dear Parents & Caregivers,

When I first started these emails to you, way back in Term 1, your replies made me think that there was a long-overdue conversation waiting to be had. Now, eight months later, I think we're starting to find the heart of it. This letter comes to you as a challenge. I want you to find your voice and use it.

Many of you agreed with me when I suggested that schools seem to be doing too much. Your parent-hearts sang in harmony with mine when you said you were tired of all the gold-coin donations and the dress-up days and special occasions and invitations to attend events and join committees and volunteer. You talked about the guilt you feel when you don't make it to something at school, and the pressure you feel to turn up to these things so you can 'support your child'. I understand these feelings of guilt and pressure, but this idea I'm talking about is bigger than our individual feelings as parents. This is our education system! This is the system that teaches our children, that creates their future. It's the system that will teach your grandkids! If it's overcrowded and overburdened; if it's broken, we have a responsibility to step in and fix it. We need to ask questions, form opinions and find our voices.

When I'm teaching, especially with older kids, I'm often asking them to turn an idea inside out. Some kids need coaxing to really interrogate ideas and consider things from every angle. I want to push you to do that now. I want you to consider this overcrowded education system from new perspectives. We need to overturn this culture of *too many things and none of them well (so none of it matters)*. So let's ask ourselves:

- Why do we go to school? Is it just so our kids can graduate and get a job?
- What matters in education? Today? Right now?
- What should our children be taught? How?
- What lessons belong at home?
- What lessons belong to society?
- What is the role of our schools?
- And what's your role in all of this?

I suppose what I'm asking from you is to dive into this discussion as parents. Parents need to invest themselves in education. But before you go spouting off with your opinions, I want to challenge you to think deeply and critically, because nothing in education is straightforward or easy or clear-cut. It's important that you take time to educate yourselves on these issues, and maybe do some reading, talk to other parents and talk to teachers. And resist the temptation to reach for easy answers that begin with *When I was a kid . . .* or *My kid seems to be coping okay so there's no problem . . .* or *Teachers are paid well and I pay my taxes, let them sort it out . . .*

We need a healthy, informed discussion on our current education system that includes the voices of parents *and* teachers *and* our students.

So how do we make school a place where students can learn the things that matter and learn them well? How do we avoid this frenetic culture of rushing and 'touching on' topics?

We have so many programs and policies, procedures and practices—yet our students are still falling through the cracks, while our teachers are leaving their careers prematurely. Something has to be done. Something has to change. And there's not a politician or policy-maker in sight who seems up to the task.

Parents—it might just come down to you.

At the moment, we seem to have these repeated, almost circular conversations on education in Australia sparked by politicians and fuelled by the media, almost always focused on NAPLAN and Gonski and funding.

Who drives these conversations? And what do they have to gain?

Where's my voice—the teacher's voice—in all of this? And where's your voice, parents? Your voice needs to be in there on behalf of your child. We need to place ourselves within these conversations and insist that the discourse extends beyond a few tired topics.

What might happen to education in Australia if parents found their voice and spoke up about the things that really matter?

Gabbie

Week 4

Dear Parents & Caregivers,

I have this memory. I'm four, maybe five, and our farmhouse kitchen bench is colonised with canisters of flour, sugar and sultanas. A large wad of butter softens slowly by the stove. There's no recipe book. The Mixmaster stands to one side, the heaviest beater, a capital K, locked in place. Smells of lamb and mint cloud the air—lunch for the shearers is underway. But their morning tea is the task at hand. A box filled with fruit, cordial and thermoses stands ready by the door. Once these biscuits are made, we will trundle it over the paddocks to the shearing shed.

'Can I lick the beater?' I ask, watching as Mum rubs butter into flour.

'We'll see. Get me two eggs, can you?'

I choose two that are big and almost brown. There's a smear of chook shit on one. Mum cracks them deftly and sets the Mixmaster going. I watch as the beater whips around the bowl. It seems like a miracle, but it is also dangerous, and Mum warns my curious fingers not to touch.

She uncurls a cylinder of plastic (a recent Tupperware purchase) and sprinkles it with flour. She sets the rolling pin beside the matting and switches the mixer to stop.

'Hey, Mum? 'Member how I'm gunna lick the beaters?'

'Hmmm.' Mum reaches past me and produces a butter knife, scraping dough from every crevice of the beater.

'Leave some for me!' I beg as she drags the knife again and again over the blade.

She hands me the beater. It's almost clean. I press it against my tongue and taste metal.

'Could I have some dough?' I ask hopefully as Mum lumps the mixture from the bowl to the mat.

'It'll blow up in your stomach,' she says.

She rubs flour on the rolling pin and dusts it on her hands. Some of it falls on me like snow, but softer, warmer. Mum presses her hands against the dough and another puff of flour moves in the air. She palms at the mass, kneading and stretching it before reaching for the rolling pin and smoothing it out. I watch as sultanas peek up through the thick white surface.

From the tin of cutters, I try offering Mum the gingerbread man hoping that this might just be the year, but she reaches into the tin and produces the same circle as always.

'Can I do it?' Again it is a hope, a wish.

With her hands guiding mine, we cut and lift, placing circles of dough onto the baking tray.

'Granny taught me how to make these,' Mum says. 'She called them Hard Timers.'

'Hard Timers!' I laugh. 'Were they hard to eat?'

'Sometimes.' Mum smiles. 'They were different every time. Just depended what she had on hand.'

When no more perfect circles can be made, Mum folds the doughy offcuts and rolls them again, making circle after circle until there's nothing much left. At the end, she gives me a tiny, marble-shaped ball.

'You can have this bit,' she says.

'It's not very much,' I complain.

'Waste not want not,' she says, sliding trays into the oven.

•

Parents, I've decided I'll stay full-time. Until the end of this year. But, after that, I can't be sure.

Your messages and emails got to me. It was something special to hear from so many of you about the impact I'm having on your child's life, the way your child thinks of me, the way my lessons have infiltrated your family. I belly-laughed when a father emailed and told me he's started thinking *fuck me sideways!* But it was the email from a mum that made me teary—a story about how her daughter has started saying 'waste not, want not'.

She's learned that from you, the mother wrote. *My daughter even told me the story about how your mum was so stingy when she was cooking! But that's how you learned to look after things and value things—to not waste and to manage your resources. We've started saying that in our house now. It's a good expression, especially since we need to be more aware of the environment and the planet and everything. Waste not, want not. You taught us that.*

When I hear those lessons have made it home with your kids I feel warm inside. But that idea—*waste not, want not*—it's not even a lesson. It's a belief of mine, a philosophy, a way of thinking about the world and how we live in it. It's a piece of me. It's something I'm sure to say on the first day of the year, as I watch them hacking into the centre of a piece of coloured paper to cut out a simple shape.

'Cut from the edge here, not the middle,' I explain. 'That way someone else can use the rest of this paper. Waste not, want not.'

I say it through Term 1 whenever they're gluing, stopping them from wetting down the paper as though it's on fire.

'Just frame the page.' I demonstrate. 'And a bit in the middle. We need our glue sticks to last a long, long time! Waste not, want not.'

When I watch their laziness, I remind them again, like a pencil thrown in the bin because it was too much effort to return it to a pencil case.

'Take it out of the bin,' I'll say. 'Put it away properly. Don't be lazy and don't be wasteful!' And by this time another student will chime, *'Waste not, want not!'*

Sure, my students come to school to learn. I've taught them to read twenty-four-hour time, to identify connections between texts and to consider factors that influence their safety. But the teaching that truly matters, the teaching my students will remember, is the way I have shown them how to *be* in this world. How to be a good person, a custodian, a friend, a creator, a listener, a thinker . . . I can stand out the front and teach them everything that's set out in those overwritten syllabus documents. But until I have the opportunity to *show them who* I am *and how they can be* . . . then my teaching is just a mechanical thing.

A teacher opens up life for students, offers them new perspectives and outlooks and ways to approach the world beyond the model that has been given to them by their parents. I love that aspect of my work. But these days it feels like I'm being squeezed out of teaching—like I don't matter. I could be replaced by the next hoop-jumping idiot and no one would even notice. Sometimes I wonder why we don't just have twenty teachers who live in Sydney and they broadcast daily lessons via YouTube, and the kids just plug in and watch the whole thing each day from their devices, submitting their responses through online portals and forum chat groups . . . That's how generic teaching can feel some days.

But your emails have reminded me that I'm still here, that my presence still matters. That my personality, my outlook, my unique take on the world still has a place here in the school and in the classroom. Thank you, parents. It's meant a great deal. *Waste not, want not.* That's the bit that got me and made me feel like I should stay full-time.

Plus there was an event with Reaxton.

My demountable classroom is opposite the Wattle Building, which includes the classrooms of Miss Douglas (Bec), Mrs Fortune and the music room (soon to be renamed the CAS). Along the length of the exterior wall of this building, right at the end, are a series of metal lockers. One locker is labelled with a small plaque that reads *Main Switchboard*, with smaller signs beneath saying things like WARNING! And DUAL SUPPLY and OPEN CIRCUIT MAX 585 V.

On Thursday morning, just as the kids went out for recess, we had what we thought was a blackout. After a series of comedic miscommunications, it was discovered that the power outage was unique to the Admin Block and the Wattle Building. This meant that not only classrooms and the front office were affected, but also the Principal's office, the Assistant Principal's office, the school phone system *and*, most importantly, the IT room. We lost the internal phone lines and the server.

The electrician was called and it was decided that the main switchboard should be opened in preparation for his arrival. That's when it was discovered Conrad's keys were missing. Panic ensued: Conrad's keys are known as The Keys to The Kingdom. They weigh a tonne and Conrad carries them everywhere.

They're more like a ball of keys that he usually has clipped to his trousers and you can hear him jangling around the Playground before you see him. Conrad has the keys for everything from the paper-towel dispensers in the toilets to the cupboards in the Principal's office. Of course, the Principal has all those keys, too, but he doesn't carry them around on a single chain; they're neatly arranged and labelled on a series of hooks at the back of his personal storeroom.

So, while Conrad's keys were officially lost, the Principal and Mrs Parnell relayed back and forth from the office, testing keys. Turned out the carefully arranged labelling system hadn't been kept up-to-date over the years, and the first set of keys the Principal confidently swaggered out with didn't fit *any* of the lockers at the end of the Wattle Building.

A few teachers backtracked through Conrad's working morning while Conrad checked his car, his pigeonhole, his lunch box, his toolbox, his garden shed . . . The electrician soon arrived, bringing with him a set of keys that he had from when he'd installed the main switchboard years ago. But, since then, the lockers had been vandalised, repaired, vandalised again and replaced, so all his keys were redundant.

It was a small kind of excitement. Teachers stood around the main switchboard, speculating while we sipped our coffee. The sounds of kids enjoying their little lunch drifted up from the Playground.

'So, the power just went out in these two buildings?' The electrician pointed to Wattle and Admin.

'Yes,' the Principal said. 'Recess had just begun.'

'And no power was lost anywhere else?' The electrician's gaze spanned my demountable, Lloydie's room and the Library.

'That's right,' the Principal said. He was still fumbling with keys. Lloydie had offered to take over, but the Principal had actually batted his hands away. 'I've got this,' he'd snapped. Lloydie glanced at me with a wry smile.

'And you didn't hear a noise or a bang or a blast? No electrical smells in any buildings?' The tradie looked at us and we all shrugged and shook our heads.

'Everything suddenly went off,' Bec said. 'Just like a blackout, I guess.'

'I was in the staffroom already,' Lloydie added.

'Of course you were,' I muttered and he jabbed me with his elbow.

'I heard the hum from the internet cupboard power down,' Lloydie went on. Then he imitated the noise, sounding like a small aircraft landing.

'The internet cupboard?' The electrician looked puzzled.

'*IT room*,' barked the Principal. He was sweating, even though the morning air was chilly. 'He means the server. He heard the server lose power.'

'Right,' the sparkie said and consulted his phone.

'He's cute,' Lloydie whispered, leaning in to me. 'You should ask him out.'

'Right now?' I giggled.

'Yes,' Lloydie hissed. 'Right now.'

'The boss'd love that.'

'I know.' Lloydie was hopping from foot to foot with excitement. 'Do it!'

The Principal rattled a handful of keys and turned to face us, his staff, who were watching him flounder.

'We probably don't need everyone here,' he said irritably. 'Ms Stroud and Mr Lloyd, could you go down and tell Mrs

Fortune we're extending recess for ten minutes. The rest of you should enjoy your break as usual.'

I wandered to the playing fields with Lloydie, joking about the cute tradie.

'What would our first date be?' I asked. 'What could I invite him along to?'

'School concert,' Lloydie offered. 'No, wait!' He stopped walking, created a dramatic pause. 'Invite him to accompany you to the grand reopening and official naming of the CAS.'

'You're brilliant,' I said breathlessly, widening my eyes. 'Now, what to wear . . .'

We were still gabbing like schoolgirls and thrilling ourselves with ridiculous humour when I became aware of Reaxton trailing behind us. He was singing strands of lyrics from a song by The Living End.

'Reaxton,' I said, slowing my walk and making space for him to fit between Lloydie and me.

'What up?' the kid said.

'You should have your hat on,' I told him, as I did every day.

We kept walking, our feet somehow falling into step.

Ax continued to sing and Lloydie joined him. They rounded out the chorus and then stopped. 'Prisoner Of Society,' Lloydie sighed. 'Love that song.'

'Me too,' Ax said. He belted out a few more lines, jumping about as he did it.

Lloydie glanced at me with a look that read, *Seriously?* The unmistakable sound of Conrad's keys could be heard jangling in the pockets of Reaxton's polar fleece jacket. I shook my head slightly and we continued to walk.

'Have youse fixed the power yet?' Reaxton asked as we approached the playing fields.

'How'd you know about that?' I asked, and he shrugged.

'Some kid told me. Some kid that went up to the office.'

'Oh, well, we're not worried about that right now,' I said. 'We've just had to call the police because someone's stolen Conrad's keys. Mr Lloyd and I have been told to come down here and line up all the students in alphabetical order so they can be questioned and their schoolbags searched.'

'That's right,' Lloydie confirmed. 'My little Kindy kids are going to freak out. Police can be so scary.'

Reaxton kept walking. He whistled a few more strands and Lloydie mumbled lyrics.

'Alright, you two motherfuckers,' Reaxton said, stopping abruptly. 'I know what's happening. You know I've got the keys and you're trying to freak me out about cops and little kids having nightmares. You're both tampons, the pair of you.'

Lloydie laughed and once he started I couldn't stop myself.

'*Tampons?*' Lloydie asked. 'Really, Ax?'

'It's her fault,' Ax said, nodding at me. 'She's told me not to swear. But then everyone gets all hectic because I'm saying things like *tampon* and *sperm duct*.' He plunged a hand into his pockets and pulled out the bunch of keys. Lloydie accepted it with hasty thanks and trotted back towards the Wattle Building.

I stood with Reaxton, watched and waited for his next move.

'Come on, Ax,' I said eventually. 'Have you had something to eat?'

He didn't move. He was like a statue, fixed to the concrete path. I moved closer to him, put my hand against his back.

'You did the right thing to hand the keys in.'

I felt his shoulders move, a familiar rise and fall I'd felt from so many children over the years—but never from Reaxton.

'Hey,' I said, letting my arm curve around his shoulders. 'It's okay, mate. You were right, the police *aren't* coming. You're not in trouble with the cops.'

A little sob escaped from him and I felt awful for tricking him the way I did. *He's a trauma kid*, I berated myself. *Cops are not a joke to him.* I bit my lip and wondered what kind of trouble I'd created.

'Ax, I'm sorry I mentioned the cops. That was the wrong thing for me to do. Please don't worry. We'll sort this out together. I'll help you make this right.'

'I don't want you to go,' he said, his voice husky and raw like I'd never it heard before.

'What?' I pressed my head closer to his. 'What are you on about?'

'I don't want you to go.' He was crying steadily, deep, shuddering breaths of sadness pouring from him.

'I'm not going anywhere.' I rubbed my hand across his back, felt the pebbles of his spine, the heat of his body.

'But Dante told me.' He sniffed. 'Dante said you're going to leave our school. You wrote it in an email. And then Quentin said it's because I'm a shithead. So I took the keys and switched off the power. Because if you want to go, just go already. Just fuck off.' He tried to shrug me off, but it was a half-hearted attempt.

'None of that makes any sense,' I said. '*If* I was leaving *because* you were a shithead—and let's be honest, Reaxton, sometimes you are—wouldn't you try to be a good kid and entice me to stay?'

'No,' he said, swiping his sleeve across his nose. ''Cause if I stay a bad kid, then you have to stay and make me a good kid. That's how it works. That's how teachers think. You think you're saving the world.' He sniffed again and swabbed at his eyes.

The bell was sounding and kids were about to stream past us, channelling their way towards their classrooms. I prompted him to start walking, directing him around the back of the buildings, taking a path that was out of bounds for students.

'For a start,' I said quietly, 'you are not a bad kid. You just behave badly *sometimes*.' I scruffed his hair, noticing that perfect circle of curl. 'Secondly, I'm not going anywhere. I'm going to be your teacher until the end of the year.'

As his face lit up with joy and relief, I felt the weight of each of those words settle like wet cement in my guts.

'And last of all,' I said, throwing my arm around his shoulders again and giving him a squeeze, 'teachers *do* save the world. We save it in tiny ways every single day. You are looking at a superhero, Reaxton, and you don't even know it.'

'I do know it,' he said, and for the briefest moment he hugged me, throwing his arms tight around me and pressing himself hard against me, like he was trying to grab the love right out of me.

Or press his love in.

Gabbie

Week 4
FRIDAY

Dear Parents & Caregivers,

Science Week. A week that should be important was treated like another add-on. The whole school gathered to watch a YouTube clip about deep space exploration in the hall on Monday afternoon, and on Wednesday the local pharmacist came in and spoke to all the kids. It was the Principal's attempt at encouraging more students into STEM careers, although at this age kids aren't really thinking too seriously about the workforce, though the pharmacist was female, which might've given extra encouragement to the girls. On Thursday afternoon we had The Afternoon of Science—I'm sure you were invited to come along via SkoolSaid. The whole school was put into mixed-aged groups and they rotated through a series of Science and Tech activities, each one organised by a different teacher.

I was assigned Robotics, which would have been fun if I had been trained in how to use the equipment. But I wasn't; I'd only just got my head roughly around things the night before. The school has a set of 'robots'—they're balls, linked to an app on an iPad. You can create code to make the ball roll, stop, spin, turn, change colour and light up. (It probably does more than this, but I haven't yet had time to figure out what.)

The Afternoon of Science featured all the usual dramas. I had foolishly made the presumption that each numbered ball would match with each numbered device—ball 1 would go with device 1 and so on. But, no, whoever set the robots up didn't think about this . . . Also, one ball didn't work. Like it just flat out would not do anything. So my first group spent the entire session fiddling with the ball that didn't work and matching balls with devices. By the time the second group arrived, some students managed to have a bit of a play. However, it was soon discovered that we were missing an iPad and three kids from *that* group spent the entire time searching the school for iPad number 2.

By the time the third group arrived, iPad number 2 had been located, but it was being used by the Principal for pictures of The Afternoon of Science. This meant that ball 7 couldn't be used, so I was down two balls. (Don't make jokes, please. Reaxton was in that group and I actually began the session by saying, 'I'm down two balls,' and Reaxton looked at me and said, 'I like you Stroudy, so I'm going to leave that one alone.') I had thirty kids, ranging in age from six to twelve, trying to share thirteen balls, and control them using code on digital devices. I'd buddied them up and created groups, but behaviour management quickly became the issue: too many kids were left waiting for a turn. Then iPad 4 lost all power and we were down another ball.

'Three balls down, Stroudy,' Ax said to me and winked.

The bell rang for the groups to rotate and that's when the Principal arrived. While a fresh lot of excited kids buzzed around us ready to start their Robotics activity, I explained that I'd need iPad 2 back so I had enough resources.

'No, sorry,' he said, placing a ball in a child's hand and snapping a few pictures. 'I'm uploading straight to Swing-Set so parents at home are virtually getting a live feed.'

'Couldn't you use your phone?' I begged. 'Use *my* phone! I'll go get it.'

'Gabbie,' he said firmly. 'We have to stop using our personal things to do our professional work. We won't be using anyone's phone.'

He took two more pictures of kids on devices and moved on to Mrs Fortune's floating-potato experiment.

You know what annoyed me the most about that? The kids weren't even using the Robotics coding app when he photographed them! They were playing some spelling game while they waited for me to give them directions.

That was The Afternoon of Science. Just enough to tick the box, not enough to learn anything new. The day left me feeling angry and frustrated. *What was the point of that?* I kept thinking as I drove home. Learning about digital technology is crucial for our students, especially when you consider the world they're growing up in. These kids will have known Google and Siri their entire lives. They're being raised on the edge of an information superhighway, and school should definitely be a place that educates them about this landscape. But I'm not trained. It doesn't matter how important I think this stuff is—if I'm not trained, I'm just learning alongside the kids, playing catch-up while they make discoveries. Learning together can be an awesome experience, but given our already overcrowded curriculum, learning on the go with students is not ideal. To learn together, we need the luxury of time. In this way, I can guide how we synthesise these new discoveries with what we already know, and pose new questions and challenges.

We need to get smart about how we're handling technology in our schools. A day or two of professional development isn't enough for teachers. I need to learn the skills, be given time to understand the concepts. Our students deserve better than a teacher fumbling their way through her lessons. We're always encouraged to take the robots home and have a play with them, but I object to that. I should be trained properly, as a professional, and paid for the time it takes me to learn these new programs and skills. If my time and work was valued in that way, I'd probably be more inclined to take the things home and have a play with them. But right now, when I'm asked to do more work at home, it feels like they're asking for a pound of flesh that I don't have left to give.

While we're talking about technology, can I just share my experiences with Swing-Set so far? First up, I get it. I can see why parents would like it. I've logged on and had a good ol' stickybeak at what Olivia and Sophie have been doing in their classroom, and I have talked to my girls about it. But the novelty of that has already worn off and the conversation I had with my girls wasn't any richer or more revealing than when I just talk to them about their day. I'm still not convinced parents need Swing-Set as a means of communicating with their own child about school.

The other issue with Swing-Set is that it takes up my time to record videos and snap pictures during lessons! It takes time to upload them and label them, and it takes time to read *and* reply to your messages. (I mean, seriously, parents? I communicate with you a lot more than I've ever communicated with parents before and *still* some of you want to message with me on Swing-Set! What is that about?)

All this *time* that Swing-Set takes from me has to come from somewhere, and usually that's lesson preparation. I spend less time now preparing my lessons than ever before. It's lucky I'm an experienced teacher and can glance at a program, see the words, *add mixed numerals with same denominator* and make something up from there. It's teaching, but I'm flying by the seat of my pants. I do a lot of chalk and talk out the front explaining things, but I'm never as prepared as I'd like to be with resources and materials and open-ended questions. Soon my time for lesson planning will be non-existent. And maybe I've been getting away with it because I've been doing this for a while now. But I wonder about teachers like Bec who don't have experience to fall back on. When is she getting time to prepare her lessons?

I'm shaking my head as I write this. Lesson preparation should be the core work of teachers. If they're not teaching, they should be preparing to teach by devising lessons, preparing aides to help the learners, considering questions that might arise, thinking about misconceptions that might be presented, selecting groups students will work in and creating challenging questions. God, I don't know the last time I did *any* of that.

These days, if I'm not in the act of teaching, I'm spending my time proving what I've already taught. Accountability drives my time. Data, evidence, evidence and data. Gather it all and upload it. Pix or it didn't happen. All this data collection doesn't *mean* anything, though. It's not accountability. You only have to log in and look at Mrs Jethro's Swing-Set portal to understand what I'm saying. Based on the stuff she's posted, you'd think the kids were in raptures during her Library lessons. You'd think she was an outstanding teacher, supporting her learners, tailoring her lessons. The pictures are all cheesy smiles and happy days, while her written posts make her sound like she's the most dedicated professional ever, someone who knows every child and is committed to fostering lifelong book-loving habits.

Now, you and I both know that's not true. The kids drag their feet to her lessons and I can hear her shouting well before I get back to my classroom.

Politicians and policy-makers and principals will argue that apps like Swing-Set make me accountable. But when you're a teacher, accountability isn't shown through data collection, or uploaded images, or in graphs or reports or any of those things. I become accountable the moment I form a relationship with that student, the moment I connect with them as a learner and become invested in their progress. The moment I feel that connection, I become genuinely and personally account-able. I feel it—a personal responsibility to that child and their learning.

You know what Swing-Set is? It's education's social media; it's an edited version of classroom life, cropped and filtered to show our best side.

Why do we do it? Because the technology exists. Because parents will probably like it. Because the school down the road does it.

None of these reasons seem good enough to me. Just because we can, doesn't mean we should.

Gabbie

PS No, Reaxton didn't get into trouble for stealing the keys and wreaking electrical havoc. Lloydie told the Principal he found the keys on the path near the sports shed, which turned out to be a feasible cover-up because Conrad had been repairing the shed door earlier that day. The electrician who had flicked a switch and restored all services suggested that the safety must've tripped itself, and again Conrad unwittingly provided a valid explanation: he'd been charging tools using an ancient exterior power point.

'That could do it,' the electrician said, but he was frowning.

'I reckon it would,' Lloydie said quickly. 'For sure!' He could see me rounding the corner with my arm around Reaxton's shoulders, and he used his head to indicate I should just amble on towards my classroom.

'Here come the kids!' I could hear him say. 'Nothing to see here.' He was using his teacher voice and wrangling the mob of curious students away from the main switchboard. 'Let's go, let's go.' As he moved, he was subtly herding the Principal, Conrad *and* the electrician away from the cupboards, shutting down any further conjecture.

'I've got to get to class. Nice to meet you, mate.' Lloydie clapped a hand on the electrician's back, almost giving him a push towards the Admin building. I watched, my hand still on Reaxton's shoulder, as the men moved into the office and Lloydie jogged over to us.

'Let's leave this one between us,' he said, offering Ax a fist bump.

'Yep,' Ax said, grinding his knuckles against Lloydie's.

'But, mate, promise me you won't mess with an electrical switchboard ever again?'

'Yep,' Ax said, dropping his head.

Lloydie made illegal leaps over two handrails to meet his Kindergarten class, whistling loudly as he went. That bloody Living End song was stuck in my head for ages.

PPS No! I didn't ask the electrician out!

Week 4

SATURDAY

Dear Parents & Caregivers,

So, this morning, Sophie piles into bed with me, her long, lean body stealing more doona than it's deserving of. She's talking and talking and I'm listening and listening, my ears nearly bleeding with the effort. After finishing a detailed recount of her dream, she asks what we're doing today.

'I've got lots to do,' I said. 'So you and Liv can just have a play.'

'Can we play our devices?' she asked hopefully. 'We haven't had them in ages.'

My girls love to have time on devices. They play games together, meeting up with each other online to construct and create new worlds. They also like to watch YouTube, online TV and movies.

And, let me tell ya, for a long time there I loved it, too. When everyone was glued to their device, the house was quiet. The house stayed tidy. I was free to do the things I wanted. It felt like everyone was happy. But I've been reading lots about this and I've discovered it's a pseudo kind of happiness. The same kind of happiness that only addiction can bring.

For this entire year, I've limited my girls' time with screens. We still watch movies and TV but, when we do, we do it together. Occasionally I'll let them watch some YouTube on the TV while I'm in the kitchen. Olivia still does some homework on the computer, and sometimes they'll ask to use their devices to make a movie or play music, but other than that screens are gone in my house. (What happens at their dad's house is up to him.) And you know what? They've hardly missed them.

This morning though, when Soph did ask to play the iPad, it took me a minute to answer her. I had a mountain of school work waiting to be completed. Devices would mean a blissful, quiet house for me to work in. I thought maybe I could set a timer—allow them an hour. But then I felt like a complete cop-out. I remembered letters I'd written to you about choosing The Path of Least Resistance. So I made the effort to step up.

'No,' I told Sophie. 'You've got so many other things you can do. You don't need devices. Remember how I told you: devices aren't good for your beautiful young brain, so we're not going to be using them.'

'Ughhh,' she moaned. 'I'm bored already. I've done all my toys.'

'What about Barbies?' I suggested. 'You could put clothes on them all. They're always naked with their legs poking out of their basket. They look so cold and uncomfortable.'

'Nah,' Soph said. 'Liv won't play that with me. She's gone off Barbies.'

'Alright,' I said. 'What about cafés? You could get the little toy stove out and all the pretend food? Use the soft toys?'

'We did that last weekend,' she said.

'A jigsaw puzzle?' I said. 'Colouring? Drawing? You could play outside on the trampoline? It's going to be a nice morning.'

'I've done all that.' She rolled over and pressed her face into the pillows, exasperated.

'Alright,' I said, trying to take her problem more seriously. 'Let's really think about some things you haven't played with in a while.' I paused and thought of all the toys in the cupboard. All the stuff that hasn't been touched.

'You could get out that clay you got for your birthday?' I suggested. 'Or you could do the paint-by-numbers pack that Nanny Judy bought you? What about that Meccano set from Christmas last year? You could make a car!'

Sophie looked at me, her face sceptical.

'But you always say those things are too messy,' she said. 'Plus I need help with that car set.'

'Yes,' I said, realising the trap I had set for myself. All of those activities were indeed messy and complex. She would need me to invest in her play if it was to be a sustained experience that lasted more than five minutes.

'That's okay,' I said, feeling an embarrassed kind of light dawning. 'You can do those things. It doesn't matter about the mess. We'll put down that plastic tablecloth. You can work on that. And I can help you pack away.'

'Really?' Her face lit up. 'Could I make that bath bomb kit I got for my birthday?'

'Yes,' I said, swallowing down reluctance. 'You know what else? There's a packet mix for chocolate slice in the pantry cupboard too. You could make that if you wanted to. You're old enough to do that now.'

'I'll help you,' said Olivia, wandering into my bedroom and slipping under the covers. 'And did you say we could do painting? Crafts and stuff? Mum, could you show me how to do that stitching project?'

It was a cold realisation I had there in my lovely warm bed this morning: how often do we put our kids in front of a screen, or restrict their play, because we want to keep our homes and lives clean and simple? How much are we palming off to schools and teachers because it's too hard and too messy to explore at home? Is this another facet of The Path of Least Resistance? Are we parenting in some kind of coma?

I had a lucky childhood. A farm is an incredible place for a child to grow and learn and discover. I was always allowed to help with the gardening, the wood-cutting, the sheep-shearing, the fence-checking. I remember playing in Dad's shed while he repaired something nearby. I loved making things with a dab of putty or winding the handle of the vice to crush an old can. I loved digging for vegies, hammering nails, opening gates, collecting kindling, picking mushrooms. I was learning and experiencing, discovering and exploring. My folks never stopped their work to play with me, but they let me tag along with the work they did.

When I wanted to play in my own way, they always made space for the things I wanted to do. I wasn't allowed to do 'anything and everything', but my folks encouraged me to play independently. They didn't try to control or contain my play. If I wanted to wash my dolls' clothes, or make mud pies, or build a cubby, or create a town from cardboard—I just did it.

'What are you doing?' Mum would ask, passing me on her way to the clothesline or the wood heap.

'I'm building a trap,' I might say, or:

'Making new clothes for my doll.'

'I'm designing a house for a frog and I'm gunna put a real frog in it.'

'I'm making a racetrack for these cars.'

'I'm digging for gold.'

'I want to paint this piece of wood.'

'Alright,' Mum would say. 'Go for your life!' And then she'd give a heap of stern instructions like: 'Don't use my good sewing scissors' or 'You have to do that outside' or 'Make sure you put those buckets back in the laundry.'

'And you must promise me you will pack everything away,' she would always say. 'You must clean up your mess!'

'I will, Mum,' I would say solemnly—the thought of packing up at least a hundred miles from my mind in that moment.

'Alright, then, go for your life, love!'

It makes me laugh now to remember how she would say that. *Go for your life!* And I'd feel encouraged. Empowered, even, to play and experiment and explore and have fun.

I could occupy myself for hours. My play would become creative, building momentum and morphing from washing dolls' clothes to washing rocks, where I'd clean all the stones I could find in our garden and along our driveway. Water on soil would lead to mud pies and I'd open a bakery, creating rows of decorated 'cakes' and 'pastries'. I'd imagine a cash register and customers. Good ol' Dad would always play along, arriving home from the paddocks to buy a few pies, paying for them with twigs before he went into the house for his real dinner.

My own kids are missing out on this. I curb their play to games and activities that are clean and neat and easy for me to manage. They play fairly well, but I'm often required to prompt them along when one game ends and another needs to begin. My clean, neat play doesn't give them enough scope; I need to let things get messy and let my kids be kids.

I'm not suggesting we need to play *with* our kids all the time—God, that would probably kill me. I'm not a huge fan of playing with my kids. In fact, I don't think it's a parent's role to play with their kids. When you're kicking around at home on the weekend, I don't think it's your job to keep them occupied or entertained. I'm all for regular family games together, such as board games and throwing the frisbee, colouring in together or a competitive round of cards! But I think kids should play in their own ways—on their own, and with their siblings and their friends—and parents can join in as appropriate.

But I realised this morning, when I very nearly trod The Path of Least Resistance, that I need to enable messier, exploratory, risky, child-directed play, just like my parents did. I need to let go of *keeping my house clean* and *keeping on top of the housework* and *keeping the kids quiet*. And I need to let them play in that noisy, creative, grubby way without supervising the shit out of them! Kids need those wonderful, disgusting, wild and crazy opportunities for play.

Refracting from this idea, I can see other ideas—little spots of colour and dots of shadow that might be connected. I'm wondering if maybe schools are trying to pick up the slack of so much of this clean, timetabled parenting that we're doing these days. Our schools are bringing in chooks and worm farms and meditation and growing food and recycling projects and all these other things . . . almost in an attempt to fill the hole that we've created at home.

This also makes me think about 'parenting styles' and child-rearing 'methods'. If I asked my mum what parenting style she adopted, she'd probably say, 'Oh, I think a pretty good one. You all turned out alright.' I'd hazard a guess that *the act of parenting* wasn't something Mum ever gave much thought to. It's not that she was parenting *without thought*, more that she was just busy getting on with it. Doing it, you know? Raising her kids and working the farm and getting to each of her part-time jobs.

Today it seems that we're more conscious than ever about every aspect of our lives. We're hashtagging our best selves and discussing the virtues of quinoa and mindfulness . . . We're aware of our parenting, talking about it in real life and on forums, posting pictures on socials, reading articles online, yet we're living it so unconsciously, handing our kids an iPad and letting them completely detach themselves from reality.

Gabbie

PS As an aside, while I may not think it's your job to keep your kids occupied or entertained when you're kicking around at home, let's get this straight: if you're out and about in public, at a café or a restaurant, at the shops or in a public space, it is *totally* your job to keep your child occupied and behaving in a way that allows everyone else sharing that space to enjoy themselves. This doesn't mean you whip out the device and induce a coma. But it means your child needs to be socialised in ways that allow them to be pleasant company when they're out socially. My weapon of choice is a pack of cards that I always have in my handbag. We get through at least one game of Old Maid before my cappuccino arrives. I've also been known to carry small tubs of play dough, slime, pens and notebooks because kids get bored, and if you let boredom go kids get creative. Now we want this creativity—just not at one hundred decibels, racing through our favourite coffee house.

Week 4

SATURDAY, LATER IN THE DAY

Dear Parents & Caregivers,

I'm still thinking about the things I wrote to you earlier. Sophie and Liv have had a brilliant day. Soph made her bath bombs and Livvy's partway through a scarf she's making on a knitting loom. The bath bomb kit was completed without my help—and, yeah, it didn't turn out quite right, but Soph was pleased with herself and happy with the outcome. She's in the tub right now, bombs away and giving us a running commentary on how they're dissolving and what they smell like.

It took me about ten minutes to teach Liv how to loom. I thought it would take ages, but before long she was saying, 'I get it, Mum, I get it.' She loomed for two hours straight, working until her hands got sore. She has plans to make a scarf for her teacher for Christmas and she's really proud of her work.

There was mess. But we cleaned it up.

I've thought a lot about those *Fortnite* boys who were gaming on camp. Mrs Fortune told me she has real trouble with some of them in class.

'I wonder,' Mindy suggested, 'if they're spending their school day in withdrawal. They can't concentrate, they're irritable, they just want to be doing the next thing, the next thing, the next thing, you know? Like there's no satisfaction for them in just being in the moment.'

'I guess that's why we're mindfully meditating?' was my response. But I'm worried just like Mindy. Concerned.

When we were travelling home from camp, marinating in the delicious smells of young bodies enclosed in a bus, I talked to some of the kids about gaming. It's not a world I inhabit, so I had a lot to learn.

'We all game together,' one boy explained—the same boy from Cabin 4 who had snuck his device along to camp. 'Like, me, my mum, my dad. My little sister plays her iPad.'

'Wow,' I replied, truly wowed by this information. 'So you all log on and have adventures together as a team?'

'Kind of, but nah,' he said. 'So, I'm at my screen—we all have our own screens—and Dad's at his over there, and Mum's over there.' He explained the layout with his hands. 'I mostly play *Fortnite*. Mum's obsessed with *Player Unknown*. Dad mostly plays *Assassin's Creed* but sometimes *Doom*, sometimes *Grand Theft Auto*.'

The boy was animated as he spoke, his words coming out in a rush.

'I don't know much about these games,' I admitted. 'Are you online when you play? Like are other people connected to you?'

'Yeah, yeah,' he said. 'So I've got my head phones on and I can talk to others.'

'You're talking with other people? Like random strangers?'

'Well, they're not random strangers, Ms Stroud,' he said, his tone patronising. 'They're into *Fortnite*, too.'

'Yeah . . . but you don't know who they are, or what kind of person they are. You don't get to see them in real life. Do they talk nicely to you?'

'Yeah,' he nodded. 'We're mostly talking about the game, like what needs to happen next, where other players are, who's gunna be looting Dusty.'

'Do you feel safe when you're playing?'

He frowned, thinking. 'Mostly. Sometimes it gets a bit salty.'

'Salty?' I pressed.

'You know, like swearing. There's lots of swearing. Sometimes they're swearing at me because I made a mistake or stuffed up. Sometimes it's a bit creepy, like talking about rude things.'

'What do you do when that happens?' I had to remind myself I was on a bus, safely suspended in the body odour of Year 5 and 6 students. I could feel myself panicking for this kid, panicking for all the kids who were skipping along the high wire of online gaming.

The kid shrugged. 'If it's too salty, I just log out and come back in later. There's one kid I mostly game with, and he tells people off if they're rude to me.'

'How do you know it's a kid?' I asked.

The boy frowned again. 'I don't.' He shrugged. 'I just think it is.'

'Do you ever tell your mum,' I asked, 'like when things get too—' I paused, reaching for his word '—*salty*?'

'Nah.' He shook his head. 'Because she's playing her game.'

Another kid poked his head between our seats to ask what we were talking about. They had soon launched into a review of a different game, and I turned around to face the front. I wanted to ask that Cabin 4 gamer if he'd ever built a cubby or climbed a tree; I wanted to know what else he did with his family. If they ever went for bushwalks or fishing. I wondered if, right now, he was looking forward more to seeing his family or playing his game.

I don't know, parents. I'm not here to instruct you on parenting. I've fumbled along too often with my own kids to position myself as an expert. But I think you need to know and understand that the research is in. Interactive screens are highly addictive. We're exposing our kids to screens *before* their young brains are fully developed, and because of this our kids are becoming addicted to games, social media, apps . . . They're becoming disconnected from people in their real life, and as a result we're seeing higher rates of depression and anxiety than ever before!

Addiction to devices isn't something we can solve as teachers. Parents, this one has to come from you.

Schools can make rules about banning phones and they can provide 'safe' devices and install firewalls, but our kids spend more time at home with you than they do at school. You need boundaries and expectations firmly in place. Or are you okay with it, happily addicted yourself so you're just passing the bottle of scotch on to your kid?

The online world is here to stay. Even now, as we begin to understand the negative effects online spaces and screens can have on our physical, mental and emotional wellbeing, we have to accept that the internet isn't going away. And, of course, screens and the net can have amazing, positive impacts on our lives as well.

But here's the thing: there's a whole heap of teaching we need to provide for our kids about this digital landscape. How to recognise and manage screen addiction, how to use our devices and social media in legal and ethical ways, how to maintain the ability to connect with one another in real life . . . It's a list that goes on and on. Right now in schools we're not covering these topics in any great detail. Instead they're dealt with through things like the Cyber Week talk and incidentally during lessons, with occasional focused topics, though this mostly happens in high school. That means that you, as parents, need to add your voice to the conversation, talking to your kids about how we use technology in healthy, responsible ways. We can't put the genie back in the bottle, but we can always teach our kids that the genie is not our master.

Today's technology is so intuitive. Most of the time our children are figuring this stuff out faster than we can. They're jumping ahead in leaps and bounds, desperate to place themselves within this digital landscape. Our kids want to create content—Dante told me the other day that when he grows up he wants to be a 'big-as YouTuber'.

'Big as what?' I asked, and he rattled off the names of his top five most admired YouTube content creators.

'They make so much money,' he enthused. 'And they're just reviewing stuff like toys, or they're showing you how to do stuff. I think I'd be so good at it, don't you, Ms Stroud?'

'Yeah, I guess so.' I nodded, and wondered what I should teach him—*how* I should teach him—if I was to help him become a financially stable, healthy, responsible 'big-as YouTuber'.

Look, parents, I'm in wild, uncharted territory here. There's so much I don't know about technology and being online. It's a concept that thrills me with its potential, but frightens me with its dangers. As the responsible adults in our children's lives, I want us to help them navigate this experience. I want us to be setting boundaries and having opinions, educating ourselves as we educate them. We taught our kids to cross the road safely, didn't we? So we have to teach them how to safely live alongside this digital, screen-filled information superhighway.

Gabbie

Week 5

FRIDAY

Dear Parents & Caregivers,

Well, the CAS has been grandly reopened and officially renamed. What did you think of our item? I thought the Principal was going to burst with fury when we started up—a classical rendition of the punk-rock song 'Prisoner of Society'! But didn't the kids sing beautifully? We worked so hard on it. I'd had a friend of mine, a music teacher from another school, create the arrangement for us. We practised secretly, always keeping someone on lookout in case the Principal caught a sniff of what we were up to. The song itself doesn't have any explicit lyrics, but it's an ode to anarchy and rebellion, and I was confident the Principal wouldn't go for it. But, man, the kids loved it. Reaxton's energy led the entire group—he was on board for every practice, never once complaining that the song had been slowed and sweetened and stretched.

'This is gunna be awesome,' he said to me the day before the performance. 'I've told The Fosters they have to come and watch me.'

That gave me the feels because for the first time this year Reaxton was attempting to bring his school and home life together.

Other highlights from the CAS event included seeing the Principal's face when he discovered the marimba I'd wedged into the corner of the music room. He was leading a group of

276

parents around, talking about the new interactive whiteboard and the renovated cupboards, when he came upon the unsightly instrument I'd snuck inside late the night before with Lloydie's help. And, no, I didn't feel a single bit guilty about my passive-aggressive behaviour because . . . guess what . . . ?

The Principal had stolen my Direction Wheel and pinned it to the music room's front door. I shit you not! What a dog act! I was ropable when I found it there. I wanted to leave the marimba set up right in the middle of the room, so when he cut the ribbon and opened the door at his ridiculous opening ceremony the stupid marimba would be the first thing he would see. Lloydie talked me out of that.

'You need to take a chill pill, Gab. This shit's not worth it.' Then he'd run his hands along a string of chimes and pretended to sprinkle fairy dust all over me. 'Be gone spirits of stress and tension.' He frolicked around the room. 'Be gone, I say!'

Anyway, the CAS is well and truly done and opened and named and all of that. Here's hoping you parents were impressed, put pictures on your socials and told all your friends and relatives because that event was just for you! I've decided I'm going to keep calling it the music room and if I get chipped about it I'll say, 'I'll call it "the CAS" when my Direction Wheel is returned.'

Ah, the petty politics of teaching. It's tiring and exhausting and yet apparently never-ending.

In other news, Conrad has removed the traffic cone from my room. It was needed in the parking lot. This means the carpet creep is happening again. It's like the students were reunited with an old friend. I've seen many of them inch over and give it a good tug. Why can't I ignore this sort of stuff? Maybe I do need a chill pill.

Today, I finally got around to delivering a lesson I'm meant to present in Week 1 of each term. It's about Learning Goals. This is an intention that the students write down at the start of term and then spend the next ten weeks working towards it. It should be something related to a specific skill or concept they want to master or understand. It's not about being kind to others or cooperating—it's meant to be something like *learn my twelve times tables off by heart.*

It's another 'great in theory' idea that has made its way into our classrooms. True, sometimes it works, and I fully support the concept, but often the students choose goals that aren't aligned with the things I plan on teaching. They often set impossible goals and there's very little time devoted to allowing them a chance to work on achieving them. Ideally I would work with each student to create their Learning Goal, however that is time-consuming (even two minutes per child is over an hour, and as we all know: *nothing* ever takes two minutes).

Nevertheless, we've written down our Learning Goals and put them on display.

I wanted to share that with you because Reaxton's goal was a bit special.

He wrote: *I want to make a friend.*

Technically it's not a Learning Goal because it's not related to learning, and it's not measurable, and it doesn't meet the fifty thousand other criteria. But I let it be. I didn't correct him. I just took it from him and said, 'That's a great goal for you, Ax. I hope you achieve it.' And I pinned it up between Coman's and Jeff's.

Gabbie

Week 6

FRIDAY

Dear Parents & Caregivers,

Gastro. First Sophie. Then Olivia. Now me.
Death is near.

Gabbie

Week 7
TUESDAY

Dear Parents & Caregivers,

After the week from hell, with vomit and shit everywhere, I returned to school to find my class had four different relief teachers in my absence. The carpet has been pulled at in such a way that there's a long, loose thread stretching across the room, though it still somehow remains anchored at either end. It's an extraordinary tripping hazard. Desks have been moved, my glue sticks are missing, and what was left in my tiny supply cupboard is gone.

'You're away a few days and the place becomes a meth lab,' Reaxton told me as I assessed the damage this morning. Considering Ax has probably lived in a few meth labs, it was a depressing reflection on the state of my room.

The kids were thrilled to see me again, many of them attempting to hug me and telling me that they missed me.

'Don't squeeze me,' I yelped as Megan threw herself at me. 'I'm still a bit sore.'

'Oh, yeah,' Quentin said. 'From vomiting. It kills ya abs.'

Their love and enthusiasm quickly drained my energy, and by recess it felt as though I'd never been away. By lunch, I needed a nap.

At 3.30 p.m., I schlepped into the staff meeting with exhaustion sticking to me like an aura. I took a seat next to Lloydie and the Principal turned on the whiteboard screen (can't have a slide show at assembly, but we see a lot of them in meetings—just sayin'). The title read NAPLAN ANALYSIS. I felt my bowels clench. Those words alone were enough to induce a new round of gastro.

'Listen to me,' I said, passing a nearby sharpener to Lloydie. 'I want you to unscrew this blade and kill me with it. Do it now.'

Lloydie grinned and offered me a jumbo-sized packet of lollies that was being shared around.

'I'm gunna need something harder than this,' I said, taking a handful, as the Principal launched into his talk about NAPLAN and how it was a valuable assessment tool.

'It's one way we capture student learning here at Halligan,' he said, pressing the clicker to reveal a screen of graphs. He clicked and pointed. Clicked again. Clicked back. Clicked forward. Zoomed in. I felt the lollies sitting heavy in my guts.

NAPLAN doesn't represent anything of my students, I thought as he rambled on, pointing at spikes with a pleased look on his face. *It does not represent their learning.* I took another snake from the packet. *Their learning is shown to me each day through the effort they exert in their tasks, in the progress they make with their work, in the new skills and understandings they demon-strate.* I stretched the snake between my hands, watched as it turned white. *Their learning is shown through the ideas we exchange in the Magic Moment.* The snake snapped.

'You know the most frustrating thing?' My voice came slicing through the Principal's monologue. 'I collect data about this learning all the time!' My voice sounded too loud. 'But, for some reason, it's only the NAPLAN data that gets discussed and held up and considered. Only the NAPLAN data leads to funding. Only the NAPLAN data is used as the measure of success.' I stopped, feeling my stomach churn.

'Well,' the Principal said, 'only the NAPLAN data is considered reliable.'

'That's the most insulting thing you can say to an experienced, professional teacher,' I said. 'Now I'm going to be sick.' I leapt from my seat and rushed to the bathroom.

Colourful pieces of jelly snakes spewed out of my mouth and into the toilet bowl, splattering dots on pristine white. Just like a NAPLAN graph, I thought.

I didn't go back to the meeting. Just signed myself out and went straight home. I'm taking the rest of the week off.

Gabbie

Week 7

FRIDAY

Dear Parents & Caregivers,

Yeah, I'm getting better. Thanks for checking in on me. Obviously I went back to work too soon. (Either that, or NAPLAN really does give me the shits—haha.) I hope I didn't infect any students. I had an email from the relief teacher who took my class for the last part of this week. Reaxton was absent Wednesday, Thursday and Friday, so that would've made things easier. He had to go to Canberra with The Fosters. His foster mum hasn't been well, apparently. The relief teacher described my class as *mostly delightful* with some *busy personalities*. Her email also included the expressions *a handful, challenging group, keep you on your toes* and *carpet pullers*. Imagine what she would have written if she'd encountered The Axe!

I'm certain to be back at work on Monday. The only thing I'm really suffering from now is demoralisation. I was genuinely hurt and angered by the Principal's statement that NAPLAN is more reliable than a teacher's judgement. You know there was a question on the NAPLAN numeracy test for Year 5 this year that zero kids in the state answered correctly. *Zero*. That doesn't show a reliable collection of data; that shows a test designed to trick kids, confuse them and sort them into file and rank.

Look, I know that I've laboured the NAPLAN point in the past, but I still have more to say. First up, the delay between the NAPLAN test and the results is preposterous! Any teacher will tell you that quality assessment, especially a standardised test, should have a reasonably short turnaround time. What I mean by this is that the assessment task is issued, the student completes it, and then shortly after this results are established and feedback is given. It's in this beautiful, critical space that learners *actually learn*. Feedback is that brilliant moment where a teacher looks at what is already understood and provides direction towards the next level of understanding. It's the soft, fertile soil where learning really happens.

With NAPLAN, the results aren't given back until months later. Months! What's the good of that? The students have forgotten the questions, they can't go back and consider the response they gave—they can't even remember what the tests were about. In the time it takes for NAPLAN results to be returned to schools, the soil where learning might have taken place has become dry and hard and completely barren. Not even weeds would grow in the space between a NAPLAN test and the results being issued.

But here's another thing—and this is where we really do a disservice to our learners—NAPLAN forces us to focus our attention on two (just two) subjects! And those two subjects are held up as *the only things that matter*.

Literacy and Numeracy.

What happens to all the other subjects when we start putting the weight of the world on those two learning areas? What happens to History? What happens to Music? What happens to Sport? What happens to Art? Let me tell you: they get neglected. They get shelved. They get dropped off because we're busy preparing our students for tests.

What does that say about the things we value? Okay, sure, it says that we value Literacy and Numeracy. And I concede these are two foundational and highly important subject areas. But I could make an equally strong case for the Arts or Human Movement or History or Science. Those subjects actually *feed into* our ability to become literate and numerate. Through music, we find the heartbeat of mathematics. In history, we uncover the stories we want to read. In science, we discover the language of precision.

When we focus our attention only on Literacy and Numeracy, what does that tell you about our values?

It says we value academics. Reading. Writing. Maths. And that's all.

And when we test for these things, through high-stakes standardised testing, it says we value the right answer. The correct response. The single way of doing things.

Conformity.

The message from NAPLAN is clear: we value those who can read and write and solve Maths problems very, very well, despite the fact that many of the personal resources you need to do those tasks very, very well come from your home life, not from your classroom. And the message our students get from NAPLAN is that their school values Literacy and Numeracy above all other things, which means they end up believing that school's not for them; that school's not for everyone.

Too bad if you're great at Art or singing or booting a footy. Too bad if you're an innovator, a thinker, a questioner. Too bad if you're from a low socio-economic household or living with a disability. Too bad if you're from a culture that's not grounded in English.

Too bad, so sad.

I keep asking you, parents, to consider the big issues around education. This NAPLAN testing represents a philosophy about learning that now underpins Australia's education system. We need to interrogate that, question that, and turn that idea inside out.

Here's my question for you: *Why do we learn?*

Is it so that we can score well on tests and go to uni and get a great job and earn a ton of money and become a good, compliant consumer and taxpayer? And then have a bunch of kids and repeat the cycle? Is that now our circle of life? Is that the answer? *We learn in order to work.*

Something about that feels wrong for me. Underpinning that answer is the idea that the only thing we value is money. That's it. Like the whole endgame is to get money in the bank. Like the whole purpose of school and education is to keep the big wheel of economics turning. Like our only language of value is money.

No. We have other languages of value:

- Kindness
- Creativity
- Innovation
- Compassion
- Questioning
- Curiosity
- Culture
- Loyalty
- Generosity
- Integrity

Surely we value these things as much as the almighty dollar? Surely we value music and singing? Surely we value individual pursuits and team sports? And why can't we value map-reading and science experiments, research and critical thinking, personal wellbeing and happiness?

What would our schools look like if we really valued these things? How would our students feel about school? What kind of young adults would be graduating?

I want you to understand how incredibly frustrating NAPLAN is for teachers and for schools. On the one hand, politicians and policy-makers want us to believe that this is merely a 'snapshot' of student performance—you'll often hear them saying this on the news . . . And yet that snapshot is held up again and again as the single reliable measure of our school, linked to the My School website and distributed to parents as the measure they can depend on. But it can't be both. It can't be a 'snapshot' *and* the complete summary of our school.

Gabbie

PS Who wants a chocolate? Nanny Maud visited yesterday and brought me a very lovely and expensive box of chocs from Switzerland! I like the ones with hazelnut inside. So good.

PPS You know what NAPLAN's like? It's like a third party coming to your home on one particular day and literally taking a photo of your family eating breakfast. Then that same third party compares your picture to pictures of other families and makes judgements about the quality of your *entire family life*— based on that one snapshot—and then publishes the collective family results online for public scrutiny.

Week 7
SUNDAY

Dear Parents & Caregivers,

Sophie's birth was much like Liv's. Fast and furious. The primal, exhilarating feeling of new life pushing out of your body, only this time at 3 a.m.

'I reckon this one's a perfect ten out of ten,' I told the midwife as she took little Soph for the Apgar test.

'How about a nine?' the midwife suggested.

'That'll do. What'd she lose marks on?'

'Colour. It's always colour.'

'Her first impossible test,' I laughed. 'That's alright. Her colour's perfect to me.'

'You're a teacher, aren't you?'

'Yeah. I am.'

Sometimes, when I think about NAPLAN, this memory floats back to me. NAPLAN results pretty much reflect a child's socio-economic status: their ability to access resources and participate in society. I have this absurd idea that we could measure NAPLAN at birth. A few simple questions for the parents and we could pretty much predict the child's NAPLAN score.

Some of you will argue that many people rise above the social status they were born into. I know. I have watched many of my students do just that. But it's not NAPLAN testing that helps them with this, it's education. And relationships. Connections with teachers. Recognising themselves as learners with an ability to improve and grow and better themselves. Reaxton, I hope, will be a classic example of that.

So what happens now that the NAPLAN results are in?

As a teacher, I don't pay much attention to the NAPLAN scores of the children in my class. The results, when they finally arrive, almost always tell me things I already know about my learners; things I have established from other standardised tests I've administered, from my ongoing assessment tasks, from observing my students, talking with them and marking their books.

Years ago, I made a conscious decision not to invest my teaching efforts into 'improving NAPLAN scores' because if I do that my attention focuses on the test rather than the needs of my students. But, whether I like it or not, our results will be analysed by the staff and the Principal. If spelling results are low, there'll be talk of a new school spelling program. If numeracy's down, we'll have a massive review of our Maths programming. The Principal will shuffle staff around, hoping one teacher might provide a magic bullet. Our best results might be used to promote and market the school on the website.

In varied ways NAPLAN is tied to funding, and I think that's one of the main reasons no schools opt out of the testing altogether. To be honest with you, I can never get my head around funding as it relates to NAPLAN, or school funding more broadly. The parameters that govern it frequently change, and it seems to be something kept deliberately complex at both federal and state level, perhaps so we won't ask too many questions.

We have money thrown at us here at Halligan and I understand that is primarily because our school has been consistently underperforming on NAPLAN. For Halligan this means we have some funds for extra teaching allocation which is incredibly useful but it's nowhere near enough (it doesn't even fund a full-time teacher). From what I can see, the money is mostly used for Professional Development of various kinds that 'builds teacher capacity'. We have several literacy and numeracy 'experts' who come into the school and work intensively with teachers in an attempt to improve our teaching so results will lift. It can be galling to endure because these people come in with all their wisdom, but they're rarely telling you something you don't already know. They arrive at class to deliver demonstration lessons, yet some can barely manage the classroom behaviour, let alone deliver instructions. Sometimes it's productive but it depends on the quality and experience of the 'teacher-expert' teaching the teacher. There are two things that this strategy seems to misunderstand:

1. Just because my students' results are low on some faulty national test doesn't mean the teacher is the thing that needs improving. How about looking at the test? The student's lived experiences? The resources I've got to work with? The overcrowded curriculum?
2. Just because you're an expert in reading or writing or mathematics doesn't make you an expert *teacher* of that subject.

Tying funds to NAPLAN doesn't make it any less of a blunt instrument. In my opinion, linking NAPLAN to funding is a means of making schools feel obliged to do the test. It also seems to raise the stakes of the testing and sets in motion a cycle of schools being a slave to the funding because it's so desperately needed.

Experience over the years has shown me that simply adding money to education doesn't lift results. (And we must think carefully about the results we want and the results we value.) Funding should reach the students who need it. Funding should empower teachers to do their work. Funding needs to be used in ways that will have long-term benefits for our children. Funding models ought to be sustainable <u>and funding allocation shouldn't be so bloody difficult to understand!</u>

I'm also going to be so bold as to suggest that the pursuit of school funding shouldn't mean a teacher's workload is increased. I'm deep in political-educational territory here and it's probably not necessary for me to unpack this for you as parents, but if you want to see a grown man cry, go to Lloydie and ask him how his Learning Progressions are coming along. Ask any Junior Primary teacher about them . . . they're another example of onerous, time-consuming, tracking and testing of our students so that funding can be justified and teachers kept accountable. They're another systemic brain-fart that keeps teachers from teaching and building relationships with their students.

There's something else I think about when this topic of NAPLAN and funding comes up. I wonder sometimes if it's a convenient means of politicians dodging the work that they're meant to attend to. If Literacy and Numeracy results are low, politicians quickly point their finger at schools and teachers. But they never look at the work *they're* doing and ask how they could contribute to improving Literacy and Numeracy skills. They never seem to consider that maybe they should develop a community-based initiative that educates parents about the benefits of reading to your child. Or a program that ensures all students have at least one nutritious meal per day. They never seem to discuss broader issues that impact student learning such as housing, access to resources, parenting or stability of home lives. They keep the discussion tight and narrow, sticking to words like accountability, data, student performance, teacher quality and funding. Just once I'd love to hear a politician look at the results and say, 'I am confident schools and teachers are doing all they can, I wonder *what else* could be done? *I wonder what I could do?'*

This morning, on a news show, I heard NAPLAN described as a milestone. *A milestone in each Australian student's education.* I want to object to that. NAPLAN isn't a milestone. Milestones are things like crawling and walking and talking and clapping hands. They're developmental behaviours and physical skills that our children develop *in their own time.* NAPLAN isn't a milestone.

NAPLAN is a construct.

NAPLAN is something the government made up to test and track student performance—and in turn to test and track teacher and school performance. They made it up. They decided it would be a good idea and then they created it. That's why it's a construct. It's something that's been created, designed and delivered to supposedly fulfil a need or achieve a purpose.

And you know the best thing about a construct? We can always *deconstruct* it. We can always dismantle it or implode it or do away with it or just stop using it because it's a made up thing to begin with. Teaching and learning existed before NAPLAN, and they will continue to exist after it.

I've been astonished by some parents' reactions when I suggest we do away with NAPLAN. They frown at me as though I've suggested something outrageous, like removing the Sydney Harbour Bridge. Learning is a process, not a product.

However, when we commit to high-stakes standardised tests like NAPLAN, we stop thinking about the process and start analysing the product. We need to let go of this way of thinking. We need to remember that learning has no end point. Learning doesn't produce a product. It's entirely a process.

The process is where the learning is.

The process is where the progress is.

The process is where the child is.

Gabbie

Week 8

FRIDAY

Dear Parents & Caregivers,

Concert fever has gripped the school and there's a part of me that loves it. The kids are bubbling with a unique excitement. Everyone's humming a tune. Favourite lines from the script are being quoted. Students with lead roles have become minor celebrities. The Kindergarten children look adorbs on stage. Parents have started bustling in with oversized bags full of costumes, wigs and accessories. Mundane items have become essential props. The whole thing is hard work. But it's also lots of fun.

For the past few years now, Halligan has employed a choreographer to teach dances to each class. This has been money well spent. Before that, each teacher had to come up with the routine. It was the stuff of nightmares—both during rehearsals and when it was performed for an audience. Now we work with the dance teacher who coaches each class for five days. Next week, she leaves us, and we continue practising. These dances are performed within a scripted play that frames the concert, and students in Year 5 and 6 are allocated the speaking parts.

A couple of parents were disappointed in the roles that Mrs Fortune and I assigned to the students. One mother made an appointment to speak to us about it, even inviting the Principal to sit in on the meeting. I think he might be starting to get the hang of things now because he was fairly abrupt with her.

'I just noticed my child only has six lines,' she was saying, 'but the person who plays the role of Mem will get forty lines.'

'Yes, that would feel disappointing,' the Principal said, bundling up his things like he was preparing to leave even though we'd just begun. 'However, the teachers' decision has been made and many children have already started learning their lines. I think you should encourage your child to steal the show with those six lines! And I don't think we should lose perspective. It's a primary school concert—no one's auditioning for NIDA.' He stood up then and I felt a bolt of shock course through me. *Who was this man and where had he been all year?*

'But, listen—' he turned back '—if your child's really interested in pursuing acting, you should enrol them in one of the local drama clubs. I believe there are two that operate here in Halligan.'

He thanked everyone and excused himself. As he left the room, I felt like giving him a thunderous applause.

'Well, I guess that's that then,' the mother said. 'The decision's been made.'

'Yes,' I said firmly. 'We considered many things when we made the casting decisions. We're confident that every child will have an opportunity to shine.' I followed the Principal's lead and pushed my chair back, gathering up my things.

The parent followed suit, and within minutes the entire meeting was over.

'That was easy,' Mindy said.

'I know,' I said. 'Who was that guy?' I jabbed a thumb at the seat where the Principal had been. 'Anyway, we think it's over now, but that mum's probably on the "HALLIGAN AREA MUMS" Facebook page right now posting about how her kid's been hard done by and none of us even listened to her.'

'You're right.' Mindy sighed. 'I mean, she'd counted the number of lines the lead character has. Who does that?'

'God, now I feel depressed,' I said. 'She probably *is* posting something about us. I mean, look at everything that's gone on with Bec.'

Mindy closed her eyes and nodded slowly.

A group of parents on a closed Facebook site had been discussing Miss Douglas and really dug their claws in. A sympathetic (or trouble-making?) parent had screenshot the posts and showed them to Bec and the Principal. The Principal had opted for a diplomatic approach, sending out a note via SkoolSaid reminding all parents to be mindful of the professional work teachers do and suggesting that parents with any grievances utilise the correct channels for school communication, rather than Facebook posts. After that letter was sent out, the situation escalated with the Facebook mums making appointments with the Principal to express their outrage that he had reprimanded them when he should instead be dealing with the incompetent teacher!

'It's a mess,' Mindy said. 'Bec's stressed out of her brain. The parents are really going for the jugular.'

'I know,' I said. 'And do you know how it started?'

'Something about birthday invitations?' Mindy frowned.

'Yup. A parent came to school and asked Bec if she could collect the RSVPs for her daughter's birthday party. Like, she wanted Bec to get a class list and mark off all the kids who were coming, and all those who weren't, and all those who hadn't decided. And she even asked Bec if she wouldn't mind putting a little reminder on the Swing-Set thingy for parents to RSVP!'

'You're joking?'

'Nup. For reals. Of course Bec politely said no because class time was too busy. So then the parent asked if maybe she could do it during recess!'

'No!'

'Yes!'

'That's ridiculous!' Mindy said. 'Like we're just hanging around waiting for more tasks to do in our precious thirty-minute break time.'

'I know,' I agreed. 'Surely birthday party responses fall under the broad heading of *Not My Problem*.' I put my hand in the air, claiming a space for each word. 'So, Bec says, "Unfortunately, *no*, I can't do that in my break, but your daughter is welcome to do it herself during recess." Bec even offered to run off a class list of first names.'

'My God, that's more than I would do.' Mindy sighed.

'So the parent waits around while Bec prints off the list and gives it to her daughter. Then she goes home, or probably gets about as far as her car, logs into Facebook and puts up a post in the closed group saying Bec was incompetent and disorganised and, *get this*, LAZY!'

'What?' Mindy growled and made a face. 'If they could see the hours she puts in. That makes me so angry.'

'It gets better. So then this *other* parent joined in the thread, the wife of that guy that had a go at her at the swimming carnival?'

'Of course she does.' Mindy's voice was resigned. 'And the bushfire continued from there?'

'Yep,' I said. 'The Principal's had heaps of meetings with Bec and lots of the parents who commented on the post.'

'Like a meeting's going to solve things,' Mindy scoffed. 'Show us some respect, parents!'

'Yeah,' I agreed. 'But at least it's rattled *his* cage a bit,' I nodded at the Principal's vacant seat. 'He's come out swinging. Bec said he's been quite assertive in these meetings. And did you see how he was just then?'

'I know,' Mindy said. 'Almost sexy.'

'Oh, my God.' I gagged. 'Do not make me sick.' I made a face that was both horrified and fatally ill. Mindy laughed so much she snorted.

Anyway, all we can do is support Bec and hope that these parents come to their senses. Meanwhile, my fingers are crossed that this six-lines-of-script parent doesn't go bitching about me and Mindy on that bloody Facebook page, too. It's such a hopeless, vulnerable feeling, but there's nothing more I can do about it. I don't need this drama and stress. There's enough of it occurring organically in my classroom . . .

Earlier this week, we were down in the hall rehearsing for the concert. Gina, the choreographer, has planned for me to make a cameo appearance towards the end of my class's dance. So far I've been standing back and watching, getting my head around the whole routine in order to remember it once Gina leaves and we're on our own next week.

Each time I'm meant to appear, Gina just yells above the music,

'Teacha', travellin' touch step . . . Five, six, seven, eight. Now the girls, six, seven, eight. Now the boys, six, seven, eight. Everyone! Six, seven, eight. And again, two, three, four!'

Yesterday, I actually had a crack at the 'travellin' touch step'. First attempt? Not too bad.

'Throw some arms out there, Teacha!' Gina shouted from the audience space. 'Try these ones!' And she flapped her arms in and out like a bird trying to get rid of its wings. 'From the top now!' she yelled.

The music started up again and I waited backstage, watching as the kids went through their moves, some of them counting along with Gina, others intuitively knowing where to go and how to move, and the last lot almost oblivious to the lesson, chatting to one another and playing thumb wars until someone pushed them onto the stage.

'Get ready, Teacha!' Gina hooted. 'You're comin' on right now!'

I hustled onto the stage, travelling and touching and stepping with my arms flapping around.

Next minute—*thwack*! The back of my hand belted someone fair across the face. I heard the sound of it over the music, even heard the kid groan *'Orrfff!'* with the shock of it.

'I'm so sorry!' I turned to find Reaxton clutching his cheek. 'Oh, Ax, mate.' I reached for him and he flinched. The music had stopped and the hall was quiet.

'What's happened?' Megan called from the wing.

'Ms Stroud hit Reaxton,' Coman said. 'Slapped him across the face.'

'Coman, I didn't—' I shook my head, took a step towards Reaxton. 'I'm sorry, I didn't see you.'

'It's alright, Stroudy,' he said, moving his hand from his cheek to reveal a bright-red slap. 'I probably deserved that.' He grinned at me, touching his face again. 'You got me a beauty.'

I gave a shaky laugh, felt relief flood through me. 'I'm a hopeless dancer,' I said.

'Nah, you go alright,' he said, 'for an old girl.'

Gina roared with laughter then, her big, loud voice taking up all the space and shoving out that tiny moment of hurt.

'Want me to run up to the office for an icepack?' Liza offered.

'I'll go with her,' Quentin said.

'I'll be right,' Reaxton said, rubbing his fingers gently over his skin.

I sent the kids off for an icepack anyway and asked Reaxton if I could take a closer look.

'I'm so sorry, Reaxton,' I said again as I stood close to him, my own fingers touching his face.

'It's alright,' he said, and he made a point of looking at me, his familiar, devilish eyes connecting with mine. 'I'm going to be okay.'

'I know,' I said, and against all better judgement I crushed him in a hug.

'Coulda been a lot worse,' he said when the icepack arrived. 'Coulda had a blood nose. "Member that, Stroudy?' The wretched child winked at me and I just shook my head.

Pages and pages of paperwork had to be filed after that; even Gina had to write up a statement. The whole thing was a bunch of stress and drama that I didn't need.

Gabbie

Week 9
FRIDAY

Dear Parents & Caregivers,

What's the word that means exhausted but, like, to the power of ten? I asked my class for ideas on this today, the morning after the concert.

'Super-tired?' Megan suggested.

'Worn out?' Coman offered, his head slumped on the desk.

'It's too hard to answer,' Yuki moaned. 'I'm too exhausted!'

Reaxton, who has discovered the thesaurus and doesn't *ever* experience energy loss, started firing off words, his finger trailing across the page as he read. 'Beat. Drained. Fatigued. Knackered. Spent. Weary.' He looked up. 'Knackered, that's my favourite. My dad used to say that sometimes, but mostly he'd just say he was fucked.'

'Well, that'll work too,' I said, 'but that's not the way we speak here at Halligan Primary, is it?'

They mumbled a response, lifeless, like puppets after the show.

Last night, they had been amazing! Dazzling. I had been glowing with pride as I watched them deliver their lines and fumble through unexpected mishaps. They were shining with achievement when they had their curtain call. And I'm fairly confident our dance was the best! Nanny Maud was standing on her seat shouting, 'Bravo! Bravo!' Even when the applause died down, she kept on clapping, and the rest of the audience felt compelled to support her. The kids loved it, grinning their heads off and laughing.

'I can't believe how brilliant you all were last night,' I told them, logging into the school intranet photo file where pictures had already been uploaded. 'Have a look at yourselves.'

They found some life then as the photos slid over the screen. We zoomed in and laughed, watching tiny clips that had been recorded, singing along with the songs and chorusing the funniest punchlines together.

'Go back, go back,' Dempsey insisted, 'to that photo and look at you, Ms Stroud.'

There was a shot of me, pushing through my travelling touch step, arms extended, mid-flap.

'Now zoom in on Ax,' Dempsey said. 'Zoom in. More. A bit more.'

Reaxton's face filled the screen. His expression was one of mock terror, his body leaning back to avoid another backhand.

'Hilarious!' Dempsey declared. 'You're hilarious.' He turned to Reaxton, who was sitting next to him. For the past month, they've been desk buddies—the first time Reaxton has shared a desk with anyone in my class. I'm hoping a friendship might develop, and when the pair of them get distracted, drawing and sketching when they should be listening, I turn a blind eye.

'Yes, it's hilarious,' I said in a flat voice. 'You're just hilarious, Reaxton.' The kids chuckled at my tone and then prompted me to click again.

I was glad Reaxton had been part of the performance. There had been talk of limiting his role to something backstage because of his volatile behaviour and consistently bad language (which he mostly saves these days for Mrs Jethro, the Principal and relief teachers). But Lloydie, Mindy and Bec all campaigned for his inclusion, and he was allowed to join in, and because it was something he wanted to do, there were no problems at all. He was a good little dancer, too, and became best friends with Gina in minutes.

He was away for a couple of days before the concert. Normally a Reaxton-free day is something I would celebrate, but I really wanted to see him participate in a whole school event. Turns out his foster mum had more appointments scheduled for herself and for him in Canberra, but he was back in time for the full-dress rehearsal and the live show.

Just one week left until the holidays, parents. Where has this term gone?

Gabbie

Week 10
FRIDAY

Dear Parents & Caregivers,

Week 10, you are the love of my life!

Alright, just a few things, parents, and then I'm outta here. I'm going to the coast with a couple of friends. Taking the kids. I can't wait to walk on the beach. Sleep in. Drink an entire cuppa while it's hot.

First up, I wish you all could've seen Reaxton's face yesterday. He arrived at school and came racing across the Playground.

'I've got a play date!' he announced.

I grinned, marvelling at how beautiful those childish words sounded in his mouth.

'A play date?' I said. 'Who with?'

'Dempsey!' he replied, eyes shining. 'His mum rang The Fosters and my foster mum said I could go, and so I am. On Sunday. I'm going to his place. And if I'm good there, he can come to mine.' He was breathless with happiness, the words falling clean out of him without swearing or innuendo. 'Dempsey's mum will probably stay because I think she thinks I'm a mass murderer. But, anyway, after that, if all that's good and, you know, I behave and all that, well, then, maybe we can have a sleepover.' He jumped up and down, like a preschooler being offered an ice cream.

'This is great,' I said. 'You, my friend, have achieved your Learning Goal.' I offered him a handshake.

'Yeah, I guess I have,' he said, pumping my hand. 'I reckon those Learning Goals are a bit of a wank though, don't you?'

'Language,' I warned.

'They're a bit of a masturbate,' he corrected.

'Inappropriate,' I said.

'Yeah, and it doesn't sound as good as *wank*.' He thought for a moment. 'They're a bit of a joke. But, if *you're* into them, Stroudy, then I'm into them. Hey, there's Dempsey. DEMPSEY!' he shouted. 'GUESS WHAT?'

'Yeah, I already know,' Dempsey hollered, jogging towards Ax. 'I told Mum to ring your mum.'

'My foster,' Reaxton said. 'My mum's in rehab, I think. Wanna play handball?' He fossicked in his bag. 'I found this on the bus.' Ax produced a rubber ball, popular among the boys, with a footy logo on it.

'You *found* it?' Dempsey asked as they walked towards the bag racks.

'Yeah,' I heard Reaxton say. 'In another kid's bag. It's pretty new, too.' He slammed the ball hard and they watched as it rocketed upward.

Thank you, Dempsey's mum. You're a brave lady, but I promise you he's easy to love (once you get past the threats, bribes, stealing, corruption, swearing, violence, aggression, innuendo and erratic behaviour).

Now, what about the rest of you? Yes, you, parents reading this and thinking, *What a lovely story about that shitty kid, Ax.* Where are you in this story? No, don't get on your high horse and tell me you couldn't handle time with a child like Ax, because Ax isn't the only one. My back pocket's filled with kids who live their school life on the margins. The kid with a disability, the kid who looks a bit different, the kid who's obese, the kid with the dodgy eye, the kid who's seeking asylum, the kid with the very dark skin . . . How often do you encourage your own child to build a bridge to a child who's marginalised?

Our schools are working hard to promote inclusive behaviours and we're teaching them to our students every single day. But there are still kids in my class—not Reaxton, but other kids—who haven't been invited to a birthday party since they were little, haven't been asked to a sleepover, haven't got a bestie and still stand around uncertainly when I ask the class to find a partner. Have you ever talked to your own kid about including others? What kind of messages does your child receive at home about inclusivity? Relating to people who are different to them? Here's the kicker: do you welcome difference into *your* friendship groups? Your workplace? Your home? Your family? We often expect our kids to set an example, but *we* are the example.

Now, parents, the Found Property? Seriously? I have already read you the riot act on this one. Refer to almost all the emails I sent in Term 1. I've been left with a scarf, one glove, three umbrellas, a drink bottle and a jumper. This afternoon, as I was trying to find homes for each of these items, four boys claimed to be the owner of the jumper. It had no name, but each boy insisted it was his.

'I don't have time for this,' I said. 'Take the jumper outside and sort it out.' I threw the jumper over to them and it landed on Coman's head. Out they went, each pointing out features on the jumper, saying, 'And that's how I know it's mine.' Ten minutes later, the boys were still outside, so I came out to investigate. I expected to find them faffing about, but they were still agonising over the jumper, each holding a corner of it like they were about to pitch a tent.

'Boys?' I called, my arms raised. 'What's happening?'

'Just give us one more minute, Ms Stroud,' Coman said. 'We're about to settle this once and for all.'

'Really?' My hands were now on hips. 'What's the plan?'

'Well,' Jeff said, 'we are all going to sniff it.'

'And?' I prompted.

'And if one of us recognises the smell, then we'll know who it belongs to,' Dante said. 'On my count: one, two, three.'

They thrust their noses down onto the jumper, inhaling like it was cocaine.

'It's mine,' three of them announced.

'I got nothing,' Quentin said, leaving the party.

'I can't watch this,' I said, tugging the jumper from them. 'Next thing you'll put it on the ground and call to see who it runs to. Just put your name on your stuff and we won't have this problem.' I bundled the jumper up and stalked into the classroom, tossing it onto the pile of things to be added to the Found Property cupboard.

'Calling to see who it runs to!' Dante laughed. 'You're so funny, Ms Stroud.'

And although it annoyed me at the time, it is an amusing story, so I thought I'd end the term with that.

Happy holidays, folks. Stay safe.

Gabbie

School holidays

Dear Parents & Caregivers,

Just a short note to express my outrage. Did you see that Minister for Education on the news today?

Drives me absolutely crazy to turn on the television and see yet another politician with a double degree in Law and Economics telling me how to do my job and handing down policy.

And did you hear him? Did you hear what he was saying?

'Data collection is *key* to measuring success . . .'

Fuck me sideways.

And this bit: 'We're committed to supporting our teachers and improving their practice . . .'

Ugh. Because it's always our fault. It's always because the teachers have fallen short.

It couldn't possibly be because parents are letting their kids trot off to the skate park instead of doing their homework. It couldn't be because our kids are at home enthralled by devices. It couldn't be because parents have absolved themselves of all responsibility and expect school to do *everything*.

I'm sorry, parents. I know that you guys are pretty much on board now. Your emails and your connection to my classroom show me that you've got a pretty good handle on how complex and challenging the teaching day is. I'm not trying to wallop you over the head and throw blame on to you. Sorry.

It's the politicians and policy-makers I rage at. They've created these constructs. They've enabled parents to think about school as a business model. They've positioned parents as consumers. It's almost like they act as the middleman within education, creating constructs like NAPLAN and My School, and developing policies and programs that promote standardisation and data collection. They create barriers between teachers and parents, between school and home. They've put things in place that have eroded the trust that's integral to successful teacher–parent relationships.

And now we find ourselves here. In a wasteland of standardisation, data collection and accountability, surrounded by Swing-Sets and SkoolSaids.

Ironically for these politicians, all the data they're collecting is mounting against them. The graphs are declining and they don't know what to do. Another policy should fix it. Another *commitment*. From some jerk who's likely going to move on to become Minister for Trade before the year's out.

Just remember this, parents: any program or initiative a politician delivers to education is a double-edged sword. If it's a success, they claim ownership. (*Look at what we did! Look at our commitment to education!*) But if it bombs? It's always because of those damn teachers. (*They need further instruction on how to teach. They need to be accountable. We need to raise their standards.*)

That's enough. It's holidays. I don't want to be thinking about any of this.

Gabbie

Term 4

Week 1

FRIDAY

Dear Parents & Caregivers,

Welcome back. This is it. The home stretch. Dig deep. (And, please, send glue sticks.)

Strange to think that in ten weeks half my class will be graduating primary and heading off to secondary school. Even more frightening to think that about six years later, they'll be graduating from school. I know most of Year 6 parents have already selected their child's high school. Always remember, though, you're not shopping for a new car when you make those choices. Schools aren't a product for purchase. They're living, breathing environments. Schools change. You can no more shop for a school than you can shop for a garden. Seek a healthy school, a place your child will feel like they belong; look for students who are happy; go in and meet the teachers. Walk through the school gates and see how you're welcomed. Don't be fooled by websites and social media and newsletters and advertising . . . And don't believe everything you hear—word of mouth keeps schools shackled to reputations that aren't always fair or accurate.

During the holidays, I spent time with friends who teach secondary. We had a few drinks and argued over who had the most formidable workload, each of us raising the stakes as we watched the sunset.

'I see your thirty-one students that you're stuck with all day,' my mate Stacey said, 'and I raise you three hundred report-card comments.'

'I see your three hundred report-card comments,' I said, 'and I raise you six-period days . . . times five days per week.'

'That's outrageous,' she admitted. 'I can't understand why primary teachers don't get more non-contact time. When do you do all your marking and your prep?'

'I do my marking on the weekends and I never have time to prepare anymore.' I sipped my wine and shrugged.

Stacey's husband, Jim, cracked a beer and sat down. 'Preschool teachers,' he said. 'I raise you preschool teachers.'

'Yes,' I agreed. 'Their work is hard—those little ones are energy vampires.'

'All early childhood teachers,' Stacey added. 'We should drink to them.'

We clinked our glasses.

'It's funny how we use the word "teacher" and it lumps everyone in together,' I said. 'There's tertiary teachers, TAFE teachers, secondary, primary, preschool, early-childhood, probably others, but I can't think of them because I'm on holidays and this wine tastes too nice.'

Stacey laughed. 'It's true, though, isn't it? We just say we're a "teacher", but we all have very different work to do.'

'Hmmm,' I said. We were thoughtful for a while, and then we cracked open another bottle.

'You know the main problem with secondary schools, right now?' Jim asked. 'It's that they're really not very much different to schools we had fifty years ago. But the world has changed. It's changed, Gab.' He'd drunk just enough to feel the need to convince me of things I already knew. 'These kids aren't leaving school with all the skills they need for all the different work they're going to do when they graduate.'

'I believe you,' I said, thinking of my 'big-as YouTuber'.

'What we need,' Stacey added, 'is greater flexibility. We need flexibility of delivery and flexibility in context. We're still locked in by timetables and schedules, and we're still expected to teach the same things in the same ways, even if we're out the back of Bourke or on the North Shore of Sydney.'

'Yes, context!' I snapped my fingers, pointed at her.

'Some states are different,' Jim said. 'Some states have plenty of flexibility. Especially for Year 11 and 12 kids.'

'See, I think that's weird,' I said. 'We've had this big shift to a national curriculum and yet we still have all this variation between states and territories!'

'Agreed,' Jim said. 'I think most of our schools are still operating like sausage factories. We push the student in at one end and expect them to pop out, ready to work, at the other. But it's a system that doesn't serve everyone.'

'Everything works somewhere,' I said.

'But nothing works everywhere!' they chorused.

'This system, though,' Jim said, 'it serves the white middle-class Australian that it was designed for all those years ago. It needs a dramatic overhaul.'

'But parents don't want that.' Stacey shrugged. 'They want school to look the way it's always looked. And they have quite traditional ideas about how schools should operate. In fact, parents are a whole other issue,' she moaned. 'From what I understand, they're all over you in primary school, but they just won't pick up the phone once their kid hits secondary.'

'Really?' This surprised me.

'Well, there are exceptions, but on the whole, parents get them into high school and then it's like "set and forget". Unless some shit goes down and then they're up at the school faster than you can imagine.'

'So how would you like parents to connect with you? Surely you don't need parent-helpers in secondary, do you?'

'I dunno,' Stacey said. She poured more wine. 'I think students need to feel like their parents are onside with what's happening at school, you know? Even though high school kids are older and more independent, parents still need to be . . . connected. Teachers need to be able to approach them, and parents should turn up to a few things at the school so the kid knows their parents are invested. I think teenage kids need their parents just as much as little kids do. They just need them—' she paused '—in more complex ways. Does that make sense?'

Our conversation stopped there because we were interrupted by our own kids and a barbecue had to be prepared. But I thought my friends' ideas were worth sharing with you.

It was so good to get away from school and Halligan, even if it was just for a week. I'm feeling good about rounding out the year with this class. I've sent you the 'real' *Welcome To Term 4* letter on the SkoolSaid app, so make sure you look for that. I'll try my best with Swing-Set this term, too. I'm meant to have a prac student joining me later this term. Maybe I can palm that task off to him?

Nanny Maud's back. We've planned some painting for this term, so I'll have to beg, borrow and steal from other classes to get enough supplies. Maud's incredibly generous, though. Just this week, she brought in lots of her own paints and let the students experiment with them. And she bought the class a beautiful set of brushes (don't tell anyone!). She said the school paintbrushes were 'despicable'.

Anyway, one quick anecdote from Playground duty today. I was up at the Junior Playground with all the little ones. There's one dude in Kindergarten named Harley who just melts my heart. He's such a character. He's got a bit of a problem with his speech, so you really have to concentrate when he's speaking to you.

Today, he came charging out of the toilet just wearing his shoes, jocks and school shirt.

'Urgency ants!' he said, waving his shorts like a flag. 'Urgency ants!'

I hurried over to him, trying to minimise the attention.

'Urgency ants,' he told me and pointed to the Kindergarten bags hanging on the nearby rack. He held his school shorts up by way of explanation.

'Did they get wet, mate?'

He nodded.

'Did you have an accident?'

'No.' He shook his head. 'Fom da floooor.' He pointed towards the toilet. 'Wet.'

'Okay,' I said, 'your shorts got wet from the floor, but your undies didn't?'

He nodded again.

'New ants,' he said pronouncing each word slowly.

'New pants?' I asked, feeling like a detective. 'Urgency ants,' I said, and suddenly it was clear. '*Emergency pants!*'

Harley nodded and pointed to the bags.

'You've got emergency pants in your schoolbag?'

He nodded again.

It was beginning to feel like an episode of *Skippy* as I pulled a bag over and unzipped all the pockets, looking for a spare pair of pants for this self-made young man who wanted to solve his own problem.

'Empty,' I said, showing him the bag. 'Just a lunch box and a drink bottle.'

'Empty,' Harley agreed.

I shrugged.

Then he said, very slowly and carefully, 'That's not my bag.'

It made me laugh and laugh. The way his earnest little face broke the news to me. The way he had watched me search the bag with such confidence.

Before lunch was finished, I had him sorted with his clean, dry 'urgency ants'. And I sent his wet gear home in another bag. I spent twenty minutes documenting the entire thing after school. But I've chuckled about it for quite a while since then.

Gabbie

Week 2
FRIDAY

Dear Parents & Caregivers,

I've had a pile of questions scribbled on sticky notes sitting on my desk at home that I've pulled out from your emails. It's time I answered a few; the notes are becoming faded.

Parent Question:
Sometimes I feel really guilty after I read your emails. I don't know anything much about education in Australia and my kid's about to go to high school. So I clicked on a link in the school newsletter and read about this idea where they're talking about measuring progress as a year of growth for each child. That sounds better than NAPLAN, don't you think?

My Response:
First up, don't feel guilty. For me, the entire experience of parenting just seems to be one long guilt fest, and I don't want to add to that.

Second, always keep in mind that the Principal writes most of the newsletter. I hardly ever read it. Anyway, the idea of a year of growth? That's an idea established by a Professor named John Hattie and made popular by The Gonski Review (you can google all this). The premise is that every child should 'demonstrate a year of learning growth from a year of schooling'. It's a slightly better idea than NAPLAN, but still tricky to measure and quantify.

A year of growth looks different for every child. A year of growth for Reaxton looks different to a year of growth for, say, Coman. How do we measure this? How do we monitor it? Already teachers are tailoring all their programs to an excessive degree. I wonder how this idea will be planned for and implemented? A year of growth in which subjects? What will we do with that data? For me, a year of growth raises more questions than it answers.

Parent Question:

Ms Stroud, you're a great teacher, but you forget that you're a mum, too! It would be great to see you participating in the parent community here at Halligan. We need parents to sell raffle tickets at the supermarket on Saturday.

My Response:

I will buy all the raffle tickets if you promise to never ask me to 'volunteer' at school again.

Parent Question:

Do you think all schools are the same? If you taught at a private school in Sydney, surely it would be easier?

My Response:

A private school in Sydney would certainly be different to Halligan Primary. I've taught in lots of different contexts for many years now and I'm yet to find a teaching position that's easy. Each school is unique and each school presents unique challenges. At a private school in Sydney, I may not have a Reaxton, but I might have a Susannah who's equally demanding. I might not have an inexperienced principal, but I might have an overbearing middle manager. And, remember, schools are like gardens—they change as their community changes, sometimes flourishing and sometimes rotting away.

Parent Question:
Gabbie, I learn something about parenting from most of your letters. Thank you. What's the one piece of advice you'd give all the parents of Halligan Primary?

My Response:
Read with your kids.

That, and put your freaking phones away! Your kids want you to check in with them. They want to know you're emotionally available for them. They want you.

So put your phone away and pick up a book.

And thanks for saying those nice things. I'm no parenting expert, though. I mean, I gave my kids a karaoke machine for Christmas. Come round to my house sometime, when the kids have the bloody thing cranking. Epic parenting fail!

Gabbie

Week 3
FRIDAY

Dear Parents & Caregivers,

Reaxton's had to move away. He's left Halligan Primary.

His foster mum has become seriously ill and she requires ongoing treatment in Canberra. Things escalated quickly and decisions were made late last week. It was impossible to find a family placement for Reaxton close to Halligan, even though he's settled here and making progress, and so it was considered best for him to stay with 'The Fosters' for as long as they are able to manage him. They've got family support in Canberra, and apparently Reaxton was okay about the situation—he's hopeful he might get to see his Mum. She's in prison nearby. I think he's always known that, but he just calls it rehab.

Reaxton.

You wouldn't think you'd miss him, but I do.

I sat down and pulled a long thread of carpet when his foster dad finally called and told me what they were doing. It's funny: Reaxton never pulled on the carpet. He had bigger, more audacious fish to fry. But I just felt like doing something rebellious while my teacher heart unravelled.

Gabbie

Week 4
FRIDAY

Dear Parents & Caregivers,

Nothing to write. Nothing to say.

Gabbie

Week 5

Dear Parents & Caregivers,

Teaching hurts. When they're just suddenly lost to you. And the kids miss him, too. It's quieter. There's a space where his swearing should be.

Gabbie

Week 6
FRIDAY

Dear Parents & Caregivers,

Reaxton's new teacher called me. His first question?

How did you survive this child?

Ax has regressed; it's to be expected. He's been aggressive but not violent. Swearing like a pirate, the teacher said. We laughed about *fuck me sideways*. I gave him some clues, promised him a good return on investment, suggested that my class might write to Reaxton . . . It's a tough situation, but I'm glad Ax isn't lost to me. I've had it happen before where they move on without a trace. The nightmare suddenly becoming a simple dream, and you're left feeling tired and confused. Even Mrs Jethro, his number-one adversary, is feeling the loss. She asked me for his new address because she wants to post him a book.

'It's *Guinness World Records*,' she explained. 'His school will have a copy but he was working his way through this one. He's been highlighting it and making notes . . . defacing it,' she sighed. 'Strange how you miss them.'

My prac student has arrived: a young dude who's in the third year of his degree. Have you noticed all the Swing-Set stuff he's been uploading? The Principal even used my portal as an example for all the other teachers at staff meeting last week.

'That's how you do that,' I whispered to Lloydie, pointing at my pictures up on the screen.

'Happy for ya,' he replied. 'But I've got a date tonight and you don't!' He clicked his fingers in my face and said, 'Hashtag winning!'

I rolled my eyes and told him to stop distracting me, that I was trying to concentrate on the staff meeting.

'First time for everything, I guess,' he said.

Nanny Maud's been creating some beautiful artworks with the students. She's somehow managing to teach them to paint with watercolours *and* acrylics.

'Well, painting's painting, really,' she said when I asked her about it. 'For this age group, in this general classroom setting, let's just get them dabbing paint on a page.'

She's been encouraging the students to experiment with various ways of applying paint, and the grand plan is for them to produce a landscape on canvas.

'Nanny Maud?' Megan asked during yesterday's lesson. 'Should I put a line down here?'

Maud crossed the room to inspect the picture she was holding up.

'I'm thinking just here,' Megan said, trailing her finger just above the canvas.

'Give it a go,' Maud said, nodding. 'If you don't like it, we can always paint over it. And if that fails, you can always make it again on a fresh page.'

'Really?' Megan asked. 'Ms Stroud always says, *waste not, want not*. Isn't that a waste of paint and stuff?'

Maud laughed and the class watched her, enjoying the way she threw her head back to full throttle. We had all been so subdued since Reaxton had left; it was nice to feel some life in the classroom again.

'*Waste not, want not* is a terrific virtue to cultivate,' Maud said. 'But I live by another motto and that is, *Never die wondering*.' She trailed her eyes around the class, finally finishing with a big wink for me. 'So, Megan, let's paint that line in and see how it looks. This might be a masterpiece.'

'You think?' Megan frowned, comparing her picture with Yuki's.

'Well, I don't know yet, do I?' Maud said. 'We have to paint on to find out.'

The finished products yesterday were quite good. Maud sat with me after the lesson as we went through each child's work.

'Their sense of perspective is really improving,' she said. 'Dempsey's work with the brush is inspired!' She held up his painting. It was a perfect rendition of Halligan's distant rolling hills that we can see from our classroom window.

'Look at Coman's,' I said. 'He's done the Playground.'

'Hasn't he come along?' Maud said.

'They all have,' I agreed. 'And I've learned so much. Thank you for your help with our Art lessons, Maud.'

'It's been my pleasure.'

I held up Jeff's painting. He'd tried to replicate a landscape by van Gogh.

'This is quite good,' I said. 'A bit different to the nudes you started us off with.'

Maud laughed. 'Oh, your face, Gabbie! You were terrified.'

'I know!' I squawked. 'It felt like you were releasing hand grenades.'

'But they managed,' Maud insisted. 'They did very well, as I remember.'

'Yeah,' I said. 'They really did.' I nodded, holding back tears that suddenly wanted to overcome me.

'You're really quite heartbroken, aren't you?' Maud pulled me into her arms, the oily smell of paint wafting round me as she let me cry on her shoulder.

We ended up going out for dinner. Maud was convinced I just needed a good feed and a match on Tinder. Honestly, that woman can still shock me!

We settled on Thai and shared a bottle of wine that made me feel better about everything.

'Gabbie,' Maud said, 'since you're refusing to hand over your phone and allow me to find you the match of your wildest and dirtiest dreams, can I ask you a personal question?'

I laughed. 'Yes, Maud, of course.'

'Well, you're a bright girl, gorgeous, lots to offer, and happily divorced, from what I understand?'

I nodded, smiled and sighed. I knew where this was going.

'Why aren't you looking for love?'

'When would I fit it in?' I shrugged.

'Oh, fuck me sideways,' Maud scoffed. 'You can always fit it in!' She laughed. 'You make time for love.'

'I don't know,' I admitted, rubbing my hands over my face. 'I really don't know.' I took a sip of wine and looked at her. 'Teaching is my love.'

She rolled her eyes at me and shook her head. 'But, I wonder, does it love you back?'

Gabbie

Week 7

FRIDAY

Dear Parents & Caregivers,

My prac student's name is Derek. He's going to be a terrific teacher. One day.

Right now, his lessons are like falling down a rabbit hole. He labours through the Learning Intentions and success criteria, trying to apply everything theoretical to the real live classroom. The kids become bored, and behaviour management becomes an issue. During the lesson, Derek loses all sense of time. It's like the kids can smell his inexperience—they lead him off on tangents so he forgets the original point he wanted to make. His tasks are too hard for this class. He's still getting a sense of what an eleven- or twelve-year-old can do, still figuring the right words to use and the best way to engage them.

On the Playground, girls have started flirting with him. He's young, fit and fresh faced. His clothes are 'on trend'.

'How old are you, Mr Smith?' Yuki asked.

He tells her that he's twenty-four.

'You're eight years older than me,' Megan announces.

'That's not right!' Yuki squawks. 'You're not sixteen, Megs!' They laugh together, flicking their hair and smiling at him. He smiles back and tells them they need to brush up on their Maths.

'What's your favourite subject, Mr Smith?' Their questioning continues all through the lunch break. It's not surprising—male primary teachers are a novelty. Derek will have his work cut out, though, to establish himself as an approachable male teacher without being pegged as being too familiar, a weirdo or too strict. I've seen parents erode male teachers out of teaching positions in less than ten weeks. He's a brave guy to join the profession in the current climate. Men tend to stay away—the risk of being positioned as a paedophile is simply too great for most. And then there's the issue of pay. Whether you believe it or not, parents, for the amount of work required a primary teacher's pay is pretty ordinary. I think that keeps a lot of blokes away. It's devastating, really, because there are so many kids like Ax who need male role models in their life.

After school, Derek wants to talk to me—deep and meaningful conversations about theories of learning and philosophies on teaching. I try to answer his questions and throw fuel onto the fire of his enthusiasm. But, generally, I just want to mark the books and get home.

'Do you think kids have changed?' was the question he opened with this afternoon. 'What I mean by that is: do you think children are fundamentally different now than they were, say, thirty years ago?'

'Good question,' I said, piling a heap of writing books in front of him. 'Are you happy to mark that paragraph they wrote this morning?'

'Yes.' He grinned. 'I love marking.'

Idiot, I thought.

'The reason I'm asking,' he went on, his pen hovering over the books, 'is because when I think about how I was in primary school and compare it to these kids now, I think we're completely different. The kids at this school can be pretty naughty, like overconfident and outspoken and full-on. I've noticed it at other schools, too. Me and my friends were never that bold.'

'Hmmm,' I said, rounding out the Maths marking and looking at the clock. 'Here's what I think. I think children are essentially the same. When a baby is born today, it's the same kind of innocent, ready-to-learn bundle that arrived in the world ten, twenty, forty years ago. I think the world has changed, which means that within months that little absorbent bundle is getting messages about life that are different to what it would have received in a previous lifetime.

'So, no, our children haven't changed. They are essentially the same as they've always been, with the same needs and desires. They want to be loved and cared for. They want boundaries and stability. They want to play and express themselves. They're inherently curious and creative. These things don't change, but the world they're growing into? Yeah, it's changed. And our children respond to that world and behave in particular ways in that environment—and this might not be the same way *we* behaved and spoke and acted as children. That's why we want to make the assumption that children have changed. But it's the world that's changed, which is maybe harder to accept.'

'Totally agree,' he said. 'I have to write an assignment on it. Do you think you might have time to read it for me before I hand it in?'

'Sure, I'd love to.' It was a lie, but there's something about new-teacher enthusiasm that I find a teeny bit inspiring.

So I read his assignment and it was good. Of course, it was completely theoretical; learning about teaching can only ever be theoretical. It's not until you do it that you realise there's so much more than theory. When you begin teaching you discover that most of the work is relational.

Some parts of his essay were brimming with an idealism that I found concerning. *He's preparing himself for a job that doesn't exist anymore,* I thought grimly. It made me realise how much teaching has changed.

But even cynical old me couldn't help but be affected by Derek's writing. His work was edged with a shiny sense of hopefulness. He acknowledged the many constraints now placed on teachers and teaching but he also wrote about the incredible impact teachers continue to have on student's lives. He canvassed the many good things that were happening in classrooms today.

His assignment reminded me that we all go into teaching because we want to make a difference. We want to help and support children. We want to do something meaningful with our work.

His essay made me remember an enthusiastic, energetic young teacher I once knew. She's still inside me, I'm sure. She's just been frightened off by all the tracking and testing, the standards and accountability. I'd love to be that teacher again, I see how excited Derek is each day. He tells me he's 'pumped' to be in the classroom and it makes me laugh.

Pumped!

Gabbie

Week 8
FRIDAY

Dear Parents & Caregivers,

I can't believe the term is nearly done and the year nearly over. It's horrifying: I still have so much to do. And School Reports need to be finalised and sent home. Learning Conferences are available for those parents wanting to attend. The Year 6 students have a graduation ceremony that requires tons of practice, but that has to be planned around the various high school orientation days. Meantime the staff are trying to haul together those policies we've been working on all year. We're figuring out new classes, while Bec's nervously awaiting news on student numbers and whether she'll be able to reapply for her position next year. The entire school feels like it's galloping towards a far-off finishing line.

Derek has one more week with me and then I'll be able to complete the wad of paperwork associated with taking on a prac student. Still, his earnest and endearing ways are growing on me. He buys me a coffee each morning and brings me a pie from the hot bake on Fridays. He's created some in-class ongoing jokes with the kids, and he's taught me and the children lots about those bloody robots.

Even so, his lessons still have excruciating moments. Reaxton would have swallowed him whole. During a recent PE lesson in the hall, the students weren't listening as he tried to deliver the next instruction, bouncing their balls at random times despite his command to keep them still.

'Alright,' Derek finally announced. 'I want everyone to sit on their balls.'

The boys sniggered and I heard Coman say, 'I'd really rather not.'

Somehow Derek manages to find his way out of each situation and I haven't had to rescue him. He's got a sense of humour and a strong sense of compassion—two things that can take you a long way in teaching.

This afternoon, as I tried to churn through the marking and get into the weekend (which would be a depressing shitload of report writing anyway), Derek tried to have a heart to heart.

'All teachers should be like you,' he said.

I stopped flicking my pen across the page for a moment. 'Mmmm, thank you? I'm not sure what to say to that.'

'You're a great teacher,' he went on. 'I've seen the kids with a few teachers now and they behave the best for you. We need teachers to be just like you, Gabbie.'

'No,' I told him. 'We actually don't want that at all. That would be standardisation and that's got no place in education.'

'Yeah, I guess,' he said. He hadn't touched his marking. He seemed to prefer to take it home each evening. 'Mrs Jethro's just so mean with the kids,' he went on. 'But you're tolerant.'

'Wait a minute,' I said. 'I know everyone thinks Mrs Jethro's grumpy. I feel it, too. But have you thought about why? Is it because her husband's just lost his job? Is it because she lives with chronic pain? Or is it because her son has a gambling debt that she's working to pay off?' I paused and wrote a comment on Jeff's work. 'It's one of those reasons, but I'm not telling you which one because it doesn't matter. What you need to understand is that all behaviour serves a purpose—that's as true for the kids as it is for any person that you meet.'

Derek frowned at me. 'I don't follow,' he said.

'Look, teachers are just like our students. We're not empty vessels. We've got lives, personalities, families and beliefs. And the work we do requires that we bring ourselves to this work each day. And, for some of us, this means that a bit of impatience and frustration comes along, too. For others, like yourself—you bring fun and energy. We are humans that do very personal, professional work.'

Derek still looked unconvinced.

'Okay,' I conceded. 'So I think Jethro's a pain in the arse. But I also know she's doing it tough right now. And I know what that's like—it makes it hard to be a bright, shiny, agreeable teacher all the time. Teachers right now are in survival mode. The workload itself is unsustainable. Add in some personal life dramas and everything can begin to feel really difficult.'

'Fair enough,' Derek said. 'But you really are a great teacher. That's all I'm trying to say.'

'Naww, thanks!' I said, making a goofy face. 'You know, not everyone thinks I'm brilliant. For some kids, for some families, I'll just be that teacher they had for Year 5/6 at Halligan Primary. But then they might be completely affected by their Year 8 Science teacher. It just depends on the relationships you form with them.'

'I guess you're right,' Derek said. 'But when I grow up and start teaching, I wanna be just like you!' He began marking the books then, and I found myself watching him, smiling at his youthful innocence.

Let him have a long career, I prayed to any god that might care to listen. *Let things change in education so that he maintains this enthusiasm. Help parents understand the work that teachers do.*

I took a breath, glanced at my watch and tried to return to my marking. I haven't felt myself since Reaxton has left. I can't help wondering what it's all for, what it's all about, and why I should bother with teaching anymore. Reaxton's departure is a small thing really, in the scheme of my career. It's happened before and it'll happen again. But his loss adds to the sense of futility that often dogs my teaching days.

Does my work even matter?

'This desk has a lot of graffiti on it,' Derek said suddenly, lifting the pages he was marking to run a hand over the indentations. He leaned down close. 'Whoa!' he exclaimed. 'Does this say *fuck me sideways?*'

I laughed. 'Yes,' I said. 'It probably does.'

Gabbie

Week 9
SUNDAY

Dear Parents & Caregivers,

I'm nursing a bit of a hangover. We had our staff Christmas party last night. We have it at Mrs Fortune's place most years because when we go out to a club or a restaurant, you can be sure that parents from the school are nearby. There are kids we've taught, now standing behind the bar and selling us alcohol or standing beside us and drinking it. It's hard to cut loose when you're meant to be seen as this upstanding, professional citizen. Mindy's place has a beautiful garden and barbecue area, and her husband has this sort of man-cave garage with lounges and a pool table, so the party sprawls around those spaces. We hire caterers and everyone throws in their thirty bucks—BYO alcohol and it's happy days. Well, a happy evening.

Things didn't get too wild this year. I think we were all too tired for any serious shenanigans. Last year we did the conga down Mindy's street and the year before that we had a fashion parade starring Lloydie wearing most of Mindy's wardrobe (between you and me, that lady has some foxy lingerie!). This year was much more mellow, most people had gone home by eleven. I stayed later, along with Lloydie and Bec and, of course, Mindy. Derek was there, too, so keen to be part of a teaching staff. We drank under the night sky and tried to make sense of the year that was.

'I think I'm more tired than I've ever been at the end of a school year,' Mindy announced. 'And I've been teaching for twenty-two years.'

'It could be your age,' Lloydie said and Mindy reached across and bumped his beer, causing it to spill down the front of his shirt.

'I don't think it's age,' Bec said. She was lying on the grass, staring at the stars. 'I feel it too and I've only been teaching a few years.'

'Oh, my God, Bec!' I said, remembering. 'Did you find out about your placement for next year? Are you still with us?'

'Monday,' she said wretchedly. 'The Principal said I had to hold out until Monday. Last year I got an email from the Department telling me, but it's changed this year or something, so he said I'll find out on Monday. Not sure if it gets sent to him or me or what.'

'That sucks dogs' balls,' Lloydie said. 'You sure you want to do this gig, Derek? Get out now while you can.'

Even in the dim light cast by Mindy's outdoor lanterns, I could see Derek's beaming smile.

'Yes,' he said. 'There's nothing you could say that would discourage me. I want to be a teacher.'

'Me too,' Lloydie laughed. 'And I'd be a great teacher if it weren't for all the other stuff.'

'We just need some solutions,' Derek said brightly. 'You're all very good at pointing out the problems but we need to be solutions-oriented.'

'Fuck off,' Lloydie groaned. 'You sound like a principal.'

'Or a policy-maker,' I said. 'Solutions aren't as easy to come by as you might think.'

'Why not?' Derek pressed.

Lloydie groaned again. 'Stop wrecking Christmas,' he said. 'Gab, make Derek stop being annoying.'

I stood and topped up my glass, offered Bec another beer. 'Derek,' I announced, still standing. 'There are no simple solutions to education. The problems we see now are a result of politicians and policy-makers implementing simple solutions as knee-jerk reactions to deeply complex problems. We don't need more solutions right now.'

'No, we need more alcohol,' Bec said.

'Yes,' Lloydie agreed.

'No,' I said. 'That's yet another bandaid.' I took a step onto a lovely granite rock that stood in Mindy's garden, making it my stage. 'What we need,' I went on, 'is some time to think. We need to have a good long look at what's happening in education right now and ask ourselves if it's working. We need to think about what we want our students to know and how we should teach them. We need to think about the role of schools and the work of teachers. We need to reimagine our educational paradigm.'

'Preach it,' Lloydie said, raising his beer in my direction.

'In fact it is my firm belief . . .'

'Firm belief,' Lloydie echoed.

'That we should divorce education from politics so we aren't always subject to these changes that continue to occur each time the political winds blow.' I paused, took a sip. 'And if we can't do that, we should make a rule that only people who have a teaching degree and have been a teacher can be an education minister. Oh, and only teachers can be policy-makers, too.'

Bec gave me a round of applause and I stepped down from the rock. I sat back in my seat, offered a bowl of chips to the others.

'These have gone chewy,' Lloydie announced. 'The night air's wrecked them.'

'Yep,' I agreed, still taking a handful.

'But what about NAPLAN?' Derek asked.

'Mate,' Lloydie said firmly, 'if you've been missing out on party invites I've got a few suggestions on why.'

Bec laughed. 'Go easy, Lloydie,' she said. 'We were excited young grads once, too.'

'No, I never was,' Lloydie said. 'I've been cynical my whole life.'

'It's why we're mates,' I said and we clinked our drinks. 'Okay, NAPLAN.' I got up and returned to the rock. 'I proclaim that we should abolish NAPLAN. Let's just get rid of it. For seven years let us do no high-stakes testing and then just see what happens.'

'That sounds dangerous,' Derek said.

'Is it?' I asked. 'Alright, if that's too dangerous, let's just shut down My School and phase out NAPLAN. Let's think about developing assessments that can give high-quality information to teachers and schools in an appropriate way. If we have to have a test, the intention should be that it gives information to the right people in a time span that allows them to work with it.'

'Nah, I like what you said before. Get rid of it,' Lloydie said.

'I can't believe you can still say words like *appropriate*,' Bec struggled to get the word out. 'I've drunk too much to say big words.'

'But of course we have to have a test.' Derek was frowning. 'Don't we?'

I returned to my seat while the others engaged in a short, animated argument about national testing.

'Derek,' Lloydie said, 'I hear you, brother, but I want to have this conversation with you *after* you've been teaching for five years.'

'How about,' I said, 'instead of NAPLAN . . . when a kid's in Year 3 or 5 or 7 or 9, they get sent a book?'

'A book? What? That's just weird,' Bec said.

'Stay with me,' I said, standing up and returning to the rock.

'That's not a stage, you know,' Derek said. 'It's a rock.'

'I know, I know,' I said, but I put down my wine glass and took up a nearby stick, using it as a microphone. 'What sort of message would our students be receiving if they were all sent a book instead of sitting NAPLAN?'

'Do they all get the same book?' Lloydie asked. I leaned forwards and offered him the stick, asking him to repeat the question into the microphone.

'Do they all get the same book?' Lloydie said again.

'Dunno,' I said. 'I've just thought of it. Yeah, probably. And then if teachers wanted to, they could do a unit of work around the book or read it as a class or just enjoy the book with their kids. And every year it's a different book so kids and families get excited about what book it's going to be. And then when they're older they'll be saying things like 'Oh I was in Year 3 the year that was the National School Book,' and it will be a way for people to connect and talk and read and . . .' I let my voice trail, ideas running out.

'It would be a strong message,' Derek said. I passed him the stick and he spoke into it. 'It would say that in Australian education we value reading and we want our kids to read *so much* that we give them books and we populate their homes with books.'

'Wait, who gives them the books?' It was Lloydie and I prompted him to use the stick-microphone. He sighed, took the stick from Derek and said again, 'Who gives them the books?'

'The government,' I said, snatching the stick from him. 'And we pay for it using the money we used to spend on NAPLAN.'

'They did something like this in the NT,' Bec said. She was sitting up and had found a smaller stick. She was speaking into it and I laughed as I watched her, hair standing up in wild tufts. It was still recovering from being shaved earlier in hte year. 'I remember a friend telling me. The kids got books in a backpack. But they ended up chucking the books and just keeping the backpack.'

'Oh,' I said, a little deflated. 'Everything works somewhere but nothing works everywhere.' I made to step down from the rock, but then turned back. 'I reckon that what we need is to stop asking *what works* and start asking *what matters*?'

'Yes, that's what that academic says.' Derek snapped his fingers. 'Is he from the US or the UK?' He frowned trying to reference the idea.

'It doesn't matter!' I proclaimed. 'If I say it here on the rock on this night, then it must be true and it doesn't matter.' I glanced over at Mindy. She was sound asleep in her deck chair. 'Mindy is asleep,' I announced, only slurring the words a tiny bit.

'So she is,' Lloydie laughed and we watched as he tickled her with a blade of grass and made her twitch.

'We just need more help,' I said quietly, tossing the stick aside and returning to my seat. 'Teachers need a Learning Support Officer in the room with them. Even if there are no diagnosed students in the class. Two adults in a classroom and then more if there are kids with needs. And someone to make up the first-aid kits.'

'Speaking of first-aid kits, how did you get on with that electrician?' Lloydie asked.

'Those ideas don't join together,' I said. 'And I never saw the electrician again, you lunatic. That was your crazy fantasy, not mine.'

'Do you want me to come round and pull the mains switch in your meter box,' Lloydie offered. 'Then we could call the tradie?'

'How are your Learning Progressions going?' I jabbed.

He made a fake sobbing sound. 'You just killed this party,' he said. 'Killed it.'

We called for our rides after that. Derek wanted to go clubbing but Bec was nearly asleep and Mindy was snoring.

I was home in bed by one and when I tallied up all my drinks I didn't feel that bad. At 1.15 a.m. Lloydie flicked me a text. It was a screen shot of the electrician's website and he'd circled the phone number.

He's such an idiot.

Gabbie

Week 10

FRIDAY

Dear Parents & Caregivers,

Thank you for all your gifts and cards, parents. There were some beautiful letters and notes sent to me this year. I'll treasure them and keep them and glue them into my scrapbooks. I wanted to share this one with you that came via email this afternoon just a few hours after school broke up:

> *Dear Gabbie,*
> *It's nearly 4 p.m. and my daughter's just home. She threw her bag on the lounge and hunted for food in the fridge. Then she sat at the kitchen bench and said, 'I think that was my best year of school so far.'*
> *'Wow,' I said. 'What do you think made the difference?'*
> *'My teacher,' she said.*
> *So, thank you, Gabbie. You made a difference.*

It's such a touching message to receive. I cried when I read it and I'm crying as I share it with you now.

I'm wondering, parents, if you can remember your own days at school? Do you remember a teacher who made a difference for you? Who was that teacher? What did they do that made them so memorable? What was it about them? I'm sure if you take a minute to think, you'll realise that they made you feel good about yourself. They made you feel like you had something to offer the world. That's what teachers do, especially when they're teaching at their best and not being hamstrung by politics and paperwork.

You know a tiny thing you could do that would make a teacher's day? Track down that teacher from your school days and send them a message. Let them know what they meant to you. Let them know you remember them. Let them know that you care about teachers and the work they do.

We must let teachers know that they're valued.

We need to love our teachers. We need to recognise them for the superheroes that they are.

We need to be aware that, right now, our teachers are being charged with the responsibility of carrying the weight of so many things they cannot control. We need to demand more from our politicians—demand that they step up, demand that they better support our students and our schools and, of course, our teachers. We must demand that politicians do the work they are elected to do instead of palming it all off to our overburdened schools.

We need to remember that our teachers became teachers because they want to make a difference. We need to understand that they're trying their best. Even the ones like Mrs Jethro, who are hurting inside and trying to pour from an empty cup. Even the ones like our Principal, who's learning on the job while putting up with stressed-out teachers like me and demanding students like Reaxton.

And we need to tell our teachers, 'Thank you', just as you have done for me today. But thanks shouldn't just be given on the last day of the school year. Thank a teacher, whenever you can. Thank them at the end of the school day, at the end of the

Learning Conference, at the end of the term, at the end of an email. You know what? Go over the top with the thank yous . . . the next time you're asked to *give the teachers a round of applause*, get up on your feet and give them a standing ovation. They deserve it.

Gabbie

My last letter

Dear Parents & Caregivers,

Before you had kids, what did you think parenting would be like?

I had visions of a sleeping baby snuggling in the bed beside me. Beautiful family Christmas portraits, with everyone smiling at the camera. Healthy evening meals, always eaten at the table . . . I didn't imagine anything much beyond that, even though I'd been teaching for years by then and I was familiar with the secret life of kids. I could only imagine the postcard fantasy of what *having children* would be like.

And then they arrived.

They vomit on your carpet. And they break your pretty things. They're noisy and busy and they're always touching the walls. They don't eat, they graze—all throughout the house, the car, the shops, even at other people's houses. They'll unashamedly eyeball the fruit bowl and ask for a banana. They're demanding. Their teeth fall out. They require endless attention. And their skin burns if you leave them in the sun for too long.

There's nothing picture postcard about it. And yet you love them. You wouldn't be without them.

Before you become a teacher, you have this ideal image in your mind of what it's going to be like, too. You tend to see yourself out the front with your class seated before you. You see yourself at the heart of the scene. And everyone's smiling. Everyone's agreeable. We're all ready to learn, and you're all ready to teach. It all looks so easy. It also looks like a picture postcard.

And then you start teaching.

The scene pans out to reveal lots of extra things that weren't in that initial, fantasy frame. There are meetings and parents and principals and meetings and paperwork and glue sticks and meetings and timetables and standardised tests and paperwork. Other students enter the scene, and they're not smiling and compliant. Other teachers come into view, along with politicians and more parents. Not all of them look happy. You hear yourself saying things like, 'Not enough time' and 'Band 4, he's in Band 4' and 'I'm sorry, that wasn't my intention'.

There's nothing picture postcard about it. And yet you love it. You wouldn't do anything else.

No one can tell you what it's really like to be a parent until you become a parent.

In the same way, no one can tell you what it's really like to be a teacher until you become one.

This will be my last letter. I don't have anything more to tell you. Besides, I think you understand what I've been trying to say:

Do the work of a parent at home, so I can do the work of a teacher at school.

Thank you for this permission to talk. It has meant a great deal. Teachers should be allowed to speak about their profession, they should be allowed a voice, allowed to talk about the important work they do.

Gabbie

A note from the Teacher

Dear Reader,

For the sake of clarity, it is worth explaining some key points regarding the organisation of the Australian education system.

In Australia, teachers are required to follow a national curriculum known as *The Australian Curriculum*. This nation-wide curriculum was a federal government commitment that would supposedly bridge geographical boundaries and reduce 'duplication' of time, effort and resources. However, each state still governs their own education system which means that there are significant differences across the borders. For example, each state and territory has a different name for the first formal year of schooling such as 'Reception', 'Kindergarten', 'Pre-Primary' or 'Prep'. Each state and territory also develops their own syllabus documents which are aligned with the national curriculum but contain local variations.

This story is set in an imagined town within New South Wales where the first formal year of schooling is known as Kindergarten or Early Stage One. In New South Wales, children in Kindergarten must turn five by the end of July although some parents delay enrolment until their child is due to turn six within the school year.

Beyond the twelve-month course of study known as Kindergarten, the NSW curriculum becomes organised into two-year courses of study that are referred to as Stages, although the students themselves remain organised in Year levels.

Stage One is Years 1 and 2, Stage Two is Years 3 and 4, Stage Three is Years 5 and 6 and Stage Four takes us beyond primary and into the realms of high school. *Dear Parents* records the year of one teacher with her Stage 3, Year 5 and 6 class.

I trust that this explanation will clarify your understanding of the text you have read, although I am sure it also raises some questions such as *Why do we have a national curriculum at all?*

Yours in education,
Gabbie

Acknowledgements

Could the following students please stand up when their name is called:

Jane Palfreyman, Louise Cornegé, Patty di Biase-Dyson, Tom Bailey-Smith, Rebecca Starford, Christa Munns, Lisa White, Grace Heifetz, Peter Bishop, Stephanie Lovat, Karen Tarpey, Zacharey Jane, Pedro and Julianne Cavalieri, Sexy Writers United, Leanne Bateman, Kyle Wilson, Nick Thornton, Jill Francis, Janet Lee, R.W.R McDonald, Steve Hawkins, Kathy Margolis, Chris and Amy Cox, Catherine Kennedy, Louise Woods, Katie Magriplis, Dumbo Steiner, Paul and Helen Carroll, Colin Butters, Tracey Hughes-Butters, Matty Stroud, The Boozehounds, Kasia Drzewiecki, The Belmora Crew, Anni Bottom, Cheryl Toole, Jacqui Siiteri, Mum and Dad.

Now let's give all these people a massive round of applause because without them, we wouldn't have this lovely book. Thank you, everyone. Students, you may sit down now.

Olivia and Sophie Stroud—why are you standing up? Nobody asked you to stand up! No, I didn't forget your names. I am glad you're standing though. I wanted to single you out separately, because you two deserve your own thunderous applause.

About the author

GABBIE STROUD is a freelance writer, novelist and recovering teacher. After years of juggling the demands of the primary classroom, she became disenchanted and disillusioned, eventually making the painful decision to leave the profession she had loved. In 2016, her critical commentary of Australia's education system was published in *Griffith Review*'s Edition 51 *Fixing the System*, which went on to be shortlisted for a Walkley Award. Gabbie's smash-hit memoir *Teacher* was shortlisted for Biography Book of the Year at the 2018 ABIA Awards and contributed to the national dialogue on education. Gabbie lives on the far south coast of New South Wales, where she co-parents her totally awesome girls—Olivia and Sophie, aka Yaya and The Boph.